Catholics against the Church
Anti-Abortion Protest in Toronto
1969–1985

Bitter division has been a hallmark of the abortion debate in Canada for decades. On an issue that seems to offer no middle ground, the lines of division appear familiar to us all: feminists and liberals vs fundamentalists, conservatives, and Catholics. But as Michael W. Cuneo shows in this provocative study, it is not that simple. The Catholic church itself has been divided on this issue – if not over the theology of abortion, certainly over the role of the church in anti-abortion activism.

Cuneo offers the first sociological and historical investigation of the Canadian anti-abortion movement, focusing on its development in Toronto and the church's role in it. The first three chapters chart the main stages of the movement over two decades, from an enterprise of political reform to one of sacred crusade. The fourth and fifth chapters focus more closely upon the movement's internal composition, its mosaic of human shapes and world-views. The final two chapters examine the tensions the movement poses for Canadian Catholicism.

The anti-abortion movement in Canada, argues Cuneo, is a symbolic point of fracture for a widening ideological dichotomy within Canadian Catholicism. Far from promoting consensus within the Canadian church, the movement is a battlefield for competing conceptions and ideals of episcopal leadership, the meaning and requirements of Catholic belonging in a secular age, and the relationship of the church both to Canada's pluralistic ideal and to Canadian political culture.

MICHAEL W. CUNEO is Assistant Professor in the Department of Sociology and Anthropology, Fordham University. He is co-author, with Anthony J. Blasi, of *Issues in the Sociology of Religion: A Bibliography*.

MICHAEL W. CUNEO

Catholics against the Church:
Anti-Abortion Protest in Toronto 1969–1985

UNIVERSITY OF TORONTO PRESS
Toronto Buffalo London

Toronto Buffalo London
Printed in Canada

ISBN 0-8020-2726-1 (cloth)
ISBN 0-8020-6758-1 (paper)

Canadian Cataloguing in Publication Data

Cuneo, Michael W.
Catholics against the Church

Bibliography: p.
Includes index.
ISBN 0-8020-2726-1 (bound) ISBN 0-8020-6758-1 (pbk.)

1. Pro-life movement – Social aspects – Ontario – Toronto. 2. Pro-life movement – Religious aspects – Ontario – Toronto. 3. Catholic Church – Canada. 4. Pro-life movement – Social aspects – Canada. I. Title.

HQ767.3.C87 1989 306′.6′0971 C89-094551-9

This book has been published with the help of a grant from the Canadian Federation for the Humanities, using funds provided by the Social Sciences and Humanities Research Council of Canada.

MICHAEL W. CUNEO

Catholics against the Church:
Anti-Abortion Protest in Toronto 1969–1985

UNIVERSITY OF TORONTO PRESS
Toronto Buffalo London

Toronto Buffalo London
Printed in Canada

ISBN 0-8020-2726-1 (cloth)
ISBN 0-8020-6758-1 (paper)

Canadian Cataloguing in Publication Data

Cuneo, Michael W.
Catholics against the Church

Bibliography: p.
Includes index.
ISBN 0-8020-2726-1 (bound) ISBN 0-8020-6758-1 (pbk.)

1. Pro-life movement – Social aspects – Ontario – Toronto. 2. Pro-life movement – Religious aspects – Ontario – Toronto. 3. Catholic Church – Canada. 4. Pro-life movement – Social aspects – Canada. I. Title.

HQ767.3.C87 1989 306′.6′0971 C89-094551-9

This book has been published with the help of a grant from the Canadian Federation for the Humanities, using funds provided by the Social Sciences and Humanities Research Council of Canada.

For my parents, Helen and Raymond
sine quibus non

Contents

Introduction

The Canadian pro-life (or anti-abortion) movement is fraught with paradox. It is a vehicle of both unity and disunity, a symbol of both common and divergent purpose for Canadian Roman Catholicism. The movement is at once a shibboleth of Catholic identity and a fulcrum of internal conflict for the Canadian church. It is overwhelmingly Roman Catholic in composition and yet scorned by Canadian Catholic elites and scarcely tolerated by most bishops. Moreover, despite its quintessential Catholicity, many movement activists regard the institutional Canadian church with unconcealed contempt.

As the first sociological and historical investigation of the Canadian pro-life movement, this study attempts to illuminate these paradoxes. Its central thesis is that the movement is the symbolic point of fracture for a widening ideological dichotomy within Canadian Catholicism. Far from promoting consensus within the Canadian church, the movement is a battlefield for competing conceptions and ideals of episcopal leadership, the meaning and requirements of Catholic belonging in a secular age, and the relationship of the church both to Canada's pluralistic ideal and to Canadian political culture. Indeed, the movement is to a significant degree a conventicle of lay dissent against forces of change and modernization within the wider culture and, more important, within Canadian Catholicism itself.

This study, then, focuses more particularly upon the conflict which the pro-life movement poses for the Canadian Catholic church than upon that which it poses for the wider society. As the first three chapters show, the relationship between the movement and the institutional Canadian church has been plagued by embitterment and mutual estrangement. As this relationship has progressively deteriorated, the movement as a whole has become subject to a process of goal displacement. Fighting the demons of modernity within Canadian Catholicism has become almost as important to many movement participants as fighting abortion itself. Particularly in Toronto, where movement passions burn hottest, militant Catholic activists have condemned mainstream Catholicism as apostate and have defined themselves as a holy remnant destined to conserve the flame of authentic faith at a time of spiritual decay and moral apathy. These initial chapters thus chart the main stages of the movement's evolution over two decades from an enterprise of political reform to one of sacred crusade.

Despite its dominant impulsion toward religious crusade, however, the Canadian anti-abortion movement is by no means monolithic. Indeed, its internal development is comparable to a collision course of conflicting world-views. The fourth chapter attempts to convey a fuller picture of the movement's composition, its irreducible diversity, and its mosaic of human shapes. This seems especially worthwhile in light of the tendency in both the popular and scholarly media to depict anti-abortion activists in one-dimensional stereotypes. A typology of pro-life activism, consisting of three empirical types, captures the movement's main ideological contours. Most germane to the main theme of this study is the activist type which is designated as Catholic Revivalist. While manifestly directed toward the protection of unborn life, the anti-abortion protest of Catholic Revivalists is seen to be also, and perhaps as profoundly, a medium for the crystallization of a *contracultural* Catholic identity at variance with the evolving *denominational* identity of mainstream Catholicism.

The fifth chapter puts flesh on the bones of the typology elaborated in Chapter Four by profiling the activist careers of individual movement participants. This anthology of case studies is primarily evocative, and thus may be passed over or read separately without loss in continuity of the main argument.

Chapter Six undertakes a more direct and extended analysis of the ideological and organizational tensions which the abortion issue poses for Canadian Catholicism. It is argued that the abortion issue, or more precisely, anti-abortion activism, is where the battle lines are drawn between rival and mutually hostile orthodoxies within the Canadian Roman Catholic church. It is further suggested that the *screen of sep-*

aration between church and state in contemporary Canada and the politics of ecumenism are the principal factors which both condition and constrain the political involvement of the Canadian bishops in the abortion controversy.

Perhaps the most significant contribution of this study is its discovery that militant Catholic anti-abortion activists constitute a distinctive and self-confined subculture within Canadian Catholicism. Chapter Seven explores the cardinal points of reference of the Catholic Revivalist subculture, its theory of cultural decline and complementary ethic of anti-worldly asceticism, as well as the ceremonial role pro-life activism performs for it as a public ritual of cultural defiance.

The concluding chapter recapitulates the main argument and also suggests the more general value of this study toward an understanding of contemporary upheaval within the Catholic universe.

The present study is limited to the highly selective interpretive themes mentioned above. It is not an ethical treatise and therefore does not enter the ongoing philosophical and theological debate over the morality of abortion.[1] Neither is it a political discourse which presumes to propose public policy solutions to the abortion controversy. Indeed, the author attempts throughout to maintain both ideological anonymity and ethical neutrality, believing with Weber that the sociologist is called to analyse and interpret social reality without supposing that he or she is thereby qualified to adjudicate questions of ultimate value or to tell people how to live.[2] In other words, the author approaches the topic neither as missionary nor as prophet.

The study is a historical investigation only in a quite secondary sense. The story of the Canadian pro-life movement is told not for its own sake, but rather to provide scaffolding for the more interpretive sections which follow. Thus, although the fruit of original research, the first three chapters are best read as a prelude to subsequent chapters which discuss more systematically the strategic relation of the movement to current lines of ideological fissure within Canadian Catholicism. Moreover, the study rehearses only those aspects of the legal and political history of the Canadian abortion dispute which are germane to the development of its main thesis.

As its thematic pitch would suggest, this study is more directly a contribution to the sociology of Roman Catholicism than it is to the field of social movement analysis. It does, however, draw upon theoretical insights from the collective behaviour tradition and employs tools of analysis (participant observation, interviewing, content analysis) which are research staples of the sociology of social movements. The research strategies of the study are summarized in an appendix.

Because 1985 is the finishing point for its historical narrative, this study does not take into account a more contemporary event which has fundamentally altered the terms of the Canadian abortion debate. Since the mid-1960s the abortion issue has been a perennial topic of public controversy in Canada, but very recently it has captured the national spotlight with unprecedented drama. In January 1988 the Supreme Court of Canada struck down the nation's abortion law, ruling that the Charter of Rights and Freedoms does not permit the state to interfere with the personal reproductive choices of women.[3] This landmark ruling has undoubtedly given rise to an entirely new chapter in the ongoing story of the Canadian pro-life movement, but this is a chapter which is merely sketched here in a brief afterword.

One additional qualification is in order. As the title indicates, the primary focus of this study is anti-abortion protest in Toronto from 1969 to 1985. The pro-life movement in Toronto, however, is in crucial respects a microcosm of the broader English-Canadian movement. Because of this, and also because much of the discussion has pertinence beyond Toronto, reference is made throughout to the *Canadian* pro-life or anti-abortion movement. Nevertheless, it should be emphasized that a full appreciation of the national movement's regional diversity would require a more exhaustive investigation than is offered here. It should also be stressed that the movement is discussed here only in its English-Canadian dimension. The French-Canadian variant is quite different and should thus preferably be the subject of a separate study.

It is impossible today, perhaps more than ever, to speak judiciously of Roman Catholicism in the singular. Bill McSweeney has convincingly illustrated how post-conciliar Catholicism's 'search for relevance' has cast into perplexity the very notion of what the church is or should be. It is difficult to escape McSweeney's conclusion that contemporary Catholicism is a discordant chorus of contentious voices, voices which no longer speak within boundaries expressive of a common religious commitment.[4] As competing *Catholicisms* in Canada aspire to make their respective theological orientations normative for the Canadian church, the abortion issue has acquired deepened symbolic significance. Anti-abortion protest has been embraced by a discontented segment of the Canadian laity as a crucible of faith at a time when the wider church, including its bishops and professional elite, seems taken by other interests and absorbed by different passions. Thus, as this study of the English-Canadian pro-life movement demonstrates, one of the stakes in the battle over abortion is nothing less than the soul of Canadian Catholicism itself.

Like most scholarly endeavours, this one has benefited from the counsel of friends and colleagues. I wish to acknowledge particular indebtedness to Roger O'Toole whose many suggestions and criticisms have greatly enriched the final product. I am also grateful for the assistance and encouragement of Jean Louis De Lannoy, Paul Gooch, James Kelly, Margaret O'Toole, Kathie Lowes, Denyse O'Leary, Anthony Blasi, Claire Hummel, John Hannigan, Don Wiebe, John Simpson, Muna Salloum, Ronald Sweet, Ravi Ravindra, and Tom Sinclair-Faulkner. Completion of the book would not have been possible without the inestimable support of Paul Attallah. Nor could it have been done apart from the happy and necessary distractions provided by Rebecca, Shane, and Brenda. I am happy also to express gratitude to my wife Margaret, who typed and edited the final manuscript and furnished intellectual inspiration throughout its writing. The book has been greatly improved by the editorial acumen of Virgil Duff, and by the copy-editing of Jim Polk. The Social Sciences and Humanities Research Council of Canada and the Killam Trust have given my research generous financial support. I extend warm thanks, finally, to the numerous individuals who kindly consented to be interviewed for this study.

CATHOLICS AGAINST THE CHURCH: ANTI-ABORTION PROTEST IN TORONTO 1969–1985

1

The Canadian Pro-Life Movement: A Fragile Alliance

Certain events and circumstances more than others in the development of a social movement are decisive for shaping its career, for giving it a distinctive stamp. A record of these can thus serve as a chronology of the movement's 'personality-formation.' It is toward this end that this and the following two chapters are written. Rather than a thorough history of the Canadian pro-life movement, they provide a series of snapshots which chronicle its metamorphosis over two decades from a movement of political reform to one of religious crusade. Such a schematic approach is of necessity highly selective, and others more intimate than the author with the movement would undoubtedly choose different snapshots, or at least prefer a larger collection. Nevertheless, although incomplete, the snapshots chosen for presentation here do manage to illustrate the basic permutations undergone by the movement since its inception almost twenty years ago.

Particular attention is paid in this chapter to the internecine conflict with which the movement has been riddled over its short history. The polytheism of values of which the movement has been composed, while potentially its greatest natural resource, has consistently been translated into internal factionalism. As one veteran activist put it: 'There has always been a tendency for us to draw up the wagons in a circle, but with not all the guns pointed outwards.'

THE 1969 ABORTION LEGISLATION

Abortion was a statutory offence under the Canadian Criminal Code when the federal government, in December 1967, introduced an omnibus bill to Parliament which included reform of Canada's abortion law among its more than one hundred items.[1] The specific amendment to the Criminal Code's section on abortion, approved by the House of Commons in May 1969, authorized that abortions could be performed for broadly therapeutic reasons in accredited Canadian hospitals after approval by a therapeutic abortion committee (TAC).[2] According to the new law, abortion would be permitted if, in the opinion of a duly constituted TAC, 'the continuation of the pregnancy' of the female seeking abortion 'would or would be likely to endanger her life or health ...'[3]

This 1969 legislation purported to be a compromise solution to the abortion controversy.[4] By making legal abortion contingent upon the decision of a TAC that continuation of pregnancy might endanger the woman's 'life or health,' ostensible recognition was accorded the independent value of intra-uterine life. In other words, implicit in the amendment was the assumption that 'termination of pregnancy' should not be allowed without demonstration of a proportionately grave cause. Speaking in defence of the bill in third reading, the then minister of justice, John Turner, said: 'The Bill has rejected the eugenic, sociological, or criminal offence reasons. The Bill limits the possibility of therapeutic abortion to these circumstances: It is to be performed by a medical practitioner who is supported by a therapeutic abortion committee of medical practitioners in a certified or approved hospital, and the abortion is to be performed only where the health or life of the mother is in danger.'[5] Nevertheless, despite Mr Turner's restrictive interpretation of it before Parliament, the bill's wording was generously ambiguous and, once passed into law, would accommodate abortions for a wide spectrum of medical *and* social circumstances.

The 1969 legislation met the disapproval of both sides of the controversy. Anti-abortionists complained that the 'life or health' provision of the law was both vague and expansive, thus giving TACs carte blanche to approve abortions for an unlimited, and perhaps frivolous, range of circumstances. In the subsequent two decades, they would persistently protest that TACs functioned merely to 'rubber-stamp' applications for abortion, and thus rode roughshod over the intent of the legislation.[6] The pro-abortion (or pro-choice) side, conversely, criticized the legislation for not going far enough, for creating a burdensome bureaucratic process that impeded the exercise of women's self-determination. The decision whether or not to complete a pregnancy, they insisted, should properly reside with the pregnant woman alone; anything short of unfettered access to abortion is an unwarranted interference in the life courses of women. In addition, since the 1969 amendment did not compel hospitals to perform abortions, pro-choice advocates, by the early 1970s, were arguing that women in certain parts of the country were ipso facto denied the right of 'reproductive choice.' Their frustration would be further compounded in 1973, when the epochal *Roe* v. *Wade* decision of the American Supreme Court abolished state laws restricting abortion, thereby effectively opening the door in the United States to abortion-on-demand.[7] In comparison with the American case, and in view of the international trend toward 'abortion freedom,' Canada's legislation seemed to pro-choice advocates to be neanderthal and onerous.[8]

Thus, by the early 1970s both sides had staked out a polemical ground which has remained irreconcilably frozen until the present. Pro-life supporters, convinced that abortion under almost any circumstance is an unjustified taking of human life, have argued that the 1969 legislation is too lenient and the 'thin edge of the wedge' for a more widespread societal disrespect for the sanctity of life. As they understand it, liberalized abortion reflects a 'shrinking circle of common human decency' in Western civilization.[9] The pro-choice side, in contrast, has argued that legal restrictions on the availability of abortion serve to perpetuate a traditional pattern of female biological enslavement and socio-cultural subservience.[10]

THE MOVEMENT'S EARLY YEARS

The Canadian pro-life movement originated in response to the 1969 abortion legislation. Actually, the earliest evidence of pro-life activity was in 1967 when a group of Catholic laypeople, principally from Ottawa and Toronto, decided to submit a brief to the Commons Committee on Health and Welfare, which was conducting hearings on the proposed amendment to Section 251 of the Criminal Code. Calling themselves the Emergency Organization for the Defense of Unborn Life, these Catholics appeared before the parliamentary committee on 7 November to argue that a more liberal abortion law would foster an insouciance toward all vulnerable forms of human life and thereby plummet Canada into a 'second Dark Ages.'[11] This earlier group evolved into the Alliance for Life, Canada's first national anti-abortion organization, which was founded in 1968 by Philip Cooper of Ottawa. The fledgling movement multiplied in membership and determination after the Alliance headquarters was moved in 1970 from Ottawa to Toronto, the hub of cultural life and major population centre of English Canada.

In *Abortion and the Politics of Motherhood*, Kristin Luker concludes that the majority of American pro-life activists are housewives who view abortion as a threat to the traditional vocation, and concomitant social prestige, of motherhood.[12] To whatever extent this may be true of the American movement, it is important to recognize the social diversity of Canadian activists, especially in the Canadian movement's incipient years. Pioneer activists in Canada were a roughly equal proportion of men and women, the majority of whom were Catholic and already established in professional careers. Among women holding pivotal leadership roles in the movement's early stages were, for example, the following: a Jewish obstetrician who would become the first woman president of her synagogue; an agnostic graduate student; the first Canadian woman to be ordained a Pentecostal minister; a lapsed Catholic and left-wing social activist; and a Catholic mother, eventually of four children, who was also a lawyer. Outside of their shared commitment to anti-abortion protest, it would be futile to seek a common sociological denominator among these women.

Primary support for the movement in the late 1960s and early 1970s derived in large measure from middle-class Catholic women whose husbands were professionals, most often in law, medicine, or academia, and who were likewise staunchly opposed to abortion. Most of these women were university-educated and mothers of at least three children, and would not have felt free to pursue a career of their own. Involvement in the pro-life movement, which not infrequently consumed as much as forty hours per week, represented for them a meritorious avocation outside of the home, one which was commensurate with their domestic and religious values. These women, in concert with their husbands' professional influence, were the backbone of the movement during its first several years of existence, organizing local right-to-life educational groups in their communities and promoting the pro-life gospel throughout the Catholic parish-school network. Their message was persistent and always clear: besides posing an immediate threat to fetal life, liberalized abortion legislation would inevitably spawn a callousness toward all forms of human life deemed disposable or inconvenient.

The early movement, then, was almost entirely orchestrated by middle-class Catholic laity, of heterogeneous ethnic backgrounds and political beliefs, who saw the abortion issue as simultaneously a moral and social concern of the highest order. Far from discouraging lay initiative on this matter, the Canadian Catholic bishops seemed pleased to be relieved of the responsibility of defending a position that was clearly controversial and socially divisive. Moreover, the movement contained only a sprinkling of clergy and religious, thus confirming at an early date its identity as an essentially lay Catholic enterprise. Partly through coverage of the abortion issue in the secular news media and *The Catholic Register*, a national Catholic weekly, partly through the energetic educational programs of pro-life stalwarts, and, to a lesser extent, because of publicity given the cause via the Sunday pulpit, the movement swelled within Catholic circles in the early 1970s and could count the support of the Knights of Columbus and the Catholic Women's League, as well as a mélange of parochial organizations. Correspondingly, the social spectrum of the movement broadened considerably to include many working-class Catholics as well as Catholic high school and university students.

Despite popular impression, the movement has never been generously financed by the institutional Catholic church. Groups such as the Catholic Women's League, Knights of Columbus, and episcopally administered charities have sporadically channelled modest funds (never exceeding several thousand dollars) into pro-life coffers, but the church's main staple of support for the movement, apart from being a reservoir of potential recruits, has been donations 'in kind.'[13] The movement's Catholic connection has delivered resources such as space and refreshments for meetings, volunteer clerical work performed by high school students, the use of vehicles for transporting literature and educational aids, discounted office space and supplies, and reconditioned office equipment. Thus, despite the lukewarmness of the Canadian hierarchy to the movement, its roots were richly nourished in the parish-school infrastructure of Canadian Catholicism, and as it continued to develop it assumed, quite effortlessly, a distinctly Catholic texture.

The complete autonomy of the movement from the Canadian hierarchy warrants special emphasis, considering that pro-life activists have elsewhere been portrayed as manipulated pawns of Catholic 'prelates,' themselves afflicted with fetal fetishism.[14] New members in the movement were for the greater part either self-recruited or introduced to the anti-abortion cause by family members or friends. Although there is no reason to doubt that the Canadian bishops were, and still are, adamantly opposed to abortion, they very early adopted a hands-off policy toward the movement. The bishops believed, first of all, that the pro-life cause was a lay apostolate that could be managed quite well without their interference and, secondly, they feared that too close an identification of the movement with the official church would constrict its appeal to the larger society.[15] Perhaps the most visible gesture of public support for the cause from the church establishment, at least prior to the 1980s, occurred in March 1976 when Archbishop Pocock of Toronto protested the inclusion of Planned Parenthood, the leading abortion referral agency in the country, as a beneficiary of the annual United Way charity drive. Pocock subsequently withdrew Catholic support from the United Way and instituted Share Life as an independent Catholic charitable foundation.[16]

Just how far removed the Canadian bishops have been from the movement may be comparatively illustrated by observing the prominent activist role played by their American counterparts since the 1973 pro-abortion decision (*Roe* v. *Wade*) of the American Supreme Court. As James Kelly points out, the American bishops have inserted their own internal structures into the right-to-life movement, including the Bishops' Prolife Action Committee which sponsors educational material, and the separately incorporated National Committee for a Human Life Amendment which actively lobbies in support of various pro-life legislation. Through these structures, and also with their 'Respect Life' program, the American bishops have succeeded in giving the pro-life gospel a much higher profile at the parish level than has been the case in Canada.[17] The Canadian bishops did not (nor have they yet to) develop structures remotely equivalent to these, and in the years ahead they would be accused by angry Catholic activists of crossing the line from arm's length support of the pro-life cause to actual desertion of it.

The Alliance for Life was for several years the principal organizational force of the Canadian movement. As the national umbrella for all right-to-life groups, the Alliance was responsible for conducting research, disseminating educational materials, formulating political strategy, and in general co-ordinating the varied activities of the movement's scattered troops. The organization adopted a rotating provincial office system, and was administered nationally by an elected board and a skeletal office staff located in Ottawa, the Alliance's first national seat, and subsequently in Toronto and then Winnipeg. Throughout its checkered history, the Alliance has been funded entirely by affiliation fees and private donations. An Annual General Meeting has provided delegates from right-to-life groups across the country with an opportunity to overview the organization's performance as well as to plot its future course. *Pro-Life News Canada*, a low-key journal still published six times annually by the Alliance, was for several years the movement's most important informational organ.[18]

The first evidence of intra-movement fissure actually occurred several months after the founding of the Alliance, when in November 1968 Louise Summerhill opened the first Birthright pregnancy centre in Toronto. Mrs Summerhill believed that the aggressive political posture of the Alliance distracted attention from the economic and emotional plight of many women facing unplanned pregnancies. Birthright, according to her design, would completely dissociate itself from political lobbying and public controversy and function exclusively as a pregnancy help resource. 'I was convinced that abortion is entirely destructive, but it is so easy to become deeply and emotionally involved in "lobbying" against the legalization of abortion in government, and overlook the humane concern of our opponents for the suffering and despair of distraught pregnant women.'[19]

Undergirded by the feminine-mystical spirituality of its foundress, Birthright has remained both intensely Catholic and apolitical. Its volunteer counsellors are strictly forbidden to discuss contraceptive practice with clients or to share office with right-to-life groups. The total separation that Mrs Summerhill attempted to enforce, as well as her gently autocratic style of leadership, caused some consternation within pro-life ranks. Nevertheless, Birthright stands alone as a success story of the Canadian movement. Besides being the only pro-life organization to receive a favourable review from the Canadian news media,[20] hundreds of Birthright centres have mushroomed throughout North America, all of which are expected to adhere to Mrs Summerhill's philosophy of Catholic altruism.

According to Canadian law, charitable organizations that engage in political lobbying are thereby disqualified from tax-deductible status. Following the 1972 federal election, the Alliance executive, then located in Toronto, decided, in conjunction with the local right-to-life group, to establish a companion organization that would concentrate exclusively on political activities. Thus, in 1973 the Coalition for Life (in 1978 renamed Coalition for the Protection of Human Life) was formed to undertake explicitly political functions such as lobbying, canvassing of politicians, and designing election strategies. Despite the boast of a predominantly Catholic membership, the main driving force behind the Coalition in its inaugural year was an Anglican.[21] The Alliance and Coalition, representing respectively the educational and political arms of the movement, were incorporated separately but worked closely and co-operatively together. The Coalition was likewise organized along the pattern of provincial chapters. This arrangement, however, proved rather spotty; several of its regional chapters were administrative creations with a dearth of popular support, and the organization drew its vigour chiefly from Toronto.

The Coalition possessed an undeniable academic stamp: its architects and most influential members were professors, their spouses, and university students. It very early gained a reputation within the movement's burgeoning grass roots sector as a pro-life 'ivory tower,' an epithet which would haunt the Coalition in the ensuing years of organizational schism. Despite a fairly uniform social base, Coalition leaders had diverse political views and affiliations, though more identified with Canada's left-leaning New Democratic Party (NDP) than with the centrist Liberals or Conservatives. Some Coalitionists in fact attempted to serve as an anti-abortion ginger group within the federal NDP. All Coalitionists were, in any event, refugees from their respective parties on the abortion issue, and would eventually surrender hope of bringing the pro-life position into the mainstream of Canadian politics. By 1986, for example, thoroughly frustrated by the New Democratic Party's continued advocacy of abortion-on-demand, all of the NDP supporters within the Coalition had resigned their memberships in the party.

As the movement continued to expand throughout the 1970s it subtly took on a demographic complexion significantly different from that represented by its mainly urban and professional founders. While its campaigns continued to be co-ordinated from urban centres, the primary engine of pro-life activity was local right-to-life groups whose stronghold was in rural districts and small cities. The congregational principle held sway in these local groups. They were aggressively territorial, protective of their autonomy, and they resisted too close an identification with the Alliance's national office.[22] Moreover, they were populated for the most part by working-class and lower-middle-class housewives for whom abortion was a composite symbol of general cultural decadence as well as a threat to traditional family values. Thus, corresponding to the movement's shifting centre of gravity was the emergence of a new pro-life mentality, one which linked the fight against abortion to a defence of cherished yet beleaguered norms of sexual and family life.

The altered social face of the movement had by the mid-1970s engendered a polarization between its professional elite who preferred to address the abortion issue within a strictly civil rights frame of reference, and its flourishing grass roots supporters for whom anti-abortionism was inextricably a crusade against feminism, secularism, and the rise of moral permissiveness in Canadian society. As the latter became ever more ascendant throughout the 1970s, the movement's more 'progressive' members found themselves increasingly on the defensive with reduced leverage to influence movement ideology or strategy. Perhaps the most telling episode occurred in 1974 when Dr Heather Morris, a well-known Toronto obstetrician respected even beyond pro-life circles for her moderate policies and balanced exposition of the issue, was ousted as Alliance president. Dr Morris had incurred the wrath of many activists for, among other things, refusing to see abortion as the linchpin of a pervasive cultural immorality and showing reluctance to lead the Alliance into a headlong tackle of Planned Parenthood. Planned Parenthood, with its neo-Malthusian ideology, stood together with feminism and homosexuality as a trinity of social evil for grass roots activists. Far from being isolated, this incident was symptomatic of a more far-reaching cleavage which would leave a deep impress upon the movement in subsequent years. Grass roots pro-lifers knew exactly what kind of a movement they wanted, and were fully prepared to savage 'progressives' in positions of leadership who would not oblige their wishes.

A more positive development in 1974 was the publishing debut of *The Uncertified Human*, a monthly newspaper founded on the principle that 'every individual human being has the right to exist and attain human fulfillment.'[23] Under the adroit editorship of Denyse Handler, *The Uncertified Human* (in 1981 renamed *The Human*) would come to represent the harvest of Canadian pro-life reflection. In addition to the standard pro-life trilogy of abortion, euthanasia, and infanticide, it addressed a wide range of human rights questions concerning, among others, the elderly, handicapped, and racial minorities in Canada. The paper's left-of-centre editorial thrust, however, did not suit the taste of most grass roots activists, and it was never able to shed its image as the 'in-house' organ of Toronto's intellectual pro-life faction.

Despite the incestuous turmoil of the previous year, 1975 represented a high-water mark of organization for the movement. Buoyed by the success of a 1973 campaign, in which 350,000 signatures were collected on a petition of protest against legalized abortion, the Alliance organized the Petition of One Million campaign which garnered 1,017,000 signatures. These, along with the brief entitled *Stop the Killing*, were presented to the federal government by MP Ursula Appolloni following a mass rally on Parliament Hill. While this endeavour momentarily bolstered its esprit de corps, it also underscored the movement's political naïvety. Many pro-lifers seriously believed that the ground swell of support reflected by the 1975 petition would lead to a reversal of the 1969 legislation. But given the patently divisive nature of the abortion issue, as well as the impressive clout of the pro-choice forces, it was predictable that the petition would be greeted by respectful political silence. As it turned out, the political dead-end of the 1975 campaign was a watershed in the movement's history, setting the stage for disillusionment, the growth of extremism, and heightened organizational panic.

For its first decade of existence the movement was overwhelmingly Roman Catholic in composition. The thickly Catholic atmosphere of right-to-life groups and an ingrained theological suspicion of political involvement discouraged most Protestant evangelicals from translating their anti-abortion sentiments into activism. By about 1977, however, perhaps emboldened by the dramatic entrance of American evangelicalism into the political theatre, more Canadian evangelicals set aside theological scruples and joined the anti-abortion fray. Some of these started independent pro-life groups, such as Christians Concerned for Life (Calgary), some operated crisis pregnancy centres, and others joined already established right-to-life groups. Evangelicals turned activist belonged to smaller denominations such as the Christian Missionary Alliance, the Pentecostal Assemblies of Canada, the Convention and Fellowship Baptist churches, and the Canadian Reformed Church. The last denomination, not evangelical in the strict sense,[24] would in future years play a role in the movement far disproportionate to its size or influence within the spectrum of Canadian Protestantism. In addition, the Christian Action Council, a consortium of anti-abortion evangelicals which originated in the United States, would, by the late 1970s, make a modest dent in the movement. And finally, Choose Life Canada, an anti-abortion outgrowth of evangelical preacher Ken Campbell's Renaissance Canada ministry, would be launched in 1985 with the purpose of bringing more evangelicals into the pro-life fold.[25]

Still, despite this upsurge of pro-life interest among Canadian evangelicals, the movement would retain its distinctively Catholic stamp. Several factors account for this. 'Fire and brimstone' evangelicalism, especially in its newly politicized American guise, has yet to find a secure niche in the Canadian imagination. Indeed, nothing even passably akin to the American Moral Majority exists in Canada. Canadian evangelicalism is a distinctly minority phenomenon with an underdeveloped tradition of social engagement.[26] It has even been argued that evangelicalism's most lasting contribution to public life in Canada, given its propensity toward stressing the hereafter at the expense of the fleshly present, has been the encouragement of a political illiteracy among its devotees.[27] The doctrine of strict separation between church and state, which has been interwoven into the evangelical fabric, has posed an additional deterrent to the acceptance of a role of political activism. Thus, given evangelicalism's minority social base and heritage of political quiescence, it is not surprising that the Canadian movement has remained predominantly Roman Catholic in membership.

If evangelicals did not significantly change the basic topography of the movement, they nonetheless helped to accentuate its basic line of ideological fissure. Most evangelicals who arrived on the activist scene shared with grass roots Catholic pro-lifers a profound cultural conservatism and also a mistrust of the more liberal Coalitionists.

Of less consequence than evangelicalism for the movement's evolving identity have been Canada's main line Protestant denominations. The Anglican, United, and Presbyterian churches have adopted positions vis-à-vis abortion which, making allowance for minor variation, are alike in tenor: in a less-than-perfect world abortion is at times an imperfect yet permissible response to situations of duress, and though the decision to abort should never be taken lightly, it should reside ultimately in the hands of the pregnant woman.[28] In the early 1970s two denominationally based groups – Anglicans for Life and United Church People for Life – were formed, but neither exerted a significant impact upon the larger movement or upon their respective religious communities. The membership of these groups was always small, and was characterized by a doctrinal conservatism quaintly out of touch with the liberalizing tendencies of their parent denominations. Many of the members of Anglicans for Life converted either to Roman Catholicism or to some variant of evangelicalism, though the group has maintained into the 1980s a prickly presence within Canadian Anglicanism. Most present-day proponents of the pro-life cause from these churches belong to such evangelical wings as the Anglican Renewal Fellowship and the United Church Renewal Fellowship.

Also formed in the early 1970s were sporadic Nurses for Life groups, primarily in response to incidents of conscientious objection at assisting in abortion procedures. Since the mid-1970s, however, hospital administrators have not forced unwilling nurses to participate in abortions, thereby removing the edge from this grievance, and most Nurses for Life groups have been in hiatus. Canadian Physicians for Life was founded in 1975 to function as a pro-life ginger group within the prevalently pro-choice climate of the medical profession. Though this organization has survived into the 1980s with a membership of roughly 1500 mainly Catholic and evangelical doctors, it has maintained a placid profile and avoided public controversy.

THE 1977 COALITION BRIEF

Throughout the early 1970s the anti-abortion movement had been able to contain its different factions and thus maintain at least a semblance of coherency. In 1977, however, the movement's smouldering ideological tensions erupted into an open conflict that would render it fragmented and psychologically scarred.

A renewed public interest in the abortion question was aroused following the release in 1977 of the Badgley Report, which was the fruit of a committee established by the federal government in 1975 to study the operation of the 1969 abortion law. While this study supported the contention of pro-choice advocates that there existed an inequable access to abortion across Canada, it also confirmed several perennial grievances of pro-life activists: first, that a majority of the therapeutic abortions reported by Statistics Canada were justified for vague and mostly dubious reasons of mental health;[29] second, that therapeutic abortion committees in Ontario were in the habit of giving blanket approval to abortion applications; and third, that a minority of hospitals continued to discriminate against medical personnel who had moral qualms about participating in abortion procedures.[30]

In light of these revelations, the Coalition executive, then based in Toronto, wrote a brief intended for presentation to the Ontario Legislature on a day of lobbying scheduled for 27 October 1977. The first of its four recommendations, which addressed the Badgley Report's finding that specious diagnoses of mental health were commonly used to expedite abortions, shocked and scandalized pro-lifers across the country. The offending recommendation read as follows: 'Coalition for Life recommends that a set of guidelines be drawn up to include both serious physical and serious mental illnesses as the only conditions under which abortions may be performed. Such guidelines should include only specific medical conditions such as serious heart conditions, cancer of the cervix, kidney disease, previously diagnosed mental illness or major mental illness for which abortion is therapeutic.'[31]

The intent of this recommendation, which its authors now concede was ambiguous and infelicitously phrased, was to press the Ontario government to specify and enforce strict guidelines for *therapeutic* abortions and thereby significantly to reduce the number of abortions performed in Ontario hospitals. Nevertheless, it brought a flood of indignation from right-to-life groups and Coalition chapters across Canada. Many read the recommendation as a retreat from the established pro-life position that abortion should be permitted only to save the mother's life. In seeming to grant the permissibility of abortions for a much wider range of reasons, it was argued, the Coalition executive had qualified beyond recognition the 'sanctity of life' principle, the first canon of the pro-life movement.

The criticisms were of two kinds. The presidents of a number of pro-life groups offered nuanced arguments against the wording of the first recommendation, suggesting that it was susceptible to misinterpretation and that the brief should reaffirm in precise language the unacceptability of all abortions not undertaken directly to save the mother's life. Others, however, resorted to ad hominem attack, accusing the Coalition executive of duplicity, 'woolly-headedness,' of being 'soft on abortion,' and of negotiating the lives of the unborn with a 'pro-abortion' government. In addition, because the brief had been composed without prior consultation with local pro-life groups, it was claimed that the executive betrayed itself as a snobbish elite indifferent to the concerns of grass roots activists.

Revealingly, many of the criticisms of the second kind were also directed at the brief's fourth recommendation which called for an expansion of such concrete programs of assistance to underprivileged women as subsidized nutritional supplements, increased day care facilities, and low-rental housing. In attempting to address the economic plight of many women facing unplanned pregnancies, the Coalition executive unwittingly touched a nerve of contention which would become increasingly prominent in future years. Many anti-abortionists could only deal with the issue by primitivizing reality – by conceiving abortion in starkly moral terms – and hence were unprepared to analyse the objective, structural conditions of Canadian society that contributed to the escalating abortion rate. The sociological implication of the fourth recommendation, that economic pressures and not merely moral complacency figured in the decisions of some women to acquire abortions, did not fit the tailored world-view of many in the movement. (The brief's second and third recommendations, that the Ontario minister of health monitor the applications approved by TACs and that medical personnel who were conscientious objectors to abortion be protected from discrimination, were generally found acceptable by pro-lifers.)[32]

Taken aback by this negative response, the Coalition executive postponed the lobby to 1 December and amended the brief to emphasize their 'complete opposition to induced abortion' and ultimate goal of changing the Criminal Code 'so that the unborn child will be given the same protection afforded all citizens.'[33] In addition, appended to the first recommendation was the following disclaimer: 'The Coalition for Life does not condone induced abortion. However, we are confident that if the above guidelines are implemented, the vast majority of those abortions currently being performed would be eliminated.'[34] And to further minimize any chance of misinterpretation, it was stressed that the 'Coalition for Life is committed to removing the word "health" from the Criminal Code (Section 251 (4c)), so that unborn children may enjoy the same legal protection as other citizens.'[35]

These clarifications failed to console the brief's detractors, and the Edmonton Coalition group declared it would present a vote of non-confidence in the national executive at the next annual meeting. At this point, the executive attempted to mollify their critics by drafting a third and final version of the brief, in which was reiterated the desirability of at least restricting abortion practice to conformity with the purported intent of the 1969 federal law. Accompanying this final draft, circulated to pro-life groups throughout Ontario, was a statement by Philip Pocock, then archbishop of Toronto, which commended the brief as a 'humanitarian and Christian approach': 'Coalition for Life, while not defending the law, attempts to have our legislators reduce its effect by pleading for the strictest interpretation of the law and for recourse to other alternatives for treating an unwanted pregnancy.'[36]

Despite this high-level endorsement from the Catholic hierarchy, opposition to the brief remained intransigent, and the 1 December lobby of the Ontario Legislature was boycotted by dissident anti-abortion groups.[37] The troubles of the beleaguered Coalition executive were compounded a week later when the Ontario State Board of the Knights of Columbus decided, 'due to Coalition's position expressed in a recent brief ... which compromised the Pro-Life stand that we hold,' to sever all connections with the Coalition, thus depriving the organization of an important source of funding.[38]

The 1977 brief did not engender the movement's internal divisions, but rather presented the opportunity for them to become transparent and more deeply entrenched. The brief was the final stake in the fence dividing the movement because it made vivid the divergent *Weltanschauungen* among pro-life activists. As indicated earlier, Coalition leaders were urban professionals who preferred an irenic and Fabian approach to the issue. As is reflected by the brief, they had no expectation of a dramatic victory on the anti-abortion front; rather, they believed that the political and cultural realities of Canadian society dictated a protracted campaign based on scoring modest political successes and slowly making a dent in public opinion. They thought of strategy in terms of the art of the possible; rather than quixotically striving to create in one fell swoop an abortion-free society, and finding as a result nothing to show for their efforts but purity of intention, they set themselves limited and proximate goals.

What Coalitionists regarded as a pragmatic, gradualist approach was interpreted by the movement's grass roots sector as equivocation and compromise on the part of intellectuals afraid to stick their necks out for the unborn. Grass roots pro-lifers demanded a brook-no-compromise strategy that would make no concession either to popular taste or to considerations of political expediency. In their view, the Coalitionist strategy was one of appeasement, of sacrificing the absolutist pro-life ethic at the altar of secularism in the hope of winning greater public support for the anti-abortion cause. Rather than seeking merely to lower the abortion rate, they insisted, it was imperative that the movement speak the unvarnished, unexceptionable truth: all abortions not undertaken directly to save the life of the mother ought to be outlawed.

Coalitionists believed that the movement was destined for political impotency unless it attempted to communicate in measured tones with the ambivalent, unconverted sectors of Canadian society. The 'middle ground,' they argued, would not be captured, and indeed would be alienated, by an unflinching, doctrinaire rhetoric. The 'middle ground' is, in fact, the place where the majority of Canadians may be found on the abortion issue. Most surveys from 1967 onward reveal, with only minor variation, that most Canadians approve of legal abortion on selective grounds, and that only a minority endorse either the pro-life or pro-choice position. Gallup polls taken on abortion in 1975, 1978, and 1983 found that only approximately 20 per cent of Canadians favour making abortion legal under any circumstances, and only roughly 16 per cent favour making it illegal under all circumstances.[39] Whereas the majority of Canadians think that a pregnant woman should have the option of a legal abortion in situations involving a serious birth defect, rape, or danger to her health, support for legal abortion drops significantly when the reasons are economic or related to life-style. (It is interesting to note that more male than female survey respondents favour abortion on request.) A. Romaniuc summarizes the survey results: 'A majority of the public supports legalization of abortion on selective grounds. The following grounds appear in descending order in most surveys: danger to the mother's life, danger to the mother's health, the risk of child deformity and pregnancy as a result of rape. But public acceptance of abortion undergoes a rapid attrition if economic circumstances or other personal motives are invoked. Finally, those who favour the idea of rendering abortion legal on any grounds form only a minority of public opinion, as do those who reject it on any grounds.'[40] The Coalition executive thought that its 1977 brief would resonate favourably with mainstream public opinion, and would thus stand a good chance of receiving a fair political hearing. Its opponents were concerned not with public opinion but with truth.

This conflict over strategy between *pragmatists* and *purists* was the most manifest cause of the movement's widening rift. What it in fact revealed was that activists were approaching the abortion issue from contrary directions. For grass roots Catholics and evangelicals, who had become numerically ascendant when the movement assumed populist proportions, relaxed abortion legislation was the death rale of Canadian society. Mannheim has observed the pronounced tendency among conservatives to view society as an organism which, accordingly, may be diagnosed as either 'healthy' or 'sick.'[41] The reality of legal abortion meant to grass roots activists that Canadian society was thoroughly diseased. And the Coalition brief seemed to them to be like a doctor recommending cosmetic surgery when only a massive transfusion could hope to save the patient's life. In contrast to this 'tip-of-the-iceberg' mentality, where abortion is a metaphor for widespread social decay, the Coalitionists attributed liberalized abortion to a lack of public knowledge regarding the nature of intra-uterine life. In this perspective, what is to be overcome is not a basic moral defect in the larger society, but a 'zone of ignorance' which has denied the unborn due recognition as members of humanity. Coalitionists, thus, believed that education, coupled with improved social assistance for pregnant women, would gradually inculcate in the wider society an appreciation of, and corresponding commitment to protect, fetal life.

Activists who gravitated to the Coalition, and particularly its echelon of leadership, tended to be intellectuals who were comfortable with most aspects of contemporary urban life. They felt no urge to be drawn into the invective against feminism, sexual permissiveness, and secularism that was the standard rhetorical fare of grass roots activists. As a fundamental violation of human rights, they preferred to argue, abortion contradicts the best impulses of modern society for justice and equality. The 1977 brief confirmed to many grass roots pro-lifers that Coalitionists inhabited a social world strikingly different from their own. They could not accept the sincerity or legitimacy of an anti-abortion position that failed to include anti-feminism and anti-secularism as part of its ideological package. Abortion was viewed by the grass roots sector as one of a constellation of causally related issues: the reluctance of Coalitionists to deal with the issue on these terms was attributed to a combination of *mauvaise foi* and intellectual 'fuzzy-headedness.'[42] The desire of Coalitionists to cultivate for the movement a reputation for reasonableness and moderation was thus viewed with contempt by those in the movement who longed to clash openly with what they were convinced was an evil establishment.

To a large extent, these competing 'definitions of the situation'[43] correspond to the distinction raised by Neil Smelser between reform (or 'norm-oriented') and revolutionary (or 'value-oriented') movements.[44] Whereas the liberal Catholics saw abortion as a discrete social problem that could, hopefully, be resolved by piecemeal political and educational reforms, their opponents believed that the existing social order was itself in need of radical transformation. What was then not readily evident, but would become so by the close of the decade, was that some of the Coalition's most vociferous critics were fervent Catholics who had invested pro-life activism with apocalyptic meaning. They were not simply concerned, as were Coalitionists, with winning the issue, but also with playing out a personal drama of salvation. They could afford to take an all-or-nothing approach to the matter because in their minds the abortion issue superseded politics. What it signified was the eternal conflict between Good and Evil. Anti-abortionism was foremost for them a religious crusade, only secondarily a political project. And as is characteristic of crusaders, they felt called 'to defeat an evil, not merely to solve a social problem.'[45] Against such virtue the Coalitionists could not hope to compete.

THE BIRTH OF CAMPAIGN LIFE

Dissatisfaction with the Coalition had actually been brewing for over a year prior to the 1977 brief. Common and partly justifiable complaints were that the Coalition leadership lacked the requisite administrative skills to make the organization financially viable, that it had failed to implement a fully national political strategy, that it was overly contemplative and thus remiss in translating plans into action, and that as a coterie of (mainly Toronto-based) intellectuals it was arrogantly out of touch with the movement's prevailing grass roots sentiments. Signs of schism had become visible in the autumn of 1977 when the Western Regional Coalition for Life was formed to coordinate strategy in the four western provinces for the 1978 federal election.[46] Though ostensibly intended to work in concert with the national Coalition, this regional group very early exhibited a separatist inclination.

In November 1977, Paul Formby, a former union organizer turned Catholic seminarian, began work for the national Coalition, presumably for the purpose of galvanizing pro-life support across the country in preparation for the upcoming federal election. Almost immediately, however, he joined forces with those who were accusing the Coalition's national executive of ideological laxity to form a new anti-abortion political organization. Unveiled in Toronto on 26 February 1978, Campaign Life advertised itself as the only authentic political voice of Canadian pro-lifers, and denounced the Coalition as an anti-abortion halfway house for phlegmatic intellectuals. Campaign Life gained strongholds in southwestern and northern Ontario, the Metropolitan Toronto area, and the three westernmost provinces where it absorbed the Western Regional Coalition for Life. Though severely weakened by the success of its new rival, the Coalition was able to maintain a national identity, with solid chapters in Quebec, the Maritimes, and Manitoba.

The establishment of Campaign Life gave solid organizational shape to the movement's ideological dichotomy. It also meant that the Coalition, divested of much of its former influence, would be consigned a spectator role as the movement plunged more deeply into a one-dimensional conservatism. In both its understanding of the abortion issue and its modus operandi, Campaign Life was the antithesis of the

Coalition: confrontational, politically absolutist, and unrepentantly hostile to post-1950s Canadian culture. Considered self-condemned by the 1977 brief, the Coalition lost over the next few years the support of many right-to-life groups, including Canada's flagship pro-life group in Toronto which elected in March 1978 to align itself with the proven orthodoxy of Campaign Life. Relations between the respective executives of the Coalition and the Alliance for Life, the national umbrella for right-to-life groups, systematically deteriorated to the point where the latter decided in April 1978 to completely dissociate from the Coalition and to ban Coalitionists from the Alliance's Toronto headquarters. Since the two executives occupied adjoining suites in the same office building, this act of shunning was not easily carried off.[47] Moreover, zealots on the Alliance executive undertook a witch-hunt in order to purge the organization of Coalition sympathizers.

An additional factor implicit in this power struggle may be described as a clash of female leadership models. Women who played key activist roles in the Coalition tended to adhere to a business-oriented model: they valued efficiency, palpable achievements, and teamwork. Moreover, most of them had no more than two children and were combining anti-abortion activism with a professional career. As the movement became heavily populated in the mid-1970s with conservative Catholic and Protestant women who were committed to a traditional domestic role, abortion increasingly came to be viewed as a life-style issue, as a contest between the competing definitions of womanhood afforded by motherhood and careerism. Feminism was vilified by rank-and-file activists as an ideology which, under the guise of a liberationist rhetoric, promotes female egocentricity, disdain for traditional family values, and a self-interested moral relativism. Within this context leading Coalitionist women were a discomfiting anomaly; despite professions of anti-abortionism, their life-style and social disposition suggested that they had one foot in the enemy camp and hence could not be trusted. Moreover, the Coalition leadership was friendly with the editorial staff of *The Uncertified Human*, the feminist-coloured paper which aspired to integrate the anti-abortion cause with a critical ethic of social change. All of this chafed those – by this point a commanding majority – who sought to make the movement coextensive with a mentality at enmity with the modern world. Perhaps revealing in this regard is that the three women most dedicated to the campaign to discredit the

Coalition would, in the 1980s, play prominent roles in founding two ultra-conservative, anti-feminist organizations: Women for Life, Faith, and Family; and REAL Women of Canada.

In 1977–8 two successive executive directors of the Coalition, both professional women, resigned their positions after feeling the brunt of grass roots resentment and perhaps realizing that many activists would accept female leadership only from a Catholic mother of six. Thus was established a pattern that would become familiar over the next several years: women (and also sometimes men) suspected of pro-life heterodoxy were hounded from positions of leadership and their roles were filled by people of an acceptably conservative stamp. In weeding itself of its impure moderates, the movement threatened to lapse into entropy.

Despite overtures of reconciliation from the Coalition executive, a ceasefire was not forthcoming and toward the close of 1978 both sides were predisposed to think the worst of each other.[48] All Coalition people who had a hand in the 1977 brief are regarded even to the present by the movement's conservative majority as personae non gratae and of doubtful pro-life credentials.

The movement's penchant for masochism, however, was still not quite spent. In 1979 a rupture in the Alliance for Life caused its frayed threads of unity to come completely undone. The few surviving moderates on the Alliance's Toronto-based board rebelled against the organization's incumbent president, claiming that her 'dictatorial and paranoid' style of leadership had become insufferable and, if left unchecked, would bring the Alliance to self-strangulation. The ensuing constitutional crisis, which resulted in the president's eviction from office, consummated the process of polarization which had been underway since the early 1970s. The powerful Toronto right-to-life group, as well as neighbouring groups in Halton, Barrie, and elsewhere, seceded from the Alliance in a demonstration of allegiance to the deposed president and her right-wing policies. Thus, by the end of 1979 the balkanized movement consisted of the following configurations: a quasi-national educational organization enervated by three years of internal jousting (the Alliance); a dispirited political organization in process of relocating its national office from Toronto to Ottawa (the Coalition); and a maverick Toronto right-to-life group which, together with its affiliated groups and the fiercely energetic

Campaign Life, would effectively set the tone of the movement for the next seven years.

The Alliance national office was moved to Winnipeg in 1979, explicitly to break the hold of the embroiled Toronto executive. The move was also an attempt by moderates in the Alliance to stem the reactionary tide in Toronto that threatened to engulf the organization. In deserting the media centre and cultural capital of English Canada, however, the Alliance would lose much of its former dynamism and become reduced to basically a regional organization. More significantly, the removal of the Alliance and Coalition national offices from Toronto – the epicentre of anti-abortionism in Canada – meant that Campaign Life would have the field to itself as the temperature of the abortion debate rose dramatically in the 1980s. The separatism of the Toronto right-to-life group, as well as the rise to dominance of Campaign Life, was like a bisection of the movement's brain into right and left hemispheres. On the one side were Coalition for Life people and moderates within the Alliance, sensitive, bright, nuanced, but with limited will and drive; on the other were the activists represented by Toronto right-to-life and Campaign Life, mountains of will and drive, but unsophisticated, obstinate, and inflexible.

Virtually the same conflicts that preoccupied the Canadian movement throughout the 1970s have been replayed south of the border. James Kelly's study of the American pro-life movement shows that it too has been faced with persistent disputes among its centralizing agencies and grass roots organizations, fractionation, conflictual claims for leadership, and tension between ideological purity and political realism.[49] The factor that perhaps enhanced, or aggravated, these conflicts in Canada is the suspicion that most Canadians seem naturally to feel for anything, in this case the Coalition, that comes out of Toronto.

A decisive difference between the two movements, however, has been the role played in each of them by the institutional Catholic church. Whereas the American bishops responded to *Roe* v. *Wade* with uninhibited activism, and in fact greatly facilitated the development of an organized anti-abortion front, the Canadian bishops have left the movement entirely to its own devices. By the late 1970s certain segments of the Canadian movement were in fact fully convinced that the Catholic bishops were traitors to the anti-abortion cause. The following chapter interrupts the historical narrative for the purpose of examining the specific role played by the Canadian hierarchy in the national abortion debate of the 1960s and 1970s.

2

The Catholic Bishops and the Abortion Issue

That the Canadian bishops are at best tepid in their support of the pro-life cause, and at worst traitors to it, has become an established belief within Catholic anti-abortion circles. It is a belief into which new recruits to the movement are solidly socialized and one that has acquired more the feeling of certainty with each passing year. While it partly reflects the frustration of a movement seemingly doomed to political marginality, and thus desperate for a scapegoat, it would not have survived so long without a prima facie plausibility. In order to trace the genesis of this belief, and therefore to appreciate the bitterness felt by many Catholic pro-lifers toward the Canadian church hierarchy, it is necessary to backtrack to the 1960s, when the bishops themselves were confronted with the formal secularization of Canadian political culture.

SACRED LAW AND CIVIL LAW

In 1966, from 1 March until 28 April, the House of Commons Standing Committee on Health and Welfare held public hearings to determine whether or not the legal prohibition against contraceptives, found under Article 150 of the Criminal Code, should be repealed.[1] In October 1966, six months after the close of the hearings, the Canadian bishops submitted a brief to the Committee which announced that they would not oppose the legalization of contraceptives.[2] The existing law, the bishops said, was incapable of enforcement and thus injurious to the common good.[3]

In their October brief the bishops attempted to clarify the 'distinction between Catholic teaching and the attitude of the church towards legislation in a pluralistic society' such as Canada.[4] They accorded explicit recognition to the autonomy of the political sphere and emphasized the ill-advisability of facilely attempting to translate moral law into civil laws. 'That which the Church teaches to be morally reprehensible should not necessarily be considered as indictable by the criminal code of a country.'[5]

The bishops, furthermore, asserted that Catholic legislators are not bound to vote only for laws that are in conformity with the teaching of the church. While responsibly acknowledging their dual obligations as members of both the church and the civil community, Catholic legislators 'should not stand idly by waiting for the Church to tell [them] what to do in the political order.'[6] Matters of politics, the bishops continued, are properly the jurisdiction of the laity, and while the Catholic legislator should be cognizant of what the church teaches on a subject such as contraception, his 'ultimate responsible conclusions are his own as he fulfills the task he has along with all other legislators.'[7] This principle of the self-responsibility of the laity in the temporal sphere, the bishops advised, has been explicitly affirmed in Vatican II's *Decree on the Apostolate of the Laity*. Here the church teaches that '[Lay Catholics] must co-operate with other citizens, using their own particular skills and acting on their own responsibility.'[8] Thus, concluded the bishops, the rights and duties of Catholic legislators in Canada are oriented toward the common good and 'do not flow from the fact that [legislators] belong to the Church.'[9]

The bishops stressed that their decision not to oppose a change in the law on contraceptives should not be construed as a tacit approval of 'all methods of regulation of births.'[10] Rather, it stemmed from their view of the inadequacy of the existing law, a view which had been arrived at 'independently of the morality or immorality of various methods of birth prevention.'[11]

This distinction made by the bishops between civil and moral law, and the prudential separation of the two in a pluralistic society, was given even clearer expression in the press release which heralded the submission of their brief: 'The question that may come before Parliament is not whether the use of contraceptives is morally right or morally wrong. It is not up to Parliament to decide such a question.'[12] The bishops did warn, however, that they would perceive the matter quite differently if the question under consideration were abortion. 'It is our clear understanding, of course, that the modification of the law in question is not to extend to that part of it which has to do with abortion. For our conclusions would be quite different were there question of such direct destruction of human life.'[13]

The principles rehearsed in the October brief – that what is forbidden by the church should not necessarily be forbidden by civil law, that the Catholic legislator should follow his or her individual conscience in respect to the formulation of public law, and that politics is the proper purview of the laity – also provided the framework of a statement issued by the bishops in April 1967 on the subject of proposed changes to Canada's divorce law. In this statement, addressed to the Special Joint Committee of the Senate and the House of Commons on Divorce, the bishops reaffirmed the Catholic position on the indissolubility of marriage, and also acknowledged the impossibility in a pluralistic society of enforcing the Catholic marital ideal as a public norm. 'Canada is a country of many religious beliefs. Since other citizens, desiring as we do the promotion of the common good, believe that it is less injurious to the individual and to society that divorce be permitted in certain circumstances, we would not object to some revision of Canadian divorce laws that is truly directed to advancing the common good of civil society.'[14] Thus, concluded the bishops, Catholics could tolerate, 'out of respect for freedom of conscience,' a relaxation of Canadian legal codes pertaining to marriage.[15]

Affecting as they did sensitive areas of family and sexual life, areas traditionally close to the heart of Catholic ethical thinking, the proposed revisions to the Canadian Criminal Code forced the bishops to show their political hand. They were expected to make some kind of response, and the Toronto *Globe and Mail* was not alone in awaiting it as a test of the bishops' Canadianism.[16] Would the bishops place their religious beliefs above Canada's pluralistic ideal, or would they give Catholic politicians free rein to make laws strictly on their presumed social merit? In acknowledging the inapplicability of Catholic moral principles to the political process, the bishops passed this initial test. They had suitably recognized that the Canada of the 1960s was happy to grant Catholic bishops the right to pious opinion, but not political influence.

In conceding the diminished social significance of religious values and practices, Catholic or otherwise, in contemporary Canada, these two episcopal statements reflected 'the steady process of secularization' which, according to John Webster Grant, has permeated the Canadian national consciousness in the post-World War II years.[17] The banishment of religion to the private sphere, and the corresponding disenchantment of Canadian political culture, is a stark contrast to an earlier era, Grant reminisces, 'when religion was a major and even decisive factor in the lives of Canadian individuals and communities.'[18] The new secular vision of Canada, to which the bishops had tacitly deferred, was given ceremonial expression on 15 December 1967 when Pierre Trudeau, then federal minister of justice, addressed Parliament at the second reading of the bill to widen grounds for divorce: 'We are now living in a social climate in which people are beginning to realize, perhaps for the first time in the history of this country, that we are not entitled to impose the concepts which belong to a sacred society upon a civil or profane society. The concepts of a civil society in which we live are pluralistic and I think ... it would be a mistake for us to legislate into this society concepts which belong to a theological or sacred order.'[19]

That the bishops accepted and, in a certain sense, anticipated the thrust of Mr Trudeau's remarks regarding the separation of church and state is not surprising in light of Canadian Catholicism's well-adjusted denominational character. As Andrew Greeley has pointed out, Canada is one of only a few countries in the Western world to have a tradition of denominational pluralism.[20] Partly because it has never enjoyed the privilege of formal establishment, the English-speaking church in the post-confederation era has seldom been tempted to indulge a specifically Catholic theocratic vision for Canada. Moreover, with at most a sporadic tradition of anti-Catholicism, Canada has been a congenial territory for the church's expansion and regional consolidation. Despite occasional turbulence, usually generated by debates over the legal status of Catholic schools, the church has been confident that it shares a common language and sense of national purpose with other denominations and with Canadians generally.

The 1950s and 1960s were a time when English-speaking Catholics joined with most Canadians in celebrating the 'good life' of Canadian democracy, civility, and ordered affluence.[21] Though they likely had reservations about the proposed changes to the laws governing contraceptives and divorce, the bishops were understandably reluctant to drive a partisan wedge into this national spirit of optimism and progress. Moreover, the new era of secular emancipation proclaimed by Trudeau likely struck some bishops as a natural stage of Canada's evolution from a Protestant dominion to a multicultural mosaic.[22] The church had in the past been a beneficiary of this momentum toward greater pluralism and toleration, and there seemed little reason to greet the Trudeau manifesto with consternation.

But there is an additional factor behind the conciliatory stance adopted by the bishops on the matters of contraceptives and divorce. The 1960s were exhilarating for Canadian Catholics, as the Second Vatican Council seemed to herald an unprecedented openness of the church to those parts of the world unconverted by or untouched by Rome. It was at this time also that Canada attained a new and more confident sense of national purpose, and the country no doubt appeared to some bishops as an ideal laboratory for implementing the rapprochement with the modern world which seemed to be suggested by the council. The bishops clearly had no desire to puncture this mood of ecumenical freshness by resurrecting the spectre of triumphalism, and thus their statements on contraceptives and divorce were marked by deferential caution. This point is ruefully noted by Alphonse de Valk, the foremost Catholic critic of the bishops' approach to the Canadian political process, who characterizes the 'spirit of optimism' at the end of Vatican II as 'a spirit marked by a desire to turn over a new leaf and abandon old ways, to seek harmony both within the Church and without, especially with the newly discovered "separated brethren", a spirit marked by a willingness on the part of Catholics to sacrifice or temporarily forego legitimate points of their own in order to meet others more than half way, not only in Church affairs but also in political-legal affairs.'[23]

The questions of contraception and divorce, however, were far easier to submit to the court of ethical pluralism than would be abortion. And yet reform of Canada's abortion law was next on the parliamentary agenda. By calling into question the very meaning of humanity and sexuality, abortion cuts to the nerve of Catholic cosmology, and thus the proposed amendment to legalize abortion posed a quandary for the Catholic bishops. Although they clearly found abortion abhorrent, they could not directly – qua Catholic bishops – oppose legalization without straining the political code of conduct they had set themselves in the brief on contraception.

The *Globe and Mail* was quick to point out that the separation of civil and moral law earlier recommended by the bishops was a formula that should also be applied to the question of abortion.[24] And in a later editorial, the *Globe and Mail* contended that in cases of conflicting moralities, the 'State should ... leave the choice to individual conscience.'[25] The prevailing attitude of Canada's mainstream Protestant churches regarding the conflict between Catholic belief and abortion law reform was tersely summarized in the Anglican monthly *Canadian Churchman*: 'In the area of abortion, contraception and homosexuality the choice is government by the individual's conscience. If his church is opposed then he has a moral obligation to obey his church's rules but he has no right to impose these rules on people of other faiths or no faith at all. There is a clear distinction between moral and civil law.'[26]

The gravity with which the Catholic bishops viewed abortion was demonstrated by their pastoral letter of 7 February 1968, over one month after the draft amendment which would liberalize Canada's abortion law had been introduced in the House of Commons.[27] The Catholic church as recently as Vatican II, the bishops wrote, has reaffirmed its traditional condemnation of infanticide and abortion as 'unspeakable crimes.'[28] Moreover, they continued, the biblical interdict against killing necessarily supersedes laws that would contradict it. 'It is clear that this commandment of God obliges in conscience, no matter what legislation may be in force in a country.'[29] Progress in civilization, the bishops exhorted, 'consists in the increasingly clear recognition of the dignity, sacredness and absolute inviolability of the human person, on both the theoretical and practical levels.'[30]

On 5 March 1968 a delegation from the Canadian Catholic Conference (CCC), led by Bishop Remi De Roo of Victoria, BC, appeared before the Parliamentary Committee responsible for reviewing the abortion law. The CCC's presentation, at once firm and deferential, established the characteristic tone for all subsequent statements by the Canadian hierarchy on the subject of abortion. Bishop De Roo's opening remarks stressed that the delegation had come 'in a spirit of dialogue' and did not want 'to impose a particular point of view' upon a 'complex and difficult question.'[31] The bishops' profound concern with the proposed abortion legislation, explained the Reverend E.F. Sheridan, SJ, stemmed from their conviction that it was 'a bad law ... that introduces ... a fundamental disrespect for life' and thus militates against 'the common good.'[32] And far from intending to obfuscate the distinction between divine law and civil law, Fr Sheridan concluded, the bishops respected the autonomy of the political sphere and did 'not believe that our moral principle must be enshrined in criminal law.'[33]

The *Globe and Mail* responded to the CCC's presentation by denouncing the bishops for ecclesiastical meddling. 'The bishops are now opposing abortion reform not because it threatens public order or the common good. They oppose it on essentially moral and theological grounds. Their imposition of Catholic morality and dogma on the rest of Canada is incompatible with their own distinction between moral and civil law ... At stake here is ... a certain high conception of liberal democracy. That means a tolerant respect for the conscience of all – not just the consciences of the most dogmatic.'[34]

In their March 1968 presentation the bishops tried to strike a balance between their obligations as Catholic pastors and their responsibilities as citizens in a pluralistic democracy. Clearly, they did not desire to convey an impression of moral superiority or of contempt toward attitudes on abortion at variance with their own. Nor did they wish the abortion issue to become a deep communal fission that would jeopardize Canada's denominational equilibrium. When the legal grounds for abortion were broadened by the 1969 amendment to the Criminal Code, however, the bishops were vulnerable to the charge of delinquency which would be made repeatedly over the ensuing years by Catholic pro-lifers. In expressing sentiments shared by many Catholic activists, for example, Fr Alphonse de Valk chastises the bishops for submissiveness and failure to intervene more directly in the political process. 'The post–Vatican II spirit ... of optimism, harmony and goodwill, of being the first to make concessions wherever possible, of being the first to make a gesture of reconciliation, was too pervasive and too dominant even for the issue of abortion to disturb it.'[35]

The distinction articulated by the bishops between moral and civil law, de Valk concedes, was motivated by a sincere and honourable respect for Canadian democracy and the diversity of ethical views that inevitably exist in a heterogeneous society. But, he argues, the bishops misplayed this distinction into the hands of cultural elites who advocated the total secularization of Canadian society and, concomitantly, the total withdrawal of the Catholic church from the political forum. Thus, apologetic and defensive at the hour of decision, the bishops offered 'no prophetic stand,' but instead stood by meekly as the 'legalization of abortion was introduced, defended and pushed through by a heavily Catholic party, thereby making Canada the only country in the world where Catholics bear this responsibility.'[36] The price paid by the bishops for their irenic approach to the Canadian political process, bemoans de Valk, has been the relegation of Catholic moral principles to a sectarian, socially irrelevant backwater. 'Let us ask once more: why did the Bishops withdraw their opposition to legalizing contraceptives and widening the grounds for divorce, and why did many Catholics do the same to abortion? Answer: because they had come to accept, willingly or unwillingly, consciously or unconsciously, what was being hammered into their heads by the secular media and a wide variety of spokesmen and women for the new ethic, namely, that opposition in these matters was purely theological and denominational, in short, for Catholics only.'[37]

There is merit to de Valk's suggestion that the state of ferment induced by Vatican II contributed to the bishops' tentativeness. As a pastoral council dedicated in large measure to clarifying the relationship of the church to the modern world, Vatican II signalled a dramatic break from the church's long record of clericalism and triumphalism. Thus, for example, the *Pastoral Constitution on the Church in the Modern World (Gaudium et Spes)* included a section on 'The Life of the Political Community' that was patently influential in the reflections of the Canadian bishops upon the autonomy of the political order, the special responsibilities of the laity in the 'earthly city,' and the distinctive provinces of church and state. On the latter topic, *Gaudium et Spes* taught that 'It is highly important, especially in pluralistic societies, that a proper view exist of the relation between the political community and the Church. Thus the faithful will be able to make a clear distinction between what a Christian conscience leads them to do in their own name as citizens, whether as individuals or in association, and what they do in the name of the Church and in union with her shepherds ... In their proper spheres, the political community and the Church are mutually independent and self-governing.'[38]

The Canadian bishops were no doubt similarly mindful of Vatican II's *Declaration on Religious Liberty* which, in stark contrast to Pius IX's *Syllabus of Errors* a century earlier, affirmed the inherent dignity of women and men and their right to pursue truth free of external coercion, even at the expense of falling into error.[39] To someone like Fr de Valk, whose views are representative of many Catholic pro-lifers, the application of these teachings by the Canadian bishops to the questions of contraception and divorce was at least pardonable, if not an occasion for applause. But when it came to the matter of abortion, where 'the supreme values of life are at stake,'[40] many Catholic activists expected from their bishops nothing less than an implacable campaign for truth. In a country where in 1969 almost half the population professed membership in the Catholic church and the governing Liberal party was composed predominantly of Catholics, they reasoned, the bishops should have been able to mount sufficient electoral pressure to prevent passage of the law.[41] That they failed to do so, it was surmised, indicated the extent to which the Canadian hierarchy had capitulated to the secularizing agenda of pro-choice supporters.

Their March 1968 Ottawa presentation would not be the bishops' last word on the subject. On 5 December 1968 the Executive Committee of the CCC released a tough-minded statement which emphasized that 'abortion cannot be taken as a purely personal and private question, as if another person's right to life were not involved.' In addition, the bishops reminded Canadian Catholics that 'they must follow the teaching of the Church [on abortion] no matter what the law may be in a pluralistic society.'[42] Again, in a further statement issued on 9 October 1970, the bishops tried to settle all doubt as to where they stood on the matter. After describing abortion as 'a most grievous moral wrong [that] involves the ending of developing human life,' they wrote that 'No matter what the civil law may say, to procure an abortion is to be involved in an act that is objectively evil from a moral point of view.'[43]

These statements, however, did not quell the disgruntlement that had become commonplace among Catholic pro-lifers. The bishops were accused of engaging in an ex post facto damage control, trying to mitigate the consequences of the 1969 legislation without bringing embarrassment to themselves or divisiveness to the larger Canadian community. Some activists, notably those who would later form the

Coalition, were sympathetic to the inherent difficulty of translating absolute moral disapprobation of abortion into language that would bear some credibility in a secular social environment, and were thus able to maintain cordial relations with the bishops. But by the early 1970s a pattern of mutual mistrust between the Canadian hierarchy and the movement as a whole was already firmly established. The majority of activists were convinced that the bishops' anti-abortion commitment was limited to what the traffic would bear, and that the future of the movement belonged to lay Catholics who would be foolish to count on the support of the church hierarchy in moments of political crunch. Conversely, by seeming not to appreciate the sensitive nature of church-state relations, certain segments of the fledgling movement gained among the bishops a lasting reputation for obtuseness.

THE CANADIAN BISHOPS AND HUMANAE VITAE

It is impossible to understand the spiral of discord between the bishops and the anti-abortion movement apart from the controversy which erupted in the Canadian church following the publication of *Humanae Vitae* in July 1968. Paul VI's anti-contraceptive encyclical fell like an anvil upon many Canadian Catholics who had fully expected a softening of the church's traditional sexual discipline. A chain-reaction of protest against the encyclical, spearheaded by academics and clergy, spread immediately across the country.[44] In an obvious effort to render *Humanae Vitae* as palatable as possible to Canadian Catholics, and thus to avert a potential ground swell of dissent against it, the bishops devoted a week-long study session to the topic in Winnipeg during September 1968. The *Winnipeg Statement*, the product of this session, ambivalently exhorted Canadian Catholics to conform to the mind of Rome on the matter of contraceptives, but to also follow the dictates of their own consciences. While declaring their 'accord with the teaching of the Holy Father,' the bishops also advised that 'Whoever honestly chooses that course which seems right to him does so in good conscience.'[45] In other words, the bishops presented *Humanae Vitae* as an ideal rather than a binding requirement for Catholic sexual conduct.

The response among Canadian Catholics to the *Winnipeg Statement* was mixed. It was harshly criticized by some for presumably diluting the force of *Humanae Vitae* and for severing the responsibilities of conscience from the teaching authority of the church.[46] From most quarters, however, the *Winnipeg Statement* was applauded both as pastorally sound and as a progressive adventure in the evolving collegial role of the Canadian church.[47]

Concerned that the *Winnipeg Statement* had been taken by some as an outright endorsement for dissent from *Humanae Vitae*, the bishops in April 1969 issued a 'clarifying statement' which emphasized that their teaching on freedom of conscience was not meant to exempt Catholics from the burden of obedience to the Magisterium. *Humanae Vitae*, the bishops advised, though not formally defined as infallible by an *ex cathedra* exercise of the extraordinary magisterium, should nevertheless command the deepest respect of the faithful. 'It is false and dangerous to maintain that because this encyclical has not demanded the absolute assent of faith (n. 14), any Catholic may put it aside as if it had never appeared.'[48] The bishops moved toward even greater clarification five years later when, in *A Statement on the Formation of Conscience* (1 December 1973), they argued that the *authentic* Catholic conscience is guilty neither of an 'exaggerated subjectivism' nor a denial of the 'personal acceptance of moral responsibility.' In alluding cryptically to the controversy surrounding *Humanae Vitae*, the bishops wrote that ' "To follow one's conscience" and to remain a Catholic, one must take into account first and foremost the teaching of the magisterium. When doubt arises due to a conflict of "my" views and those of the magisterium, the presumption of truth lies on the part of the magisterium.'[49]

Catholic pro-lifers in the late 1960s and early 1970s were too engrossed in the subject of Canada's new abortion law to be overly concerned with the reception accorded *Humanae Vitae* by the Canadian bishops. Moreover, most activists at this stage still regarded abortion and contraception as unrelated issues. The *Winnipeg Statement*, however, had a delayed effect upon the movement's consciousness and would several years afterward be deployed as corroborating evidence of the bishops' 'failure of nerve' on the anti-abortion front. A combination of circumstances caused this to be so.

First, faced in the mid-1970s by steadily increasing abortion rates as well as rock-ribbed support for the pro-choice ethic among cultural elites in the media, legal and medical professions, and academia, anti-abortionists were no longer able to regard the trend toward liberalized abortion as a historical aberration or as an episode of madness that could be easily dispelled. Thus, many activists became concerned with understanding the cultural sources of changed attitudes toward abortion. How did something that to past generations seemed self-evidently wrong suddenly achieve the status of a right and even at times a moral good?

By the mid to late 1970s the 'contraceptive mentality' thesis was being adduced by more and more Catholic activists as the master explanation for this revolutionary shift in attitudes toward abortion. Donald DeMarco, the leading exponent of the thesis in Canada, reasons that the dissociation of intercourse from conception has been the primary cultural engine behind increased public acceptance of abortion. 'The "contraceptive mentality" results when this separation of intercourse from procreation is taken for granted and the contracepting partners feel that in employing contraception, they have severed themselves from all responsibility for a conception that might take place as a result of contraceptive failure ... At any rate, the "contraceptive mentality" implies that a couple has not only the means to separate intercourse from procreation, but the right or *responsibility* as well.'[50]

Although conventional wisdom holds that wider contraceptive usage would reduce abortions, DeMarco maintains, history shows that an increase in the one leads ineluctably to an increase in the other. 'Using the contraceptive mentality to fight the abortion mentality confuses cause and effect. It is like trying to put out a fire with matches.'[51] When one separates sexual pleasure from procreation, an American advocate of the thesis argues, the 'resolve to prevent a child from coming to be is often sufficiently strong that one will eliminate the child whose conception was not prevented.'[52]

The transvaluation of sexual mores in the 1960s, the rise of feminism, and a consuming anxiety concerning over-population, claims DeMarco, were the factors chiefly responsible for making the 'contraceptive mentality' dominant in Western society.[53] The challenge confronting pro-lifers, according to this perspective, is to change a distorted conception of sexuality which has permeated Western culture. 'Since abortion thrives on the contraceptive mentality, we fight abortion realistically not by doubling our efforts to intensify the contraceptive mentality, but by working to eliminate it. But this first step – is a step our society has not yet taken. Indeed, at the present moment most indications are that it would "rather be ruined than change." '[54]

The 'contraceptive mentality' thesis would encounter considerable resistance within the pro-life movement. Many activists, especially those connected with the Coalition, were unconvinced of the causal connection it implied between contraception and abortion, and some of these themselves practised artificial birth control.[55] Others who found it persuasive in varying degrees were opposed to its public transmission on the ground that an attack against contraception would almost certainly nullify whatever credibility the movement possessed. A public seemingly unprepared to consider biological evidence for the humanity of the fetus could not be expected to swallow an argument of such decidedly Catholic flavour. Nevertheless, the thesis was kept alive, and by the late 1970s it had become an *insiders' doctrine* for many activists who found it an attractive résumé for their ideology of cultural decline.

Regardless of its explanatory value, the 'contraceptive mentality' thesis imparts to the abortion issue an overwhelming, almost metaphysical, magnitude. For if abortion is the product of a fundamental sexual-spiritual disorder in modern society, it is something that transcends political solution. Only by miraculous erasure of the sexual revolution, feminism, and other nemeses of virtue might abortion be stopped. When the issue is conceived in these terms, when it ceases to be a political issue in the ordinary sense, anti-abortion protest itself takes on changed meaning. Instead of being directed to practical political accomplishment, it becomes an icon symbolizing the survival of goodness in the midst of rampant evil. For if the roots of the 'abortion mentality' run that deeply into the cultural soil, something greater than human action will be required to remove them.

It is difficult to know exactly when contraception and abortion became linked in the minds of many Catholic activists.[56] What is certain is that the thesis held its greatest appeal for those Catholics in the movement who were personally attached to *Humanae Vitae* and who regarded fidelity to the encyclical as the measure of *authentic* Catholicism in the modern world. Pro-life protest has been irresistibly attractive for such Catholics, and the thesis gained currency as they emerged in the late 1970s as the movement's most militant force. It was at this time also that the *Winnipeg Statement* was disinterred and added to the ledger of sins committed by the Canadian bishops. By appearing to balk on *Humanae Vitae*, it was concluded, the bishops had opened the gate further to the 'contraceptive mentality' and even allowed it admission into the Catholic church.[57]

Thus, by the late 1970s prevailing sentiment within the movement held the bishops and other Canadian Catholic elites partly, and strategically, responsible for the moral disorder upon which, presumably, the 'abortion crisis' was founded. By seeming to desert the political arena at critical junctures of the debates over abortion and other matters of public morality, it was thought, the bishops had participated in the secularization of Canadian political culture and the concomitant exile of religious beliefs and values to a zone of cultural irrelevance.[58] The only thing left open to question was whether the bishops had been merely unwitting accomplices to the pro-abortion tide or had in fact knowingly surrendered to it.

3

Science, Religion, and Radicalism in the Pro-Life Movement

Any social movement is engaged in a dynamic of 'impression management'[1] as it seeks the most attractive format for presentation of its views to the wider society. Success or failure, in terms of garnering more widespread support for its goals, is largely contingent upon maximizing its appeal to the prevailing cultural temperament. The social movement, then, has a strong interest in displaying its message in a package most palatable for public consumption. Its mode of discourse, or popular rhetoric, can reveal much about its perception of the broader cultural climate, the sectors of society it hopes to sway, as well as possible disjunctions between its *private* and *public* beliefs. In addition, to the extent that it projects a public image which militates against the attainment of its declared objectives, we may learn about the movement's *expressive*, or non-instrumental, dimension.[2]

Although convulsed by internal fractiousness, the Canadian pro-life movement emerged from the 1970s still largely committed to a uniform public strategy. Its activities were confined to behind-the-scenes political lobbying, educational projects sponsored by local right-to-life groups, occasional public demonstrations and rallies, and picketing outside 'abortion-intensive' hospitals. All of these activities served to remind the Canadian public of the continued existence of an organized opposition to legalized abortion, though the movement likely struck many as more a Catholic preoccupation than a serious political force.[3] Pro-lifers, for their part, were eager to prove that the Catholic face of the movement was merely an accident, that the injustice of abortion was something that could, and eventually would, be seen by all reasonable Canadians. And while pro-lifers were acutely aware of the movement's internal dissensions, they were able to paper over the cracks and thus give the movement an appearance of concertedness.

In the 1980s, however, the movement's simmering religious energy would have its cap unscrewed and anti-abortion protest would assume an unprecedented stridency. Moreover, as the decade progressed it became apparent that the battle over abortion was, at least for some activists, being fought as much for the soul of the Canadian Catholic church as it was for the souls of unborn children.

THE QUESTION OF STRATEGY

While differences of social location and of ideology festered in the 1970s into a bitter contest for control of the movement, an aggravating factor was the growing sense of political impotency felt by many activists in the face of an escalating abortion rate. During the period from 1971 to 1980, the number of therapeutic abortions obtained by Canadian residents in Canada more than doubled, from 31,000 to 65,751 or 8.5 and 17.7 per 100 births respectively.[4] And though the vast majority of these were performed for social and psychological reasons, thereby contravening the purported intent of the 1969 amendment to the abortion law, pro-lifers were unable to induce among politicians and the general public the sense of outrage they were convinced this situation warranted.[5] The failure of the massive 1975 petition campaign to bring about a re-assessment of the abortion law and an epidemic of indifference to the pro-life appeal within Canada's political parties fostered a sweeping disaffection with the national political process.[6]

Equally disturbing to pro-lifers was the seemingly cold public reception accorded their presentation of the anti-abortion message. The founders of the movement in the late 1960s had deliberately chosen to fashion their arguments on behalf of nascent life within a frame of reference they thought would resonate most favourably with Canada's secularist and pluralist climate. Thus, despite the Christian commitment of most activists, pro-life literature was notable for its avoidance of explicitly religious language or argumentation. Convinced that the canons of science and liberalism had supplanted supernaturalist religion as Canada's paramount cultural authority, they attempted to make an imprint upon the public mind by formulating the pro-life position in human rights terms and by publicizing the growing body of scientific data on the development of the fetus.[7] Catholics in these early years were especially sensitive to the popular depiction of anti-abortionism as a peculiarly Roman Catholic idiosyncrasy and were anxious to defuse the refrain that pro-life Catholics were intent on imposing their morality upon the larger Canadian population.[8]

Thus, in order to break the Catholic stigma of anti-abortionism, the religious component of the movement was compartmentalized – that is, kept underground, away from the public view – and pro-life presentations were based almost exclusively upon appeals to scientific facts, without reference to either religious dogma or confessional morality. This strategy, of liberating the pro-life position from its Catholic stereotype for the sake of winning the largest possible audience, was followed for the most part throughout the 1970s.[9] Pro-life educational materials were limited to graphic descriptions of the development of pre-natal life, and religious motives of activists were kept under tight wraps. By the close of the decade, however, signs of severe leakage appeared in this carefully orchestrated strategy, and in the 1980s the movement's religious dragon would finally escape its dungeon. Several interrelated factors were responsible for bringing the movement's religious dimension to the surface.

First, many of the grass roots Catholics and Protestants who swelled the movement's membership in the late 1970s discovered – often with astonishment – that they inhabited similar religious worlds. Their theological differences were overshadowed by a mutual feeling of estrangement from the secular character of modern Canadian society. Moreover, they tended to represent the most doctrinally conservative sides of their respective religious traditions. Conservative Protestants, many of whom initially defined their working relationship with pro-life Catholics as a co-belligerence of necessity, were delighted to learn that many Catholic activists were similarly committed to doctrines of biblical inerrancy, the historicity of the Resurrection, and the necessity of a personal relationship with Jesus Christ as a pre-condition of eternal salvation. Though they cringed at the ardent Marian piety and ultramontanism of grass roots Catholics, conservative Protestants were willing to tolerate certain excesses when so much else seemed right. Grass roots Catholics, for their part, developed a grudging respect for conservative Protestants who were able to shed their political inhibitions and join them on the anti-abortion picket line. They also saw their Protestant counterparts as valuable allies in the fight to reinstate a traditional Christianity as the guardian of the nation's morality.[10] With the more moderate Coalitionists – many of whom had been responsible for steering the movement away from a religious expression – by this time on the sidelines, pro-life discourse began to take on a more explicitly religious content. Scriptural passages appeared alongside civil rights slogans on pro-life placards and broadsheets, and public prayer, which was exceptional in the movement's earlier years, became a regular feature of pro-life rallies and demonstrations.

Complementing the bulging religious disposition of the movement in the late 1970s was a mounting dissatisfaction with a strictly factual presentation of the pro-life position. As was noted above, pro-life strategy had been premised on the assumption that the general public, and perhaps even the movement's antagonists, would be persuaded of the humanity of the fetus through exposure to nakedly physical evidence. Accordingly, the substance of pro-life educational materials concerned 'grubby little facts' pertaining to the chronology of intra-uterine life, such as the time when the embryonic heart starts beating and the time when the fetus has a clearly human form. But pro-life expositions were often greeted by an equal mixture of indifference and contempt. And, worse, pro-lifers saw the rhetorical rug pulled out from under their collective feet as the opposition shifted the argument from a biological to a metaphysical ground. Even if the fetus is demonstrably human by strictly physical criteria, pro-choice advocates asserted, it can claim personhood only when its mother lovingly affirms its existence or when it is capable of meaningful social interaction. According to this line of reasoning, the biological status of the fetus is irrelevant: society should be concerned with guaranteeing the rights only of real persons, not of potential and unwanted ones. Naturally, this logic struck pro-lifers as mystifying double-talk, and they were appalled that it was able to gain wide currency.[11] Moreover, the pictorial depictions of aborted fetuses, frankly employed by pro-lifers for their shock value, were branded as sordid sensationalism. This they found especially vexing: pictures just as gruesome depicting, for example, war atrocities or victims of botched back-street abortions were somehow deemed culturally admissible.[12] All of this drove many activists to the conclusion that they had been wrong to place all their strategic bets on scientific evidence, that there was truth in David Hume's maxim that 'facts alone will never sway people,' and thus the door was opened further to a more overtly religious approach to the issue.

In stumbling across the Weberian insight that values are not derived from science but rather have a non-rational source[13] and that biological evidence would not therefore by itself convert people to the pro-life viewpoint, the religiously devout in the movement found it harder to quell what they had always thought: the abortion issue signifies above all a spiritual conflict between a transcendent value system and a godless utilitarianism masquerading as compassionate humanism. This understanding of the abortion issue as the point of intersection for clashing cosmologies would receive its full expression only after the Coalition's fall from grace. Indeed, some of the animosity directed at Coalitionists may be interpreted as psychological fallout resulting from the movement's repressed religiosity. Prior to the advent of Campaign Life, many conservative Catholics had complained that the Coalition, by attempting to muzzle talk of God and evil, had closed off the movement from legitimate religious sentiment.[14] For many in the movement abortion was a religious issue of the highest magnitude. At stake was nothing less than the primordial meaning of life: believing as they did that all human beings, regardless of stage of development or degree of perfection, are uniquely created in the image of God and hence sacred, they regarded abortion, infanticide, and euthanasia, as well as genetic engineering, as signposts of a monstrous spiritual rebellion, in which human life is seen as endlessly manipulable and anthropocentrically ordained. By seeking a modus vivendi with the prevailing culture, the Coalition leadership had seemed to want to address the abortion issue without confronting this fundamental spiritual disorder of modern society. To many activists, this was missing the point altogether.

Thus, as the pro-life movement entered the 1980s, haunted by a fractious past, it did so with a revolutionary resolve: the entire secularist apparatus of Canadian society must be dismantled and an ethic of ultimacy installed in its place.

Despite the shaken confidence among many pro-lifers in its persuasive power, science would retain an important place in the movement's public strategy. Indeed, by the turn of the decade the movement had developed a dual personality, with complementary emphases accorded both scientific evidence and religious belief. These two faces of the movement, the scientific and the religious, seemed almost to be personified in Bernard Nathanson and Joseph Borowski, two men of enormous and contrasting influence upon Canadian pro-life ranks.

Although Bernard Nathanson is American, it is doubtful that any single individual has been a greater symbolic asset to the Canadian movement. Nathanson was an obstetrician-gynecologist in New York City when in 1969 he helped to found the National Association for Repeal of Abortion Laws (NARAL), an organization dedicated to the elimination of restrictive abortion laws in New York and elsewhere. Moreover, from February 1971 through September 1972 he served as director of the Center for Reproductive and Sexual Health in New York City, which was then the world's largest abortion clinic. In November 1974, however, Nathanson confessed his misgivings in the *New England Journal of Medicine* where he wrote: 'I am deeply troubled by my own increasing certainty that I had in fact presided over 60,000 deaths ... We are taking life, and the deliberate taking of life, even of a special order and under special circumstances, is an inexpressibly serious matter.'[15]

Dr Nathanson's change of heart would involve far more than a mere act of literary contrition. In subsequent years the former apostle of abortion freedom would become one of North America's foremost champions of the fetus, tirelessly touring the continent to dispute pro-choice arguments he himself had once helped to formulate. Dr Nathanson's defection from the enemy was an inspirational boon for the Canadian movement. Although some in the movement likened it to Paul's revelation of light on the road to Damascus, the real political value of Nathanson's conversion was precisely its lack of religious motive. An avowed atheist of Jewish background, he credited his changed evaluation of abortion entirely to the scientific testimony of fetology. Only the invincibly obtuse, he claimed, could fail to recognize the humanity of the fetus as it was shown through new diagnostic procedures such as fetoscopy.[16] Canadian pro-lifers were thus anxious to use Nathanson's frequent proselytizing visits to Canada as occasions to puncture the fanatical Catholic stereotype of their movement.

The other half of the movement's personality – its unabashedly religious side – was exemplified by Joseph Borowski. Affectionately dubbed 'Holy Joe' by admirers, and a religious kook and crackpot by detractors, Borowski had risen from prairie poverty to become a union activist and eventually a cabinet minister in the Manitoba NDP government of Ed Schreyer. In 1971 he clashed with his own cabinet colleagues over NDP policy on abortion and resigned from formal politics to carry the pro-life torch full-time. Borowski's penchant for the dramatic has led many Catholic pro-lifers to regard his personal crusade against abortion as a modern-day Stations of the Cross. In 1981, for example, he undertook a nine-month fast of protest because Canada's proposed Charter of Rights and Freedoms failed specifically to guarantee the unborn a right to life. It took a special intervention from the Pope, relayed to Borowski through the Vatican's emissary to Canada, to interrupt the fast in its eightieth day. An event of greater political note occurred in 1983 when Borowski unsuccessfully challenged the constitutionality of Canada's 1969 abortion law before the Saskatchewan Provincial Court.[17]

The inseparable connection between these public histrionics and his enthusiastic brand of Catholicism has made Borowski a plump target for the lampoons of pro-choice advocates. At the time of his 1983 trial, *Toronto Star* columnist Michele Landsberg ridiculed him as 'a man who worships in a painted shrine in his backyard and decks his body with special amulets to save him from the fires of hell.'[18] The extravagant piety which struck people such as Landsberg as ludicrous, however, captured the imagination of many Catholics in the pro-life movement. They felt a special bond with Borowski, a man who, like some of them, had re-embraced Catholicism in its most conservative rendition following a period of religious doubt, who brooked no compromise in either his spirituality or moral beliefs, and who was unafraid publicly to chastise bishops and priests for not taking a stronger stance against abortion.

But while lionized by some in the movement, to others Borowski was a source of perpetual embarrassment. The movement's intellectual stratum believed that Borowski presented a ready-made caricature to those who would discredit the movement on religious appearance alone. Wish as some pro-lifers might, however, Borowski would seldom entertain a moment of silence. Believing that existing pro-life groups would cramp his unique style, Borowski in the early 1970s established a maverick organization which he baptized Alliance against Abortion and which would serve in future years as a political outlet for his anti-abortion passion. Based in Winnipeg, the Alliance against Abortion has made Borowski's name virtually synonymous with the pro-life cause in western Canada.

THE ENEMY WITHIN

As the movement in the 1980s became radicalized and took on the quality of a religious crusade, it did so chiefly through the instigation of militant lay Catholics who looked upon anti-abortion protest as the fulcrum of a genuine Catholic piety in the modern world. Because the abortion issue was freighted in their minds with apocalyptic significance, these Catholics demanded that their bishops and the Canadian church in general demonstrate a like-minded commitment to the pro-life campaign. When this commitment failed to materialize, many Catholic activists became convinced that the institutional church had lapsed into obliquity. Thus was erected the constant backdrop for the pro-life drama (at least in its militant Catholic dimension) in the 1980s: anti-abortionism for many activists had become a definitive badge of Catholic authenticity and of countercultural spirituality, and any Catholic who did not wear this badge proudly was branded a traitor to the faith.

The Canadian movement is fully national and exhibits the regional diversity typical of Canadian cultural life. Nevertheless, several episodes that occurred in Toronto in the 1980s encapsulate its recent impulses, foibles as well as strengths. By casting a searchlight on these, it is possible to illuminate both its evolving Catholic extremism and its mood of political desperation.[19]

The politics of polarization practised by Campaign Life, the main organizational home for the movement's militant Catholics, was exemplified by the 1981 imbroglio which erupted in Toronto over Canada's projected new Constitution and Charter of Rights and Freedoms. At this time the premier of Ontario, William Davis, attempted to break the log-jam of provincial opposition to Prime Minister Trudeau's proposed constitutional package by publicly declaring his support of it. Campaign Life, which was lobbying fiercely for inclusion of the rights of the unborn in the proposed Charter of Rights, was incensed that Davis would lend his support to a document that had nothing to say about pre-natal life.[20]

Campaign Life conveyed its displeasure through literature distributed at Catholic parishes as well as advertisements placed in the *Catholic Register*, which called on Catholic voters to reject candidates from Davis's Progressive Conservative party in the forthcoming 19 March provincial election. 'For PC [Progressive Conservative] candidates that are pro-life we advise you tell them that you would like to vote for them, but that a vote for the PCs is also a vote for Mr. Davis and his support for the Charter of "Injustice." ' Especially worrisome to Campaign Life was the section of the proposed charter that guaranteed equality rights for women. Entrenchment of this in the new constitution, the organization warned in its *Catholic Register* advertisement, would open the floodgates to abortion-on-demand. 'Any restriction on abortion would be considered as sex discrimination as abortion affects one sex only.'[21]

Campaign Life's strategy of targeting Progressive Conservative candidates for defeat at the polls had no appreciable impact on the 19 March election; the Davis government was returned to power with a resounding majority. It did, however, accentuate the crusading mentality by which the organization was gripped. Considering that the Progressive Conservatives boasted more self-professed anti-abortion candidates than the other two major parties combined, the strategy of working for their defeat seemed particularly awkward. Campaign Life, however, was not operating according to a prosaic political logic.

Even more awkward for Campaign Life was the response of Cardinal Carter, archbishop of Toronto, who claimed to resent the organization's use of the church for partisan political purposes. Characterizing Campaign Life's methods and strategy as unacceptable, Carter issued an order to diocesan priests that henceforward '*no* information prepared and published by Campaign Life be circulated in any parishes either directly or indirectly through parish bulletins.'[22]

The Campaign Life leadership did not take this reproof passively. Fr Alphonse de Valk, one of the very few clergymen active in the organization, protested in the *Globe and Mail* that 'The attack upon Campaign Life by means of ecclesiastical prohibition ... seems to indicate that the Cardinal would like his archdiocese to believe that his opinion on the charter is the only legitimate one ...'[23] And Laura McArthur, president of Toronto Right-to-Life, claiming to represent the views of over ten thousand organization members in Metropolitan Toronto, insisted that the 'Cardinal was absolutely wrong' to support the charter and censure Campaign Life. 'It's something pro-life people won't buy. We didn't spend 10 years of our lives dedicated to a cause only to have a hatchet job done on us.'[24] Paul Formby, Campaign Life's national co-ordinator, said of Cardinal Carter, 'He's entitled to his opinion, but we don't think he's entitled to smear our name.'[25]

Campaign Life raised the polemical pitch by accusing Cardinal Carter of fabricating political deals at the expense of the unborn. Carter himself had initially expressed dissatisfaction over the proposed charter's failure to recognize the rights of unborn life, but apparently experienced a change of heart following a meeting with Prime Minister Trudeau in early 1981, and thereafter pronounced the charter acceptable to Canadian Catholics in its basic principles. But Campaign Life alleged that the cardinal had agreed publicly to endorse the Trudeau constitutional package, despite its silence on the unborn, in return for the promise of full public funding for Ontario Catholic schools.[26] And since, the Campaign Life leadership contended, the cardinal was counting on Premier Davis's Progressive Conservative government to deliver this extended support to separate schools, his censure of their organization was based more on crass political interests than on a concern to preserve a proper distance between the church and the voting behaviour of Catholics.

Attempting to deflect the outrage of the militant anti-abortion faction, Cardinal Carter contributed an article to the *Catholic Register* in which he reaffirmed the commitment of the Canadian hierarchy to the pro-life cause while arguing that the bishops were obliged 'to remain apart from the political aspects of ... disputes and to intervene only on matters which touch upon Gospel values or affect the Church and its teaching.' Further, Carter disavowed any partisan political motive behind his acceptance of the proposed charter and stressed that he too would prefer that it include explicit recognition of the 'absolute right to life' of 'everyone from the moment of conception onwards.' Nevertheless, he added, though the proposed charter did not enshrine the rights of nascent life, he had been given assurance by the prime minister and various legal advisers that it was not an invitation for abortion-on-demand and, therefore, 'because of its many positive values' had elected not to oppose its passage on moral or religious grounds. The cardinal, however, left himself open to charges of equivocation when he wrote: 'However, I hold the Prime Minister and the government of Canada accountable for any diminishment to the rights of the unborn which may flow from this charter.'[27]

If the cardinal sought by this article to assuage his critics, he succeeded only in stoking the fires of controversy. Campaign Life responded with customary vehemence. The organization's principal legal counsellor, Gwendolyn Landolt, remarked in a *Toronto Star* article that 'in ten years of fighting abortion it never entered my mind a Catholic cardinal could take the stand Carter has taken. We believed we were making the only possible moral response when all of a sudden we find the huge cannons of the Catholic Church blazing at us – no warning, no dialogue, nothing. We're dumbfounded.' And raising once again the spectre of a political collusion between Carter, Prime Minister Trudeau, and Premier Davis, Landolt asked cryptically: 'Why should the cardinal be so anxious not to seem to be allied with any attack on Bill Davis?' Other Campaign Life spokespersons quoted in the same article were more pointed in attributing the cardinal's stance on the charter to a backroom political deal. As one said: 'The cardinal is in effect selling human life for aid to the [Catholic] separate schools.'[28]

The cardinal responded to these charges in a 'clarifying statement' published in all three Toronto dailies. After admonishing his critics for 'distortion and misrepresentation' and advising that there exists no 'clear religious or moral *opposition* between the Church and the Charter,' Carter stated that Canadian bishops would overstep their rightful authority if they instructed their people 'how to vote or what parties to support.' By implication, he continued, Campaign Life had no right to use or expect to use the influence of the church as a partisan political instrument. It was for this reason, and also because of Campaign Life's vindictive approach, the cardinal asserted, that he had prohibited as 'a disciplinary measure' the distribution of Campaign Life literature in parishes.[29]

On 12 May 1981 Campaign Life unleashed its heavy artillery with a letter of distress to Pope John Paul II. The Catholic-dominated Family Life Survival Fund, based in Prince George, BC, had written to the pope two weeks earlier bluntly condemning Cardinal Carter as 'a traitor' and 'a Judas' and urging the pope to change Carter's mind on the charter 'before it was too late.'[30] The Campaign Life letter, which was signed by members of the organization's Toronto and national executives, likened Cardinal Carter's apparent volte-face on the charter to an act of sabotage against the pro-life movement. 'By publicly removing his opposition to the Charter, Cardinal Carter has completely undermined the work of the pro-life movement in Canada to insure protection for the unborn in the Charter. All our efforts to encourage Members of Parliament to oppose the Charter have been nullified. The government has used the Cardinal's statement in Parliament and in special letters to constituents, to deflect enquiries and protests regarding the exclusion of the right to life for the unborn in the Charter ...'[31]

Since Campaign Life believed that the entire Canadian hierarchy was delinquent on the pro-life front, the pope was further advised that the '*precarious* situation regarding ... the leadership of the Catholic Church in Canada merits your direct attention [emphasis added].' But the sternest rebuke was reserved for Cardinal Carter. 'The Archdiocese of Toronto needs an Archbishop who will truly stand up for the right to life of the unborn. Our country needs strong and courageous religious leaders who will speak out publicly on behalf of pro-life.' The letter's closing tribute to the pope, while in line with expected protocol, indicates where Campaign Life's allegiance rested. 'We are grateful to God for giving us a Pope whose strong and courageous moral leadership has given hope and encouragement to people all over the world who are struggling to secure protection for the lives of defenseless human beings.'[32]

Expressing concern that this mounting acrimony was 'sowing disunity' among Canadian Catholics, Cardinal Carter appointed a 'committee of reconciliation' to meet with representatives of Campaign Life. The cardinal's conditions for detente, however, were a pill far too bitter for Campaign Life to swallow: the organization was forbidden to distribute political literature in parishes or to use Catholic papers 'to direct people how to vote.' Moreover, Carter advised, because Campaign Life had misrepresented his position by confusing the distinction between 'not opposing and supporting' the proposed charter, 'it would seem very difficult for us to direct any funds [to them] since the literature which they are disseminating is, de facto, erroneous.'[33] Predictably, then, the meeting between the two sides, which took place in the late spring of 1981 under the shadow of Campaign Life's hard-hitting letter to Rome, failed to calm the troubled waters, and a pattern of mutual recrimination between the cardinal and Catholic pro-life militants was firmly established.[34]

In late May 1981 Campaign Life informed the Canadian Conference of Catholic Bishops that it had appealed over the heads of the national hierarchy to 'the Holy Father concerning the Catholic Church in Canada and the proposed Charter of Rights.' By falsely describing the charter as neutral on the rights of the unborn, the bishops were told, Cardinal Carter had provided an escape-hatch for pro-life politicians who were under party pressures to vote for it. On this point Campaign Life was correct. Carter's absolution of the proposed charter had in fact been used by the federal liberal government as moral leverage to win support for it from Catholic politicians.[35] Anti-abortionists across Canada, the bishops were also told, were flabbergasted that the Catholic hierarchy had neglected to take a firm stand against the charter. 'The Charter excludes the Right to Life of the unborn child. With over 65,000 abortions each year in our hospitals the Charter can not be considered as neutral on abortion. If the Inuit or any group or class of people were excluded from the Charter all Christians would feel obliged to oppose it. They would not say that it has so many positive points that it could not be opposed for religious or moral reasons.'[36]

Campaign Life's request that the national episcopate announce its opposition to the charter 'before [it] comes to a final vote in Parliament'[37] would not be granted, and when in April 1982 the Queen proclaimed Canada's new constitution, many Catholic activists had ceased to regard their bishops as allies.

At issue here is neither the allegation of a political compromise made by Cardinal Carter nor the potential impact of the Charter of Rights upon Canada's 1969 abortion law. Rather, the present concern is to examine what this stream of events reveals about the evolving relationship of the pro-life movement to Canadian Catholicism.

1 Throughout the 1970s leading Coalitionists enjoyed an amicable relationship with the Canadian bishops, thankful for their moral support but preferring that the bishops remain in the background as a precaution against the *Catholicization* of the pro-life position in the public mind. But with the rise to dominance in the 1980s of Campaign Life and, correspondingly, the internal exile of many

prominent Coalitionists, such public relations scruples were thrown to the wind and a new political style was imparted to the movement. Convinced that abortion was a by-product of secularization, and impatient with the Fabian approach favoured by the Coalition and moderates in the Alliance, the Campaign Life leadership decided to play its 'Catholic hand' to the limit. Accordingly, Canadian Catholics were urged qua Catholics to oppose the proposed charter and bishops were exhorted (for the most part unsuccessfully) to assume a high-profile activist role. Given their emerging theocratic political vision, Campaign Life leaders were less concerned than had been Coalitionists with bruising the feelings of non-Catholics or with crossing any presumed boundary of separation between church and state.

With the release of the movement's latent religious energy, there developed a tendency among many Catholic activists to define anti-abortionism as much in *vocational* as in *humanitarian* terms. By the late 1970s anti-abortionism had come to be regarded as the pivotal point for a repudiation of secularism, liberalism, and individualism.[38] It had become synonymous with Catholic virtue, and appeals for greater support from the Canadian church were expressly made on this basis. In other words, the abortion issue had taken on embellished significance: at stake was not only unborn life but also the meaning of Catholic belief and commitment in a secular age.

Paradoxically, paralleling the unharnessing of the movement's religious energy in the early 1980s was a growing tendency for pro-life Catholics to view the institutional church with a mistrust which would at times border on hostility. Far from being anomalous, the conflict with Cardinal Carter over the charter only confirmed the suspicion of Catholic militants that their bishops were laggards on the abortion issue. Throughout the 1970s there had been intermittent complaints from right-to-life groups that the Canadian hierarchy was parsimonious in its financial support of the movement, but the actual pro-life commitment of the bishops had only rarely been questioned. By the close of the charter debate, however, this grumbling had grown to a roar, and accusations that the bishops and, by insinuation, most Canadian clergy and laity were indifferent to the plight of the unborn had become commonplace. It was at this time too that the past pro-life sins of the bishops rebounded into the movement's consciousness. Looking back to the response of the bishops to the 1969 legislation and also to *Humanae Vitae*, it became clear to Catholic militants, now fitting together the whole picture, that the hierarchy had from the start been guilty of complicity in the trend toward social acceptance of abortion. Given this definition of the situation, Catholic militants began to conceive themselves as a holy conventicle within a national church that was too immersed in mainstream secular life to make opposition to abortion a chief priority.

In attempting to enlist the support of Pope John Paul II, Campaign Life drew the battle lines for what was fast becoming a cold war within Canadian Catholicism. From this point onward militant Catholics would make little effort to disguise either their disgust with the Canadian Catholic establishment or their determination to look directly to Rome for moral and spiritual leadership.

Besides illustrating the divisiveness which the abortion issue posed for Canadian Catholicism, the charter affair also underscored the intractable political idealism of Campaign Life. Throughout 1981 both the Coalition and Campaign Life lobbied vigorously in Ottawa to have protection for the unborn specifically written into the charter. By year's end, however, Coalition leaders recognized that this was a virtual impossibility owing to insufficient support in the House of Commons. Reading the handwriting on the wall, the Coalition shifted gears and aimed instead for inclusion within the charter of a clause that would give Parliament ultimate power over Canada's abortion law. What the Coalition had in mind was the epochal 1973 decision (*Roe* v. *Wade*) in the United States wherein the American Supreme Court declared first and second trimester abortions to be a constitutional right, thereby abolishing state laws restricting abortion and effectively legalizing abortion-on-demand.[39] Coalition leaders realized that patriation of Canada's new constitution, with an entrenched Charter of Rights and Freedoms, would likely lead to numerous constitutional challenges of Canadian laws and thus to an expanded role for the courts. Specifically, they were concerned that the Supreme Court of Canada might in the future rule that any legislation restricting abortion availability was discriminatory and hence in contravention of the equality guarantees contained in section 15 of the charter. By campaigning for a provision in the charter granting Canada's elected representatives final say on abortion-related laws, then, they hoped to obviate in Canada the scenario which transpired in the United States when existing abortion laws were rendered invalid by judicial decree. While Coalition leaders recognized that such a provision would not serve the interests of the unborn as decisively as would explicit constitutional protection, they nevertheless saw it as a worthy and, more important, a *feasible* objective.

The Campaign Life leadership, however, regarded this altered strategy as further indication of the Coalition's lack of resolve, and refused to budge from the original game plan of attempting to secure entrenched rights for the unborn in the charter. In any event, neither of the proposed pro-life amendments found their way into the charter that was eventually approved by Parliament, thereby accentuating the feeling of powerlessness among anti-abortionists that had been building since the mid-1970s.

The charter debate represented the maximum expression of Campaign Life's unforgiving political style: if a politician was not prepared to walk the straight and narrow pro-life path, he or she was excoriated as anti-life. Thus, when MP Ursula Appolloni, a long-time friend of the movement, registered her approval of the proposed charter before the Liberal caucus, she was immediately denounced as a backslider and excised from the ranks of 'bona fide' pro-life MPs.[40] Indeed, as time passed it became increasingly more difficult for Canadian politicians to qualify as 'bona fide' pro-lifers. For Campaign Life demanded of politicians a degree of commitment to the cause that even those opposed to abortion found difficult to espouse. The politician was expected to take the hard and pure line on abortion, to buck party discipline and sacrifice opportunities for cabinet promotion by serving as a pro-life prophet. Explicit identification with the anti-abortion cause had come to be perceived among parliamentarians as a political albatross, a tell-tale sign of cultural cretinism, and thus very few politicians were prepared to meet Campaign Life's demands more than halfway.[41] One Liberal MP confided that he fell into disfavour with Campaign Life during the charter affair precisely because of his reluctance to commit political suicide.

You've got to understand the terrific party pressure we were under to say yes to the Charter. Some of us have serious misgivings about the way the abortion law's been interpreted. What was supposed to be rare and precisely therapeutic is now just a matter of course for any or no reason. So we say to the pro-lifers – the Campaign Life people – sure, we're concerned. This is a big problem. We're committed to working on it. But give us time and let us be an influence within the system. Because we have so many interests to juggle. We have to satisfy the women's movement, too. But no way. They march onto Parliament Hill like moral storm troopers, telling us to do it exactly their way or else bear the burden of guilt for the ongoing destruction of babies. If we do it their way, we're through, written off as fanatics. So they told me I was anti-life. They've lost a lot of allies this way. The Coalition tries to understand the political dilemma we're in. They're patient. 'Okay,' they would say, 'we know it's tough, but do what you can do. Keep the issue alive in caucus and when an opportunity arises, act on it.' This we can handle. I know I didn't go to all the trouble to get to the Hill to be a martyr for the unborn. And, shit, I know it's a worthy cause. But things are more complex here than they like to admit.

The stern and uncompromising approach of Campaign Life reflected the moral outrage of its membership. But it involved more than this. In scorning political delicacy as well as the bartering process which is the stock-in-trade of Canadian politics, the Campaign Life leadership showed that the demeanour of anti-abortion activism had become almost as important to it as the actual resolution of the issue. Contemptuous of the realities of political negotiation, and unwilling to forfeit anything of its ideological purity, Campaign Life had elevated anti-abortionism from the realm of political conflict to a plateau of religious righteousness. This point was expressed by a retired pro-life activist as follows: 'I have this image of many of the Campaign Life people appearing before St Peter at the Pearly Gates. Peter says to them, "So you good people were pro-lifers. Tell me, how many abortions did you prevent?" And they reply, "Well, actually, none. But, damn it, we never once compromised." '

While the movement as a whole foundered without tangible political accomplishment, Campaign Life and its supporters received a boost with the March 1983 publishing debut of *The Interim*. As the monthly newspaper of Campaign Life, *The Interim* promised in its inaugural editorial to adhere unwaveringly to a philosophy of 'no compromise on abortion.' 'We may not be successful at all times, but rest easy, we will be, *always faithful*!'

Not only would *The Interim* subsequently keep its pledge, but it would do so with a torrid tone and 'bar-no-holds' editorial policy which matched the militant temperament of its mainly Catholic readers. It, furthermore, would provide a regular forum where old grievances against the Canadian bishops could be recalled and new ones hatched. On very rare occasions, *The Interim* would even find reason for applause. The following notice from the September 1983 edition, for example, salutes Adam Exner, one of the few outspoken opponents of abortion from within the Canadian hierarchy: 'We understand that Archbishop Adam Exner of Winnipeg has sustained a certain amount of criticism (negative) regarding his warning to anyone involved directly or indirectly in an abortion that the church intends to act and enforce Canon Law provisions. Bishop Exner is the only Bishop in Canada who has spoken up loud and clear on the subject of abortion, and as you might guess, much of the criticism has come from complacent catholics and weak clergy.'

THE MORGENTALER CLINIC

The next major passage for the movement, beginning in June 1983 with the opening in Toronto of English Canada's first elective abortion clinic, further convinced pro-lifers that the 'powers and principalities' of Canadian society were arrayed against them. Dr Henry Morgentaler, the clinic's proprietor, had been a public figure in Canada since 1968 when he opened his first of several free-standing abortion clinics in the Montreal area. Charged on three occasions with conspiracy to commit an abortion and procuring of an abortion, and acquitted by three different juries, Morgentaler was now looking to expand his operations beyond Quebec.[42] Until 1983 the anglophone movement had been spared the *scourge* of elective clinics, and thus had been able to concentrate its protest against abortions performed in accredited hospitals. But by making abortion unconditionally available on a strictly supply and demand basis, and thus brazenly defying the strictures of the 1969 legislation, Dr Morgentaler sent shock waves throughout pro-life ranks.

The furore surrounding the opening of the Toronto clinic induced the movement to suspend its fissiparous tendencies and temporarily to close ranks. For the first time since the release of the Badgley Report, the abortion issue was accorded celebrity status by the Canadian news media, and the ensuing spectacle of publicity brought in its trail a swarm of new recruits to the movement. Far more than did hospital-restricted abortions, the clinic constituted an egregious contradiction of the pro-life ethic. Whereas abortions performed within the antiseptic confines of hospitals could at least be grimly tolerated, if only because the ritual of approval by TACs created an illusion of attendant solemnity, the moral nonchalance of the clinic seemed to put abortion in the same league as any other elective surgery, more of a nuisance perhaps than having a hangnail removed but of less consequence than gallstones. In other words, the inherent value of unborn life, given at least ostensible recognition by the 1969 legislation, seemed jettisoned by the 'open market' principle of the clinic.

Compounding this affront to the anti-abortion ethic was the rhetoric of Morgentaler himself: in his media pronouncements and speeches all opponents of abortion-on-demand appeared to be reduced to 'fanatical fetus-worshippers' and 'religious freaks,' the embryo was adjudged to be 'a cluster of cells' of no more human significance than 'a tadpole,' and the 'termination of unwanted fetuses' was commended as a favour both to themselves and to society.[43] For many of those in the movement accustomed to viewing reality through a religious lens, Morgentaler was a demonic sledge-hammer poised to pulverize any loitering sense of sacredness in Canadian society.

The early history of the Toronto clinic is a legal labyrinth. Shut down by Metro Toronto police on 15 June 1983 when Dr Morgentaler and two colleagues were charged with abortion-related offences, it reopened on 10 December 1984 following the acquittal of the three doctors by a Supreme Court of Ontario jury. The Ontario government launched an appeal of the acquittals and the clinic was closed again on 20 December 1984 when fresh charges were laid against Morgentaler and an associate. After a three-week hiatus the clinic opened once again, on 7 January 1985, and has since remained in full operation, protected and under constant surveillance by the Metro Toronto police. Following its resumption of business in January 1985, the clinic existed in a legal limbo: pro-lifers were angry that the province allowed it to remain open despite Criminal Code statutes stipulating that abortions may be performed only in accredited hospitals after approval by a therapeutic abortion committee; pro-choice advocates were disturbed that the legality of the clinic remained in doubt even though its operators had been acquitted by a Supreme Court of Ontario jury on charges of conspiring to procure a miscarriage. (The Crown appeal of this verdict was scheduled to be heard on 29 April 1985.)[44]

Throughout all of this the clinic was picketed daily by anti-abortionists. At the beginning of February 1985 the Toronto-based Campaign Life, which was responsible for organizing the pickets, received an unexpected boost when Cardinal Carter announced in the archdiocesan newsletter plans for an intensive show of pro-life strength outside the clinic during the period of 18–21 February between 3:30 pm and 5:30 pm each day. Instructing the pastors of the archdiocese's 196 parishes to encourage their congregations to attend the demonstrations, the cardinal wrote: 'This is a strategically important time to let officials know that there is support for applying the law to prevent abortion on demand that Morgentaler and his associates seek.' The 'strategically important time' mentioned by Carter referred to the possibility that the newly elected Progressive Conservative government, with Frank Miller as premier, might be pressured into closing the clinic. The cardinal's directive, as well as his hard-hitting pastoral letter of November 1984 which had urged all Christians to co-operate 'to curb and, if possible, eliminate this abomination,' once again placed Carter in the limelight of the abortion controversy.[45]

Campaign Life welcomed the cardinal's support, though at least several of the organization's leaders interpreted it as an attempt by Carter to atone for previous indiscretions. From the other side of the fence, the cardinal's intervention was immediately denounced by pro-choice advocates and by leaders from Toronto's liberal Protestant and Jewish communities. Criticisms of the cardinal's involvement fastened upon one or more of the following three themes:

1 Anti-abortionists are moral terrorists who will stoop to the lowest tactics to deprive women of a necessary medical service.
2 The separation of church and state is a valuable feature of contemporary Canada, and thus the Catholic church has no legitimate place in the public forum.

3 Catholics who disapprove of abortion have no right to impose their morality upon the Canadian population.

The diatribe against Carter issued by Judy Rebick, spokeswoman for the Ontario Coalition for Abortion Clinics, combined all three themes and thus epitomized the complaints that would be echoed often in the Toronto media during the following month. Quoted in the *Globe and Mail*, Rebick said that 'it's shocking that responsible leaders of the church would call to support this picket line, whose only function is to harass women using the clinic.' Professing outrage that Carter would endorse the actions of 'a band of ruffians,' Rebick asserted that 'the church has no business trying to impose its moral values on the rest of us through government action.' Further, Rebick insisted that the 'formidable organization' of the Catholic church must be kept out of the abortion dispute. 'To me, it's stepping over the line of the division between church and state. Abortion is a moral issue, and Catholics have the right to their views. They're against abortion and don't have to use them.'[46]

In a similar vein, an editorial in the *Toronto Star* decried the spectacle of hundreds of Catholics converging on the clinic site 'to harass and frighten women who have made their own decision to seek an abortion.'[47] Very Reverend Bruce McLeod, a former United Church moderator, claimed that the demonstrations would only create divisiveness in the community and 'harass women who are availing themselves of a legal opportunity [to have an abortion].'[48] And a statement issued by fourteen Reform rabbis from across Canada likewise deplored calls from the 'pulpit urging people on to greater militancy' over the abortion issue. 'Religious leaders,' the statement read, 'should continue to instruct their communities in the truths of their tradition. But they must not upset the delicate balance of society by threatening to impose their values on other communities.'[49]

The scheduled week of demonstrations was actually orchestrated by the Pro-Life Action Committee, an ad hoc group formed specifically to pressure the provincial government to close the clinic permanently.[50] Although the Action Committee was broadly ecumenical in composition, its main driving force were Catholics who had once played prominent leadership roles in the Coalition for Life.[51] Because the Coalition had in previous years enjoyed a generally warm relationship with the Canadian hierarchy, these Catholics were in a better position than would have been the Campaign Life leadership to persuade Cardinal Carter to lend his authority to the demonstrations.

Reverend John Gallagher, principal spokesperson for the Pro-Life Action Committee, informed the press that Catholic high schools had been invited to participate in the four days of protest, which would culminate in a mass rally on Thursday, 21 February. Meanwhile, supporters of the clinic announced that they would stage a counter-demonstration on Friday, 22 February. 'We feel it's just outrageous that the Church is using religion for political ends,' said Judy Rebick of the Ontario Coalition for Abortion Clinics.[52] And Norma Scarborough of the Canadian Abortion Rights Action League remarked: 'I simply do not understand how they [the protesters] can assume they can control the lives of other people. It won't make any difference at all to a woman facing an unplanned pregnancy.'[53]

Monday, 18 February, the curtain raiser for the demonstrations, produced a turnout considerably less than anticipated by organizers. Approximately 150 placard-carrying marchers somberly traversed the Harbord Street sidewalk in front of the Morgentaler clinic. The protesters were mostly Roman Catholic, ethnically diverse, and were composed of roughly equal numbers of women and men. The temper of the demonstration was unabashedly religious, with small groups breaking away from the line of marchers to recite the rosary and the entire assembly combining to sing a hymn adapted from Deutero-Isaiah 49.

I will never forget you, my people
I have carved you on the palm of my hand
I will never forget you, I will not leave you orphaned
I will never forget my own.

Does a mother forget her baby?
Or a woman the child within her womb?
Yet, even if these forget
Yet, even if these forget
I will never forget my own.

Both media and police personnel were out in full force, perhaps anticipating a clash between pro-life and pro-choice factions, but though the demonstration bristled with energy it remained uneventful. The clinic was prudently closed for the week.[54]

The demonstration the following day was slightly larger and also free of violent confrontation. A protest marshal with a megaphone led the crowd in shouting slogans:

We Want Justice!
Premier Miller Uphold the Law!
Stop Killing Babies!
We Shall Overcome!
Close This Morgue![55]

Anti-abortion organizers, deeply disappointed by the modest turnouts of the first two days, were heartened by the 1000 to 1200 picketers who arrived on Wednesday, 20 February. Bolstered by busloads of demonstrators from thirty right-to-life groups across Ontario as well as contingents from Metro-area Catholic high schools, the picket line stretched for three city blocks and at one time engulfed the street itself, blocking traffic and creating a sea of placards and banners. Still, several demonstration leaders expressed concern that the vast majority of picketers were lay Catholics already committed to anti-abortion protest through their local pro-life groups: the event seemed not to have attracted many non-Catholics or previously uninvolved Catholics, and thus was essentially a convocation of the already converted. Considering that the ranks of protesters included only five identifiable priests, some leaders questioned whether the demonstrations had been duly publicized in Catholic parishes. (The author's poll of twenty parishes revealed that in only six had word of the demonstrations been broadcast from the Sunday pulpit; in the remainder it had been consigned a perfunctory space in the church bulletin.)[56]

The rally of Thursday, 21 February, meant to climax the week of demonstrations, was alternately buoyant, meditative, and surly. An impressive throng of roughly 3000 clogged the narrow sidewalks and alleyways surrounding the clinic, shuffling in a circling motion and joining the chorus of slogans prompted by marshals equipped with bullhorns:

Abortion's Got to Go – Hey Hey – Ho Ho!

Let Them Live!
Arrest Those Criminals!
Arrest That Murderer!
Praise the Lord!

The chanting and hymn-singing had a biting ring that had been absent the first three days. Hundreds of placards bore messages that confirmed the picketers' common purpose:

Adoption Not Abortion!
Your Choice Cost Me My Life!
It Could Have Been You!
Tiny Babies Are Being Killed in Here!
Abortion Exploits Women!
Unborn Women Have Rights Too!
10 Weeks after Conception – A Tiny Perfect Human Person!
Stop This Silent Holocaust!
Stop the Slaughter of the Innocents!
He's Not Heavy – He's My Brother!
Back Alley Butchers!
Father Forgive Them – They Do Not Know What They Are Doing.

The week's first incident of civil disobedience occurred at approximately 4:30 pm when three demonstrators sat down on the road and refused to allow traffic to pass. The mounted police reacted swiftly, escorting the three to a paddy wagon behind the clinic where they were charged with obstructing traffic. This incident reinforced the crowd's sense of militancy, the chants became louder and more vociferous, and a further fifty demonstrators defied the sidewalk barriers and spilled onto the road. Once again the mounted police moved in and forced the protesters from the pavement to a waiting paddy wagon where several were charged. By 6:00 pm the crowd had declined to about 1000 demonstrators and the rally came to an end at 6:30 pm. A dozen people remained to pray the rosary in front of the clinic's main doors where a huge banner had been unfurled, bearing the message: 'House of the Silent Scream – 85 Harbord.'[57]

The contagious excitement of the rally surpassed the crowd-induced emotion normally occasioned by political protests. With its predominantly Roman Catholic composition and consciousness, the gathering possessed the distinctive flavour of a religious revival. The incessant hymn-singing ('Kum-ba-yah' was the crowd favourite), overt Marian piety, and the emotively charged placards with pictures of bloody fetuses gave the demonstration an effervescent mood which underscored the common religious identity of its participants.

From the viewpoint of the anti-abortion movement, the public support given the demonstrations by Cardinal Carter was a double-edged sword. On the one hand, it helped to mobilize the activism of a greater number of Catholics. On the other hand, however, Carter's sanction of the protest was a blessing in disguise for the pro-choice side. Henceforth, anti-abortionism would be emblazoned in the public mind as a peculiarly Catholic hysteria and an attempt by a single religious group to control a crucial zone of decision-making. The nightmare of the movement's founders and the Coalition leadership had thus become reality: rather than being debated on grounds of empirical evidence and basic civil rights, the abortion issue had been turned into a controversy over the presumed threat posed to Canadian pluralism by intolerant Catholic zealots. The Catholic cat had finally been let out of the pro-life bag and the demonstrations would provide a constant store of ideological ammunition for the pro-choice side in the months ahead.

The cardinal's support of the demonstrations backfired for a second reason. In calling Catholics to anti-abortion protest, Carter was perhaps drawing upon a fund of authority that was already severely depleted. Of the more than one million Catholics in Metropolitan Toronto, less than two thousand made an appearance on Harbord Street between 18 and 21 February. (Several hundred of the Catholic picketers had come from outside the Metropolitan Toronto area.) This lukewarm response could be interpreted as evidence either of the political timidity of the vast majority of Catholics or that an astonishing number of Catholics had themselves become 'soft on abortion.' In any event, the lingering perception was that the mighty Catholic church had flexed its pro-life muscles only to be exposed as a lightweight. Thus, Cardinal Carter had gambled and lost at the 'abortion numbers game.' This observation was duly exploited at the pro-choice rally at Queen's Park on Friday of the same week. In alluding to the hundreds of thousands of Catholics who were notable by their absence from the

Harbord Street demonstrations, Judy Rebick assured her audience that the pro-choice ethic had thoroughly infiltrated even Catholicism.[58]

The Harbord Street demonstrations reconfirmed the essentially Catholic character of the pro-life movement. Despite appeals to 250 conservative Protestant congregations across Southern Ontario, the evangelical presence at the four days of protest was minimal.[59] (The 100 picketers covered by the author's informal survey, undertaken during the four days of protest, included 94 Catholics, 3 Canadian Reformed, 1 Baptist, and 2 protesters who identified themselves as 'Socialists against Nihilist Ethics.')

Despite its cosmopolitan texture, Toronto arguably still retains, in addition to an undercurrent of anti-Catholicism, an Anglo-Canadian disdain for outbursts of religious passion. Glimpses of this surfaced at the rally of 21 February. A reporter for a Toronto daily newspaper, when asked by the author for her impressions of the event, replied that 'As far as I'm concerned, it's just a bunch of Catholics making assholes of themselves again.' Similar sentiments were expressed by jeering motorists and pedestrians as they passed the protest. One policeman, mistaking the author for a reporter, remarked: 'It's always the same with these papist bastards. They want to take over the fucking country. Do these pricks think they can run my life?' A young man, taking field notes of the rally for a university project, described the demonstrators as 'Catholic nazis who'll flush the country down the toilet if we give them the chance.' And a United Church minister took several picketers aside for a stern lecture: 'Don't you realize that the whole country's laughing at you? You think you're making a point, but we're all in stitches. You're worshipping the Roman fetus-god, but this isn't Rome. Abortion has nothing to do with true religion. Consider this an invitation to the twentieth century.'

Cardinal Carter took a pummelling in the news media over his sponsorship of the demonstrations. In letters to the editor published by the Toronto dailies, Carter was variously accused of obscurantism, fanaticism, misogyny, hate-mongering, and child exploitation.[60] The sardonic tenor of most commentaries on the cardinal's involvement, in both the electronic and print media, was a lesson likely not lost on the fraternity of Canadian bishops: outright identification with the pro-life movement was a certain road toward social derision.[61] As a consequence, it appeared that Cardinal Carter's initial foray into anti-abortion militancy would likely also be his last. A high-ranking diocesan official confided to the author that the cardinal would be ill-advised to support any further demonstrations. 'I doubt you will see that again. The animus against the Cardinal's role in the picketing was tremendous. The media had a heyday bashing the Church. In reality the Cardinal played only a minor role in the whole thing, but I think it would be counterproductive for him to do anything similar in the future. The response from the Anglican and United Churches, and most segments of the Jewish community, was totally negative. This really hurts our ecumenical efforts.'[62]

Much of the enthusiasm among pro-lifers generated by the 21 February rally was deflated by the success of the pro-choice march the following day. Anti-abortionists had for years consoled themselves with the belief that the pro-choice position, while that of cultural cognoscenti, was instinctively loathsome to most Canadians. Accordingly, the bruises afflicted by repeated political setbacks were suffered in the hope that a future popular referendum would resoundingly vindicate their views. The demonstrations of February 1985 were regarded by many pro-lifers as just such a forum for measuring the respective numerical strength enjoyed by each side. Most activists interviewed by the author at the 21 February rally sincerely doubted that the pro-choice march scheduled for the next day would attract more than a handful of supporters. As one young woman put it: 'We're here marching for life, for the rights of unborn babies. This is solid. People must know that this is the truth. Who could actually stomach to march for the right to commit death? How could anyone do this? I'm going to be at Queen's Park tomorrow just so I can laugh at them. There won't be more than a few diehards there.'

On 22 February, however, approximately 5500 people, some carrying placards that read 'Saint Henry,' assembled at Queen's Park to demand that all charges against Morgentaler be dropped and that the Ontario government legalize elective abortion clinics. Bolstered by chants of

What do We Want? Choice! Now!
Not the Church – Not the State – Women Must Control Their Fate!

the crowd marched under police escort from the Parliament Buildings to the Harbord Street clinic. Included in the demonstration was a small group which carried a sign reading 'Catholics for Choice.' Also present was a contingent of about thirty United Church of Canada members. Alluding to the pro-life demonstrations of the previous four days, a retired United Church minister said: 'It's untenable in this modern world for one Christian denomination to try to force its opinion on the rest of us.'[63]

Judy Rebick boasted to cheering supporters that the rally had effectively 'blown [the opposition] out of the water' and exposed 'the anti-choice side as a tiny isolated minority.' While these claims were exaggerated, it did appear that the pro-life movement had been outgunned at a showdown it had felt certain to win. This massive show of pro-choice strength introduced an element of 'cognitive dissonance'[64] into pro-life ranks. The belief that the pro-choice movement could not possibly match the pro-life side in a duel of numbers, for many years a psychological salve for pro-lifers, had been severely shaken, and at least some activists surrendered the protest as a lost cause. A small band of seven pro-life activists, all youthful and all bravely adorned in 'Choose Life' buttons, attended the 22 February pro-choice rally fully expecting to witness a travesty. All seven, however, came away thoroughly demoralized and all but two of them shortly afterward discontinued their activism.

Veteran activists in Campaign Life and Toronto Right-to-Life, however, enured by years of combat to political disappointment, took the events of the week as confirmation that the 'worst-case scenario' had already descended, that Canada's moral resistance to abortion had dissolved and that even most Catholics were unprepared to take a public stand on behalf of unborn life. Thus, the fateful week of demonstrations would have an unanticipated consequence for the Canadian movement: instead of being transported into the centre of Canadian cultural life, the movement would sullenly retreat to its fringes, more than ever convinced that an evil larger than abortion had blanketed the country. On the bright side for pro-lifers, the February 1985 protests did bring to the movement a fresh supply of foot soldiers, most of whom were Catholic and under the age of thirty, and thus the survival of the anti-abortion gospel seemed assured for another generation.

The excitement generated by the Morgentaler clinic gave the pro-life movement some new wrinkles. In late 1984 several self-professed 'pro-life feminists' founded the Women's Network for Life (WNFL) for the purpose of challenging the pro-choice orthodoxy of mainstream feminism. Thus, in advertising a December 1984 demonstration against the clinic, WNFL spokeswoman Denyse Handler wrote that 'Feminism and pro-life should go together. Pro-abortion feminists resent the discrimination against a whole class of humans because they happen to be female, yet they themselves discriminate against a whole class of humans because they happen to be very young. They resent that the value of a woman is determined by whether a man wants her, yet they declare that the value of an unborn child is determined by whether her mother wants her.'[65] The WNFL, loosely affiliated with the American organization Feminists for Life, is the most recent attempt by progressives in the Canadian movement to build a bridge across the chasm that divides mainstream feminism and the pro-life ethic.[66] An earlier group of similar design existed in Toronto for several years during the 1970s. The members of WNFL are a 'cognitive minority'[67] in two worlds simultaneously. Treated like political lepers by established feminism and viewed as a fifth column by many pro-lifers, they constitute at present a fragile group concerned mainly with self-preservation.

The Morgentaler clinic was also the precipitant for the launching, on 23 February 1985, of Choose Life Canada, an anti-abortion ministry sponsored by the Ken Campbell Evangelistic Association. Campbell, pastor of Emmanuel Baptist Church in Milton, Ontario, was also the founder in 1974 of Renaissance Canada, an organization which claims 15,000 supporters across Canada and which exists to promote 'traditional values in public education and public life.'[68] In the summer of 1985 Choose Life Canada purchased half ownership in 87 Harbord Street, the same building which houses the Morgentaler clinic. There, immediately adjacent to the clinic, Campbell opened The Way Inn, which advertises itself as 'a counselling and support agency for mothers with difficult pregnancies.'[69] Campbell hoped that prospective clients of the clinic could be diverted by sidewalk counsellors into The Way Inn, where they would be encouraged to complete their pregnancies with the promise of moral and material support. This strategy has apparently been modestly successful: unconfirmed reports estimate that it has circumvented roughly five scheduled abortions per month.[70]

Publicity arising from the clinic was directly related to the introduction of an entirely new slant to anti-abortion activism in Canada. In late 1985 the Catholic Foundation for Human Life, an organization dedicated to the retrieval of a traditional Catholic sexual morality, began a clandestine 'rescue mission' in downtown Toronto.[71] By ambiguously advertising itself as a pregnancy referral service, the foundation sought to lure women with troubled pregnancies who were seeking abortions. Instead of making abortion arrangements, however, the foundation would provide its 'clients' with information on fetal development and discuss alternatives to abortion. Because of the surreptitious nature of this operation, as well as the foundation's refusal to grant interviews with potential 'enemy agents,' it is difficult to gauge its success. Similarly covert operations have existed for over a decade in the United States. As is the case for its American counterparts, the foundation is tangential to, and in some respects at conflict with, the broader pro-life movement. While some Toronto anti-abortionists are appreciative of the foundation's efforts, others believe that its misleading approach is unethical and perhaps fraudulent, and still others doubt the political efficacy of its 'underground strategy.' Foundation members, however, are nonplussed by such misgivings. They understand themselves to be engaged in guerrilla warfare against a satanic force which has conquered Western society. The foundation's Toronto co-ordinator, who guardedly consented to speak to the author only by telephone, insisted that pro-lifers are obligated to be more cunning than their adversaries. 'It's beyond the point where we can attribute the rise in abortion to normal political conflict. It's the fruit of a demonic conspiracy. It's insidious and it's everywhere. The whole culture all of a sudden says it's fine and good to kill babies. This is the madness we're up against, and so we have to resort to every tactic we can. Do you know how pervasive the evil is? Maybe you're part of it. It's our responsibility to be aware of "wolves in sheep's clothing."'

Following the demonstrations of February 1985, protest against the Morgentaler clinic settled into a regular pattern that has since remained essentially unchanged. Anywhere from five to one hundred picketers are stationed daily during business hours at the front and rear entrances of the clinic. In addition, volunteer counsellors, most of whom are young Catholic women, confront women about to enter the clinic and attempt to persuade them to complete their pregnancies. Partly because this is only rarely successful, and is recognized as the most emotionally draining aspect of pro-life work, counsellors are limited to stints of one or two hours, after which they normally join the line of picketers. Those women thusly deterred from undergoing an abortion are either brought into The Way Inn or referred to Birthright or one of several other 'crisis pregnancy centres,' where arrangements may be made for maternity assistance.

More dramatic forms of protest are described by activists as 'public witness' or 'direct action.' These usually involve picketing the private residences of clinic employees and public appearances of 'pro-abortion' politicians. But the limelight of 'public witness,' engaged in mainly by the movement's elite cadre of activists, is civil disobedience at the clinic site. The Canadian movement discovered civil disobedience in 1985, and has since then held in highest esteem those who show a readiness to suffer arrest for the cause.

CIVIL DISOBEDIENCE IN THE CANADIAN AND AMERICAN PRO-LIFE MOVEMENTS

The subject of civil disobedience provides a useful point of reference for comparing the respective temperaments of the Canadian and American pro-life movements.

Unlike the American situation, where activists have received lengthy prison sentences for vandalizing abortion clinics, civil disobedience in Canada has thus far been employed primarily as a symbolic gesture: Canadian activists have staged several sit-ins at the Morgentaler clinic as well as one at the Ontario premier's Queen's Park office; they have twice obstructed vehicular traffic in front of the clinic, and have several times padlocked the clinic's rear gate. Despite frequent charges of harassment and assault brought by clinic employees against pro-lifers, only twice have Canadian activists been imprisoned for convictions related to civil disobedience, and no Canadian activist has yet to spend more than several days in jail. Still, civil disobedience has captured the imagination of the Canadian movement and its practitioners have generally been regarded as anti-abortion heroes. Indeed, given the inbred 'law and order' mentality of Canadian culture,[72] it is striking that civil disobedience has so readily been accepted within the movement as a legitimate mode of protest.[73]

In direct contrast to the Canadian situation, where Campaign Life has accorded it the status of a pro-life sacrament, civil disobedience has been a source of considerable dissension among American anti-abortionists. The executive of the influential National Right to Life Committee (NRLC), the organization which claims to represent the mainstream pro-life voice in the United States, has renounced civil disobedience and called on its membership to work solely through socially respectable channels. But snapping at the heels of the NRLC, trying to goad it into a more confrontational approach, are smaller, more volatile groups such as the Prolife Nonviolent Action Project, Father Paul Marx's Human Life International, Prolifers for Survival, the St Louis-based Pro-Life Direct Action League, and Joe Scheidler's Pro-Life Action League in Chicago.[74] These groups regard the NRLC as a ponderous, self-congratulatory body which, in trying to steer the pro-life movement into the heartland of middle-class American culture, has blunted the urgency of the abortion issue. Educational efforts, political lobbying, crisis pregnancy services, and counselling, they insist, are by themselves an inadequate response to the daily destruction of human life in abortion clinics across America. In his *No Cheap Solutions*, a booklet which has found a receptive audience among many Canadian Catholic activists, John Cavanaugh-O'Keefe writes: 'Offering alternatives to abortion is prochoice – *truly* prochoice, but *only* prochoice. Education, while urgently necessary, is extremely dangerous when it is not accompanied by action to clarify the urgency of the message. Legislation may shape the future, but children are dying now ... What is missing in the Right-to-Life Movement is the simple statement, fleshed out in action, that the unborn are our brothers and sisters. The heart of the movement is loving action to protect our unborn brothers and sisters. The future of the movement is direct action.'[75]

In like vein, Juli Loesch, founder of Prolifers for Survival, insists that pro-lifers must graduate beyond even symbolic protest such as sit-ins and engage in direct action to put an immediate stop to abortions. 'Symbolic action is very limited ... The analogy is if you had a fire and you called the fire department and they came and they picketed the fire and started chanting, "No more fire, no more fire." That's protesting fire. So we don't do [direct action] to express our inner feelings ... We do it to stop abortions in that clinic on that day.'[76]

As the militant purists of the American movement, the 'direct actionists' insist that pro-lifers are morally obligated to shut down abortion clinics, or at least to disrupt their operation. In a country where elective clinics have become a standard feature of urban ecology, a number of these activists have adopted civil disobedience as a veritable life-style and some, in the words of Charles Rice, 'have made a conscious choice to offer their lives in what amounts to a cyclical imprisonment for life.'[77]

The leadership of the NRLC has attempted to defuse the romantic allure held by the movement's militant faction by calling for a moratorium on public protest altogether (with the exception of *domesticated* street picketing) and by arguing that the best prospects for success lie with polite persuasion.[78] The NRLC is probably sincere, and also likely correct, in believing the prevailing cultural climate of the United States to be inhospitable to liberally unesthetic exhibitions of anti-abortionism. Nevertheless, its preference for a temperate mode of protest is not fully appreciated without consideration of several factors.

First, the NRLC has worked hard to cultivate a liaison with the governing Republican party in the hope of consolidating political support for the anti-abortion agenda. (For its part, by currying favour with a constituency whose numerical strength remains temptingly uncertain, the Republican party hopes to garner a store of credit which may deliver dividends in future elections.) The survival of this marriage of convenience depends in large measure upon the willingness of anti-abortionists to limit themselves to legal and institutionalized avenues of protest, and thus the NRLC has sought to fence the movement within a tame pasture.

Second, the NRLC desires to give the movement an ecumenical stamp and, in particular, to accommodate the tastes of the recently politicized force of American evangelicalism. Public defiance of the law through civil disobedience lies well beyond the scope of what most American evangelicals, weaned to show deference to *consecrated* civil authority, would deem acceptable political protest. Although some evangelicals have recently shown an openness to engage in more extreme forms of activism, the radical wing of the American movement is composed predominantly of young Irish-American Catholics. Many of these militant Catholics have neither much stake in the existing order nor much affection for the Republican party, and are prepared to demonstrate their commitment to the cause regardless of expense to themselves personally or to the movement's public reputation.[79]

And third, the public image of the broader movement has been tarnished over the past few years by the bombing of a number of abortion clinics. While the movement's extremist wing disclaims any responsibility for these bombings, and insists that there is no 'conspiracy of violence' against clinics, it refuses to condemn as immoral any actions, if merely destructive of private property, that are intended to save unborn life. But the NRLC leadership is concerned that *any* illegal activities by anti-abortionists are grist for the mill of a news media eager to vilify the movement as a clearing house for social misfits and religious fanatics. Accordingly, it has appealed to its membership to wash its hands of civil disobedience in order that the movement might better foster a reputation as the stoic conscience of middle-class America.[80]

Mainly because elective abortion clinics have only recently been introduced in English Canada, civil disobedience has thus far been conducted on a much less dramatic scale than in the United States. And yet, in contrast to the American case, civil disobedience (activists prefer to call it 'holy disobedience') is an uncontroversial strategy within the mainstream Canadian movement and has, in fact, been encouraged, staged, and participated in by movement leaders. Indeed, with the opening in 1986 of a second Toronto clinic by a Morgentaler associate, and given the eventuality that the Supreme Court of Canada may rule in favour of the legality of elective abortion clinics, it is not unlikely that 'direct action' will become a more prominent element of the Canadian movement's activist repertoire.[81] Many Canadian Catholic activists have already expressed impatience with more conventional modes of protest.

Why, in comparison to the American movement, has the centre of the Canadian movement become radicalized and more extreme forms of protest been given legitimacy? As discussed earlier, pro-life organizations in Canada, such as the Coalition and the Alliance, which have historically promoted a more moderate form of protest, have been pushed to the periphery by Campaign Life, which has effectively taken control of the movement's reins. And because anti-abortion activism is understood by the Campaign Life leadership as the sine qua non of authentic Catholicism in a post-Christian society, civil disobedience, with its strains of religious bravery and even martyrdom, is particularly valued as a virtuoso expression of anti-worldly spirituality. Furthermore, whereas the American movement has made inroads into the political establishment, Canadian anti-abortionists have been treated by all three national parties as a political liability and have been shunted into a bleak corner of the national political scene. The growing radicalism within the Canadian movement, then, is partly the product of frustrated expectation and an accumulated feeling of political impotency.[82]

THE CALVINIST CONNECTION

One of the more significant developments arising from the February 1985 demonstrations has been the increased presence on the Harbord Street picket line of Dutch-Canadian Protestants, most of whom are members of either the Christian Reformed Church or the smaller, more theologically conservative Canadian Reformed Church. Catholics and their Calvinist allies together constitute over 90 per cent of clinic picketers; the remainder consists of a smattering of Presbyterians, Anglicans, Baptists, Pentecostals, and others of no professed religious allegiance. Though less inclined than their Catholic counterparts to participate in civil disobedience, Reformed activists similarly espouse a 'sanctity of life' ethic and believe abortion to be a crime of the same magnitude as murder.[83] Whereas the Catholic activist contingent (which comprises roughly 70 per cent of the total number of picketers) is composed of an equal number of women and men and includes many young adults under the age of thirty, Reformed picketers are preponderantly middle-aged housewives with three or more children. There is, in addition, a corps of Reformed men, mostly farmers from a one-hundred-kilometre radius of Toronto, who make a weekly pilgrimage to the picket line.

Catholic and Calvinist activists are predominantly lay people whose theology and social values may be described as stubbornly conservative. Very few priests or ministers have joined them on the picket line, and they have discovered a commonality that cuts across religious differences. Both draw on religious traditions which make allowance for the challenge of civil authority believed to be unjust or corrupt. And perhaps even more germane to their shared activism, both have rejected the central precept of modern secularism, namely, that the religious and political spheres be circumscribed in separate, self-confined orbits.[84]

'THE SLEAZY AGREEMENT'

Cardinal Carter's support of the February 1985 demonstrations so surprised Catholic militants that some even considered a reappraisal of the institutional Canadian church's commitment to the anti-abortion cause. An August 1985 agreement struck by Ontario Attorney-General Ian Scott with Cardinal Carter and pro-choice organizer Norma Scarborough to limit the number of picketers outside the Harbord Street clinic, however, reopened old wounds and set off another round of intra-Catholic acrimony.

As the protests outside the Morgentaler clinic escalated throughout 1985, neighbourhood residents and merchants complained of unruly crowd behaviour, noise, and constant tension. When a neighbourhood association caught the ear of Attorney-General Scott with these complaints, he arranged separate meetings with Cardinal Carter and Norma Scarborough, president of the Canadian Abortion Rights Action League, to secure a means of restoring the clinic neighbourhood to its 'normal tranquillity.' Advising Carter and Scarborough that protesters outside the clinic were subjecting neighbourhood people to 'severe inconvenience and occasionally to risk to their safety,' and that the question of the clinic's legality would likely be before the courts for at least several years, Scott requested that the number of demonstrators from each side be limited at any one time to five or fewer.[85]

In his reply to the attorney-general, Cardinal Carter expressed personal sympathy with the frustration and intentions of the clinic protesters. Nevertheless, he wrote, 'all people of goodwill should deplore' the 'grave risk to public safety' and 'tendencies to violence' that had become associated with the Harbord Street pickets.

> There can be no doubt that people in a democracy who have strong convictions have the right to demonstrate those convictions and to communicate their opinion to the general public. But nothing, absolutely nothing can be achieved by violence. To endanger life in the name of life is a contradiction

which hardly bears comment ... I must urgently request all of the organizers of demonstrations in this situation to limit their action so that violence may not be incited or encouraged. I urge the pro-life groups to agree to provide not more than five picketers under any circumstances ... We must demonstrate to our own community and to the world in general that we can be law-abiding citizens no matter how passionately we feel about our convictions.[86]

On 22 August 1985 Cardinal Carter wrote to Campaign Life and Toronto Right-to-Life, requesting that they support his 'plea for a de-escalation of confrontation' and agree to limit their 'picketers to the number of five.' The cardinal entreated the picket organizers to eschew violence and to restrict their activism to legal and pacific avenues. 'Violence would very much damage our cause and create an atmosphere in which we would be virtually helpless to use the means which are available, such as legal procedures and public peaceful pressure. Violence would alienate the great majority of the community in which we live and would end up being a disservice to the very innocent children whom we are trying to protect.'[87]

The cardinal's diplomatic intervention at this juncture was plausibly motivated by sincere concern for public order and safety and the public reputation of the pro-life movement. But, in addition, having entangled himself in the protest business six months earlier, it is not unlikely that Carter desired to distance both himself and the official church from any untoward truculence on the Harbord Street picket line.

It is noteworthy that the cardinal seems to have subscribed wholesale to the popular media image of the clinic protest as menacing and violent. Throughout six months of intermittent participant observation at the clinic site, the author neither personally witnessed, nor heard reports of, acts of violence committed by anti-abortionists. Two widely publicized incidents which did occur over a year previously seem to have registered permanently on the public perception of the protest. The first, an attempted bombing of the clinic which resulted in extensive damage to a women's bookstore housed in the same building, was apparently not the responsibility of anyone formally connected to a pro-life organization. In the second, an elderly man, likewise unaffiliated except in the loosest sense with the movement, made a threatening lunge with a pair of gardening shears at Dr Morgentaler.

With the exception of these two conspicuous incidents, performed during the clinic's first year of operation by people not subject to movement control, it does not seem to be true, as both Carter and Scott suggested, that the protest constituted a 'grave risk to public safety.' Even the sporadic acts of civil disobedience were undertaken in nonviolent fashion. Although at least several activists confessed a dream of violence against the clinic, they did not seriously entertain the possibility of implementing it. Ironically, it was anti-abortionists themselves during this period who seemed to face the greater physical danger. The author saw a woman threaten three activists with a shotgun, another woman pull a knife on a middle-aged female picketer, a clinic doctor on two occasions threaten to 'kick the shit out of' activists, and a clinic employee repeatedly promise that he would 'blow the fucking brains out of [the] motherfucking Catholics.'

The daily protests undoubtedly were, however, nerve-jangling and disruptive to area residents and business people and could qualify as 'violent' if the term were given a sufficiently broad meaning. Anti-abortionists sometimes kicked the bumpers and tires and more than once draped themselves across the hoods of cars driven by clinic employees; they taunted police officers assigned to protect the clinic, and indulged in name calling, shouting, and loud chanting. Designation of a protest as either 'violent' or 'peaceful' is, of course, largely a matter of political definition, and depends to a considerable extent upon whether opinion-makers in the media and elsewhere approve of its basic goals. Thus, demonstrations of a similar range of activities and intensity may be labelled alternatively as 'spirited,' 'enthusiastic,' 'boisterous,' 'threatening,' or 'violent' according to the degree of deviance ascribed to them. The Harbord Street protest was uniformly depicted in the Toronto media as deviant, hysterical, and violent, and at least one commentator suggested that the police should suppress it entirely.[88]

Cardinal Carter's 'sleazy agreement,' which was how several activists described the accord with Attorney-General Scott and Norma Scarborough, aroused disgust within pro-life circles. Not only had Carter lent credibility to the image of the protest as violence-prone, but he had agreed to a deal in which only the anti-abortion side was expected to make concessions. The accord entailed no cost whatsoever to the pro-choice side which, as Norma Scarborough herself pointed out, had decided several months earlier to refrain from organizing pickets at the

Harbord Street site.[89] Worst of all to activists was the involvement of Scarborough in the deal. To their minds, Carter had consorted with the enemy and turned his back on innocent lives merely for the sake of reducing public conflict.

What this episode made clear was that most public actors, including the attorney-general, the media, pro-choice leaders, and perhaps Cardinal Carter himself, still did not appreciate the essentially popular, extra-institutional character of the pro-life movement. No one in the Canadian Catholic hierarchy, and perhaps least of all Cardinal Carter, was in a position to manipulate or assert authority over movement strategy. Campaign Life leaders bristled at the thought they should hand over their lay independence to an institution that had appeared from the start Janus-faced on the abortion issue. In their view Cardinal Carter and most Canadian bishops were moral inferiors, incapable of a solid commitment to the cause.

Having misread the relationship of the movement to the official church, the Toronto media expressed surprise that pro-life leaders intended to 'disobey' the 'religious leader of the city's anti-choice movement.'[90] Laura McArthur, president of Toronto Right-to-Life, gave the situation perspective when she informed the press that 'We're not bound by any wheeling and dealing between Carter and the pro-abortionists.'[91] And promising that 'It will be business as usual' in front of the Harbord Street clinic, Gwendolyn Landolt, Campaign Life's chief legal adviser, fulminated: 'Cardinal Carter may be speaking for himself, but he doesn't speak for the pro-life movement.'[92] And from the opposition, Judy Rebick of the Ontario Coalition for Abortion Clinics expressed pleasure that 'Cardinal Carter has at last condemned violence and harassment at the clinic.'[93]

Campaign Life, true to form, disregarded the agreement to limit picketers, and protest against the clinic continued unabatedly. More significant than this episode itself, which after all was just one of countless skirmishes fought by the movement, was the fallout it produced. Recent Catholic recruits to the movement, whose incubating experience had been the February 1985 demonstrations, learned that defiance of the Canadian Catholic hierarchy was part of the price to be paid for their activist spurs. As one young male activist related to the author:

I have to admit, when I first came out in the snow last winter it was partly because of what Carter said about the abortuary and the need for Catholics to oppose it. But now I realize that we're part of a very small Church, a true and faithful Church, within a huge apathetic institution that couldn't care less about what we're trying to accomplish. It seems that the unborn are close to the bottom of the bishops' list of priorities. As for us, they probably just wish we'd piss off into the wind, and that way save them a lot of aggravation and embarrassment. I've met a lot of solid Catholics on the picket line. We pray together and have become really close. What they tell me about the bishops and abortion is a horror story.

By far the most encouraging event for the movement in 1985 was the 21 September 'Justice for the Unborn' rally which took place in front of the Ontario legislative buildings and culminated in a procession past the Morgentaler clinic.[94] The turnout, estimated by organizers at between twenty and twenty-five thousand, suggested to movement leaders that the time was ripe for the formation of a 'pro-life' political party. Thus, by 1986 much of the movement's energy would be dedicated to creating a concrete alternative to Canada's 'anti-life' political consensus.[95]

4

A Typology of Anti-Abortion Activism

In an age when every ripple of social dissent is accorded instantaneous celebrity status by insatiable news media, critical observation is often sacrificed to the production of facile stereotypes, which invariably reveal more about reigning cultural biases than the social reality to which they are supposed to refer. As Turner and Killian have noted, when the media become aware of a movement they tend 'to reify it and assign it a transparent and unitary character.'[1] Thus, the image of the anti-abortionist most likely to elicit recognition among Canadians may be that of the gullible stooge of celibate priest-masters, marching naïvely with rosary in hand, and expecting every woman to emulate the Virgin at the Annunciation, greeting news of her pregnancy with a sense of reverence mixed with astonishment.[2] American anti-abortionists, James Kelly has observed, are likewise ensconced in popular stereotypes and journalistic caricature. 'Right-to-Life activists are commonly characterized as sectarian, morally naive, politically conservative, and best understood in the reductive social-psychological terms of "status politics" ... The problem, it seems, is not in the moral dilemmas of abortion, but in the misshapen psychologies of those opposing abortion.'[3]

The scholarly output on this subject is not much more enlightening. Most works purportedly intended to analyse the values and motivations of pro-life activists have been ruled by a vulgar reductionism, whereby political opposition to abortion is explained entirely according to categories of cultural maladjustment and psychological pathology.[4] What these works share is the ascription of ulterior and irrational motives to pro-life activists. Operating from the assumption that the anti-abortion stance is inherently and self-evidently unreasonable, they attempt to ascertain the personal deficiencies that would induce someone to hold it. Turner and Killian, on this score, have noted the Manichaean tendency among scholars of social movements: the goals and articulated meanings of movements the scholar approves of are taken at face value; movements that the scholar personally disparages, however, are interpreted 'as vehicles for dealing with personal frustrations while disguising pathological motives as lofty ideals.'[5]

Precisely because it is concerned more to understand the world-views of activists than to propagandize for or against them, Kristin Luker's *Abortion and the Politics of Motherhood* is the most balanced and intellectually satisfying study to yet appear on the subject.[6] Written in the demanding tradition of Weberian social science, where the point is to analyse and clarify conflicts over values rather than adjudicate them,[7] Luker's book successfully penetrates the identities of those who have created headlines by protesting abortion. Even this work, however, contains some defects similar to those discussed above.

Luker depicts American anti-abortionists as a unitary status group with a common set of demographic and ideological characteristics.

> The average pro-life woman is also a forty-four-year-old married woman who grew up in a large metropolitan area. She married at age seventeen and has three children or more. Her father was a high school graduate, and she has some college education or may have a B.A. degree. She is not employed in the paid labor force and is married to a small businessman or a lower-level white-collar worker; her family income is $30,000 a year. She is Catholic (and may have converted), and her religion is one of the most important aspects of her life: she attends church at least once a week and occasionally more often.[8]

Given this activist profile, Luker argues, anti-abortionism may be interpreted as a rearguard protest against the devalued status acclaim of motherhood in contemporary Western society. Abortion is opposed primarily because it is the most visceral symbol of a profound historical process – the transvaluation of the domestic role of women – which threatens the prestige and honour traditionally accorded motherhood. What abortion implies to pro-life women, according to Luker, is both the desanctification of motherhood and the diminished cultural significance of raising a family. 'When pregnancy is discretionary – when people are allowed to put anything else they value in front of it – then motherhood has been demoted from a sacred calling to a job.'[9]

Luker's analysis does convey an important insight. Indeed, some of the women interviewed for the present study candidly acknowledged that personal resentment over their declining status as homemakers was pivotal to their anti-abortion protest. Nevertheless, anti-abortionists, at least in Canada, are not reducible to a single sociological type. The fragmented character of the Canadian movement reflects above all the ideological diversity of its membership. While it is true that disaffected housewives are a significant component of the movement, pro-life activists in Canada exhibit a plurality of what Gusfield has aptly termed 'paradigms of experience.'[10] As evidenced by their different social backgrounds, value commitments, and aspirations, it is clear that not all activists inhabit the same cognitive and cultural world. At the most obvious level, for example, Luker's *status deprivation* thesis fails to account for the considerable pro-life involvement, in both Canada and the United States, of men and of unmarried women under the age of thirty.[11]

In addition to its Procrustean bent, Luker's thesis suffers from an implicit monocausality: the impugned status of housewives in the face of the exodus of women from homemaking into the public workplace is adduced as the primary, if not exclusive, impetus behind anti-abortionism. This explanation of pro-life activism perhaps conceals an ideological bias. In locating the roots of anti-abortionism in the sociocultural circumstances of activists, it seems to imply (though Luker does not explicitly state it) that the question of abortion itself cannot, or should not, carry sufficient moral weight to arouse people to activism. Rather than taking seriously the claims of anti-abortionists regarding the inherent value of fetal life, these claims are dismissed *tout court* as a façade for what is essentially an alarmist reaction to the realignment of gender roles in contemporary society. It may be that the social situation of some housewives is especially conducive to pro-life activism, just as that of some white middle-class students was conducive to civil rights activism in the 1950s and 1960s. There is no reason, however, to assume the motivational relevancy of conscience in the latter case while precluding it in the former.

If a reductionistic explanation of anti-abortionism is intellectually unacceptable, so too would be one that saw pro-life activism as an ethical response sui generis and, as such, one uninfluenced by activists' specific social locations, status discontents, political affinities, and religiosity. Accordingly, this study will attempt to avoid either interpreting anti-abortionism as merely a psychological pretension or in abstracting it from its social context. Such an approach seems advantageous because, while not ignoring the sociological dimension of pro-life protest, neither does it preclude the relevance of the moral concerns raised by activists.

Over a twelve-month period in 1985 and 1986 the author conducted interviews with an availability sample of one hundred and eleven anti-abortion activists. The sample represents a cross-section of the movement's various organizations as well as its ethnic, age, and gender distributions. (Fifty-five of the subjects are women.) Because all of the subjects reside in the Toronto area, however, it may reflect a regional bias and thus is perhaps not fully representative of the national movement.[12] While the uniqueness of each subject should be respected, the interviewing process did in fact yield several distinctive patterns. Opponents of abortion experience different kinds of tension with Canada's prevailing culture, which vary according to their constellation of values and the circumstances of their pro-life commitment. Thus, since anti-abortion activists are not all of a piece, it seems useful to distinguish several empirical types.

The purpose of delineating a typology of activism is simply to render the bewildering variety of individual cases in a manageable form. Specific and illustrative case studies presented in Chapter Five will bring the typology to life. It should be stressed that the typology discriminates empirically available cases of activism and, as such, is grounded in the *Lebenswelten* of the activists themselves. The empirical types outlined here, therefore, are not pure or ideal constructs devised solely for heuristic purposes.[13] (As the author understands the difference, the empirical type organizes reality whereas the ideal type analyses it.) At the same time, because they are designed to cast attention upon and to accentuate distinctive characteristics among activists, the types do not correspond exactly to any particular, concrete individuals. They are, so to speak, composite profiles that may facilitate a nuanced understanding of the complex pro-life phenomenon. Moreover, as will become apparent, the types are not mutually exclusive and they allow for significant areas of overlap.

The typology considers the following elements: activists' careers, or the social psychological background of anti-abortionism; the primary authorities by which activists legitimate the pro-life position; preferred modes of discourse for presenting this position to the wider society; attitudes toward contemporary popular culture in Canada; the role of religion in the anti-abortion world-view; and the social locations of activists.

EMERGENT NORMS IN THE CANADIAN PRO-LIFE MOVEMENT

Turner and Killian, as well as other scholars in the collective behaviour tradition inspired by Robert E. Park,[14] have underscored the role of *emergent norms* in the process whereby collective action becomes channelled into a concerted and purposive direction. In order both to justify and co-ordinate their participation in a social movement, as well as to endow it with the character of an obligatory mission, social actors require a shared definition of what is unjust about a situation and how best to resolve it. This *definition of the situation*, or *emergent norm*, in the words of Turner and Killian, 'serves to guide and coordinate behavior by providing for the actors both *meaning*, an interpretation of what is going on, and *rules* about what sorts of behavior are consistent with this definition.'[15] The emergent norm may be likened to an ideological charter whereby movement members are bound together in a common course of action for the sake of ameliorating a shared grievance. Far from being static, the emergent norm matures and crystallizes with the development of the movement.[16] And as is the case in the present context, the movement may have competing emergent norms, each of which is advanced by one of its own internal constituencies. These emergent norms may, then, have a rotating ascendancy as the power configurations within the movement change over time.

The factional conflict discussed in earlier chapters attests to the existence of competing *definitions of the situation* within the Canadian pro-life movement. Indeed, there exist within the movement three empirical types of activist which are animated and defined by three quite different *emergent norms*. These empirical types, which correspond to *actual* ideological groupings within the movement, may be designated as *civil rights* activists, *family heritage* activists, and *Catholic Revivalist* activists. The respective emergent norms of these types can be summarized as follows:

1 *Civil rights activists*. The performance of abortion for any reason other than to save the mother's life is an unjust destruction of innocent human life. If abortions cannot be eliminated entirely, they can be significantly reduced by fostering an awareness of the humanity of the fetus (educational reform), by bringing about legal protection for the fetus (legislative reform), and by changing cultural attitudes and social structures that discriminate against women with children (institutional reform). The case for the fetus should be made by appealing exclusively to scientific evidence and to basic principles of civil rights.
2 *Family heritage activists*. Besides promoting the destruction of innocent human life, the movement toward liberalized abortion is a calculated strategy on the part of cultural elites (feminists, secular humanists) to subvert both the traditional family and traditional religious values. Because pro-abortionists are determined to accomplish their goals regardless of the biological status of the fetus, it is futile and naïve to think that the issue can be resolved by tactical mechanisms of persuasion (educational reform) and facilitation (institutional reform).[17] Civil rights activists are wrong to assume the moral decency of their opponents. In addition to educational and legislative reform, therefore, it is necessary both to attack pro-choice forces at their vulnerable points and to champion traditional family and religious values. The pro-life movement is, above all else, a *moral crusade*.
3 *Revivalist Catholic activists*. In addition to the destruction of innocent human life and the endangerment of traditional religious values and family organization, what is at stake in the abortion issue is the survival of Canadian Catholicism as an authentic vessel of transcendence and eternal salvation. In an age of accelerated spiritual crisis, when the Canadian church has become a yea-sayer rather than a sign of contradiction to secular culture, it is imperative that those Catholics in fidelity to the church's ancient past demonstrate their unqualified allegiance to the unborn. For in so doing, they give

witness both to ultimate value and to the supernatural origin of all created life. To the extent that mainstream Canadian Catholicism fails to rally to the cause, it betrays itself as compromised and spiritually otiose. The pro-life movement is a sacred crusade.

The first three chapters provided an overview of the reciprocity of relationships between these three activist types and their respective emergent norms, or *value orientations*. The various permutations that have taken place in the movement's history have been due to an ongoing contest between these norms. Thus, the value orientation of civil rights activists was dominant in the movement's early years, and was only seriously challenged when it became apparent to many in the movement that liberalized abortion was symptomatic of a more general upheaval in Canadian society. Confronted by a rising abortion rate and an intransigent opposition, and convinced that liberalized abortion was a frontal assault against a traditional cultural order, many activists became dissatisfied with the earlier emergent norm. Rather than simply being abandoned, however, the civil rights norm was modified, elaborated, and thereby converted into one more consonant with the attitudes and interpretations of the majority of grass roots activists. Thus, the emphasis given the human rights of the fetus by the older norm was retained, but added to it were elements concerning family and religion.

The interaction of several factors gave the family heritage norm ascendancy in the late 1970s: an influx into the movement of stay-at-home mothers, fear and frustration brought about by political failure, the cultural establishment of feminism, and unhappiness with the leadership of the Coalition. The 1977 Coalition brief was the coup de grâce for the civil rights norm. Prominent advocates of the family heritage norm both instigated and exploited discontent with the brief in order to convince grass roots activists that the movement should reassess its purpose, its direction, and, most of all, its enemies. The refusal of most civil rights activists to subscribe to this revised norm amplified the movement's ideological disparity.

Much like the family heritage norm, the Revivalist Catholic norm existed in gestation for a number of years before a combination of circumstances induced its delivery. Although Catholics of varied theological persuasions have participated in pro-life activism, the movement historically has held a special appeal for Catholics of a profoundly conservative religious disposition, many of whom feel disinherited from the resculptured post-Vatican II church. Many of these Catholics have been unable to discern the imprint of the sacred in the reformed church, and they believe that Canadian Catholicism in particular has lost its transcendent edge and become little other than a somewhat solemnized reflection of prevailing cultural habits. Convinced that the Canadian church has sacrificed a large portion of its heritage on the altar of cultural relevance, these Catholics regard the abortion issue as a redemptive trial. By identifying with the pro-life cause, in their view, Catholics both repudiate the value system of secularism, where human decision is the measure of all things, and demonstrate their allegiance to a higher order of meaning.

The apparent failure of the bishops and Canadian Catholics generally to conceive the issue in such absolutist terms is seen by Revivalists as the final capitulation. A church unwilling to take an unequivocal stand on behalf of unborn life is one which has clearly become a mere adjunct to the world. The charter debate and the February 1985 demonstrations served as crucial 'keynoting'[18] events for the crystallization of the Revivalist norm, and by the end of 1985 many Catholic militants conceived themselves as a special elect called to revitalize Canadian Catholicism by heroic dedication to the anti-abortion cause.

Rather than displacing it, the Revivalist norm has extended and complemented the family heritage norm. It has struck a responsive chord among those in the movement who have felt, however vaguely, that something was amiss with the contemporary church. Not all pro-life Catholics, however, are ready to include the Canadian church within an encompassing theory of cultural decline. Some, and civil rights activists in particular, believe that the religiously embroidered militancy of Revivalists has obfuscated the essential purpose of the movement.

Most of the remainder of this chapter will discuss these three activist types in greater detail.

THE SCATTERED TROOPS – CIVIL RIGHTS ACTIVISTS

Civil rights activists conceive anti-abortionism as an essential aspect of a more extensive project of creating a social order in which no class of human life is denied fundamental justice. They believe that pro-life activism is comparable to such historical movements of emancipation as nineteenth-century abolitionism and the current struggle against South Africa's racist system of apartheid. And while they acknowledge the deep crevice that separates their position from that of mainstream feminism, they insist that anti-abortionism is not in principle incompatible with, and in a better world would be integral to, the expressed feminist goal of full human liberation. They aspire by their activism, in the words of one woman, 'to simply win the fetus membership in the human race.'

Civil rights activists espouse what has become known in the progressive wing of the American movement as a 'consistent' or 'seamless garment' pro-life ethic.[19] Thus, they seek to integrate anti-abortionism within an inclusive 'pro-life' conceptual framework that encompasses such concerns as world peace, economic justice, and racial equality. They claim to be especially concerned, as one woman put it, 'to bring about social change so that women will no longer be marginalized by child-bearing.'

These activists believe that the abortion issue should be addressed exclusively according to the language and logic of 'civil rights.' Thus, they speak of the aborted fetus as a victim of ultimate violence and as a social outcast which has been denied any vestige of due process. Furthermore, they attempt to turn the pro-choice argument on its head by claiming that abortion exacts an untold psychological and physical toll from women and that liberalized abortion, ironically, perpetuates and reinforces the cultural image of women as sexual playthings.[20]

The style of discourse favoured by civil rights activists – temperate, ecumenical, humanistic – is partly a reflection of their class standing. Of the twenty-one sample subjects who qualify as civil rights activists, fourteen are professionals in academia, law, medicine, or journalism and are thus better equipped than most in the movement to present the anti-abortion position at a sophisticated level of analysis. And though eleven of the twenty-one are devoted Catholics, all recognize that Christianity no longer holds a 'presidency'[21] in the public realm and prefer that the institutional Catholic church limit its involvement in the movement to occasional statements of support that might have a resonance of plausibility for the wider community. They likewise have conceded, if not celebrated, the secularization of public morality in Canada as well as changed norms of family life and sexual practice. Accordingly, they believe that the movement should squelch its talk of religion and family and focus simply upon the 'hidden humanity' of the fetus. This strategy is described by a male activist as

> the only chance we have of getting an audience for the anti-abortion viewpoint. In our situation of pluralism it is stupid to condemn abortion on the basis of morality or religious teaching. We have to give the factual evidence the floor so people will have an opportunity to see the fetus as a truly human being. Then we can appeal to a common sense of justice, and use science to cut through the mythologizing of the other side. Besides, I'm Roman Catholic, but what about non-Catholics who already share our view? We have to try to appeal to the broadest possible constituency without needlessly alienating anyone.

The *esthetics of protest* have been a principal source of internal contention for the Canadian movement, and civil rights activists are openly critical of the rigidly programmed and bellicose style of protest employed by other activists, arguing with some justification that it has succeeded mainly in reaping for the movement public scorn and political impotency. They believe that patient dialogue, rather than invective and confrontation, is the strategic road that the movement must follow. By reducing the heat of the controversy and exploring common points of intersection, they claim, the movement might induce even the staunchest pro-choice supporters to reconsider their position. Thus one activist, a university lecturer, laments that

> the shrill rhetoric on both sides of the issue stifles any chance of meaningful dialogue. The infantile black-and-white thinking of some pro-lifers just turns off pro-choice people who I personally know are compassionate. What do we gain by reviling against people of demonstrable goodwill who happen to disagree with us? What we require are forums where we can discuss – without name-calling and wrapping abortion up with so many other issues – both the basic humanity of the fetus and the legitimate concerns women have about their autonomy. Many pro-choice people have a profound respect for human life; it's our job to persuade them to extend this respect to the unborn. We can't do this when pro-lifers are blustering and condemning the opposition as evil.

This assumption of goodwill on the part of their opponents, and a corresponding desire to civilize the debate through dialogue, has contributed to the segregation of civil rights activists from the wider movement. The quest for dialogue, on this or any other issue, usually presupposes that conflict is epiphenomenal and that its resolution therefore awaits mutual clarification, or that behind polarized viewpoints there lurks an elusive core of shared truth which only needs to be discovered and pinned down. For many in the movement, however, dialogue is a luxury which only distracts attention from the ongoing destruction of unborn life. Most other activists are not interested in seeking a beatific Middle Ground, nor do they want to hear of moral dilemmas or the noble intentions of their opponents. And as the following remarks by a prominent family heritage activist suggest, it is difficult for some in the movement to regard the purveyors of abortion as anything but moral monsters:

> Look, it's so damn simple any grade-schooler should see it. Babies are being murdered and we've got to stop it. It's so frustrating to hear some pro-lifers – and I guess they mean well – saying, 'Well, let's get together with these abortion advocates and these feminists and this abortionist, let's organize a meeting so we can understand each other and work from there.' If they had their way, we'd never get beyond talking. Babies are being slaughtered daily and pious platitudes sure won't save them. It's like saying to a known child-killer like Clifford Olsen: 'Well, listen, we'd really like to hear your point of view. If we could understand you, maybe we wouldn't judge you so harshly. On the other hand, maybe you'd come to appreciate why we have problems with what you do. So let's meet over coffee in a nice broadloomed office. But do remember the number one ground rule of our conversation. Neither of us must sound judgmental, because we're both basically wonderful. We just happen to disagree.'[22]

These discrepant approaches to the issue stem in large measure from the different social locations of civil rights activists on the one hand, and family heritage and Catholic Revivalist activists on the other. The former tend to work in careers where the pro-choice position is the accepted orthodoxy of most of their peers. Professional survival and assumed norms of tasteful discourse dictate that they broach the issue with delicacy and nuance. In contrast, most of the latter are socially removed from the major cultural currents of pro-choice support and, accordingly, are constrained to a much lesser extent by conventions of polite discourse.

By favouring a strategy of accommodation to feminism and secularism, civil rights activists are accused by the movement's more militant contingent of naïvely thinking that the abortion battle can be successfully fought on enemy turf. Whereas the latter addresses the issue in terms of a deepening crisis of national morality, civil rights activists stress the necessity of reordering Canada's economic priorities in order that women might complete unexpected, and unwelcomed, pregnancies with minimal financial and emotional distress. Moreover, whereas the majority of movement participants aspire to nullify the cultural prestige of feminism and to reinstate a 'traditional' Christianity as the guardian of the nation's virtue, civil rights activists deplore the likelihood that the movement would thus become known as a Canadian version of the Moral Majority. As the following comments from a family heritage woman make clear, the progressivism of civil rights activists is regarded by the movement's conservatives as weak-kneed pandering.

> These people talk about how abortion ghettoizes women, about the need to unite pro-life and feminism, and all kinds of left-lib crap. Haven't they totally missed the point? Abortion kills babies – pure and simple – and this is what has to be said time and again. They try so hard to make pro-life look nice and liberal. This isn't nice – this is about life and death. Who gives a damn about trying to make ourselves look good when babies' lives are at stake? We have to be tough and tell it like it is instead of hiding behind trendy clichés and worrying about offending anybody. Why can't they just say it – feminists have led the way in promoting abortion, so who's our enemy? You tell me. There's no way around this if we want to be honest. The feminist agenda is aimed at wiping out the family. This is the message we have to get across, and gentleness and niceness just isn't going to do it.

The main distinguishing feature of civil rights activists, then, is their assignment of the pro-life position within a liberal reformist conceptual framework. Otherwise, however, they exhibit mixed characteristics. The twenty-one representative subjects, eleven men and ten women, include ten practising and two lapsed Catholics, two Anglicans, a

Presbyterian, two non-observant Jews, three agnostics, and one woman who describes her faith as 'mystical universalist.' All but four of them are over thirty-five years of age. Fourteen are married with at least two children, two are divorced with children, and the remainder are single. All of the women, with the exception of two university students, have full-time careers. And though ethnically diverse, they all are at least second-generation Canadians.

Unlike many of the family heritage and Catholic Revivalist activists to be discussed below, civil rights activists generally do not attribute their moral disapproval of abortion to either personal experience or religious belief. They insist that the right-to-life of the unborn is a self-legitimating proposition once people are attuned to their best moral sensibilities. Typical in this regard are these remarks by a woman whose involvement in the movement dates to the early 1970s: 'I know that abortion is wrong mainly because I'm a human being who's always tried to be attentive to the silent voices of marginalized groups. And there's no one more silent or marginalized than the unborn. I'm against abortion on the same ground that I'm against discrimination against women, the handicapped, and gays. To me the humanity of the unborn is self-evident; it results from my moral reflection and it's part of my overall concern for equality.'

It is of course possible to hold strong moral beliefs on an issue without also undertaking political action. Translation of these beliefs into political activism is often contingent upon some personal event (or events) which gives the issue an immediate sense of urgency. Civil rights activists, however, are generally reticent to discuss specific biographical circumstances which may have launched their activism. Most describe the journey toward activism as a steady path unpunctuated by any noteworthy personal experience.

Several civil rights activists, in fact, expressed frank annoyance with the author's attempt to probe personal stages of their entry into anti-abortion protest. Because they believe the humanity of the fetus and the corresponding injustice of abortion to be self-evident, they resent the implication that pro-life activism should necessarily require some extraordinary insight or conversion. In their thinking this would seem to put it in a similar category as joining an exotic religious cult or eccentric political party. The pro-life position, as they see it, is so cogent that it stands on its own rational merit, unsupplemented by either religious belief or special experience. Thus, one woman said: 'I'm uncomfortable with this line of questioning. I'm also involved in an anti-apartheid organization and a native rights group. I don't think anybody would ask me what occurred in my life to cause me to politically support these groups. They'd just take for granted that I'm concerned with injustice. It isn't some bizarre thing like joining a flat-earth society.'

The notable exceptions among civil rights activists to this *developmental* entry into anti-abortion protest are two women from the sample who themselves have undergone abortions. Both claim that this personal experience resulted in acute and perduring feelings of guilt, sorrow, and depression which were in turn their major motivation for joining the movement. Women Exploited by Abortion, American Victims of Abortion, and PACE are American organizations composed of women who similarly regret their abortions and are convinced that abortion is considerably more than an inconsequential medical procedure.[23] With the exception of one recently formed in Calgary, comparable organizations have yet to appear in Canada. The Canadian movement, however, does include an undetermined yet apparently growing number of women who claim on the basis of personal experience that abortion is destructive of both patient and fetus.

Of all anti-abortionists, the *Weltanschauung* of civil rights activists has been most sorely tried. Whereas others in the movement have viewed abortion as the product of deep-seated social decadence, they have interpreted it as a social problem that could be tackled by education and conventional political methods. If the general public could learn more about fetal development and if Canadian institutional life could be rearranged so that women were no longer economically penalized for bearing children, they have reasoned, the pro-life position would eventually make its way into the cultural mainstream. The assumption underlying this ameliorative strategy was that most women submit to having an abortion only as a last resort and under conditions of economic duress; if the structural sources of this duress could be removed, so too would be the motivation for a significant number of abortions.

Civil rights activists were initially sanguine that their analysis would strike a responsive chord among feminists, and that it would stimulate discussion on the structural changes required in Canada to justly accommodate motherhood. Many of them, however, miscalculated the degree to which mainstream North American feminism is attached to an unqualified pro-choice ethic. In insisting that motherhood must always and under every circumstance be completely discretionary, the Women's Movement has made abortion freedom the sine qua non of its agenda for cultural change. It has become the non-negotiable imperative against which dissent is forbidden. Not only has the awaited dialogue not occurred, some civil rights activists are unsure why they had entertained hope for it.[24]

Civil rights activists, furthermore, have for the most part been forced to concede the inadequacy of their analysis. As a number of studies have shown, neither economic privation nor ignorance of embryology can account for the present abortion rate. Contraceptive failure, irrespective of economic, educational, or marital status, is the reason given most often by Toronto-area women for having sought an elective abortion.[25] And studies of American abortion patients by Francke and Maxtone-Graham reveal that the decision to abort can be a complex and often befuddling process that seems to owe as much, if not sometimes more, to emotional confusion, unstable personal relationships, and the immaturity and irresponsibility of men as it does to either economic need or lack of knowledge regarding the fetus. Some of the women interviewed in the aforementioned studies frankly confided that they believed the fetus to be human, yet could not bear the personal costs of bringing it to term.[26]

Many civil rights activists, who are in general familiar with such evidence, have concluded that they had underestimated the scope of the issue and were wrong to think that it could be resolved by educational and political means. Although they remain uncomfortable with the apocalyptic scenario into which the 'abortion crisis' is painted by the movement's conservatives, they have become more receptive to the idea that increased societal acceptance of abortion reflects a loss of both community and shared values in the modern world. Some have even developed a greater sympathy for the 'contraceptive mentality' thesis which is advanced by the movement's Revivalist Catholics, thinking that the higher abortion rate might after all be causally related to changed understandings of sexuality and intimacy. Having lost confidence in a political solution to the issue, some civil rights activists fear that a stricter law would only create a flourishing underground abortion industry and an attendant minefield of health hazards for women.

Making matters worse for civil rights activists is their tenuous place within the anti-abortion movement itself where they are regarded by many as pro-life imposters. Committed to a cause defined by themselves as progressive but by many of their professional peers as reactionary, and marooned within a movement which has turned its back on the modern world, they feel enervated and are pessimistic about the movement's prospects for success. One of these activists attempted to explain why she has temporarily withdrawn from activism: 'It seems sometimes the time's just not right for accomplishing what you know needs to be done. The hostility of this culture to pro-life really wears you down. And the movement has taken a hateful direction that some of us find hard to live with. It's a combination of things.'

Throughout the 1970s civil rights activists served as the political arm of the pro-life movement and were the main driving force behind the Coalition. Following a series of intrigues on its national board, however, the Coalition was taken over by a more conservative group in 1985, and since then civil rights activists have been organizationally homeless and reduced to standing on the sidelines while others chart the movement's future course.[27] Some have attempted to maintain an active profile in the Alliance, several have taken refuge in the Human Life Research Institute, a pro-life think tank founded by a former Coalition president Ian Gentles,[28] while others have tried to be a progressive ginger group within Campaign Life. New civil rights activists continue to join the movement on a regular basis, but the life expectancy of their activism is considerably lower than that of the other types.

Ellen Tabisz, a former executive director of the Alliance for Life, may serve as an exemplar of the civil rights type.[29] Upon leaving her Alliance position to take a degree in social work, specializing in women's studies, Tabisz wrote a farewell column for *Pro-Life News* in which she implored pro-lifers to do their utmost to make common cause with feminists. 'I repeat, the feminist movement will not go away. The answer is to join it, become part of it, whether you are male or female ... Show the feminists that abortion is a male cop-out in this male-dominated world and that *abortion is not a right for women but, like wife abuse and rape, is a wrong against women.*'[30]

Sentiments such as these, however, strike most family heritage and Catholic Revivalist activists as self-indulgent and perhaps even insulting. Thus, for example, the following complaint appeared in the Action Life newspaper after a talk by Ellen Tabisz at the Ottawa-based group's annual general meeting: '... her speech and subsequent debate on Feminism [were] very off-topic and self-serving ... At the very least, it is bad manners to fire off salvos such as the devaluation of women, misogyny (woman-hating), or related terms at a captive audience, who are doing, or have done, their best to raise families and/or contribute to their society, and who have assembled to save a more defenseless form of human life.'[31]

THE SUPPORT TROOPS – FAMILY HERITAGE ACTIVISTS

Family heritage activists have provided the basic imprint and impetus for the movement since the mid-1970s. They have been the movement's major fund of vitality, working in local right-to-life groups and crisis pregnancy centres, making financial donations, participating in rallies, marches, and letter-writing campaigns, and in general spreading the pro-life gospel throughout their home communities. They are the support troops without whom there would be no recognizable and continuous anti-abortion movement in Canada. Virtually all of the movement's conservative Protestants, as well as many of its Catholics, may be classified as family heritage activists. (The representative subjects from the sample include thirteen Protestants and twenty-five Catholics.) If despondency is the prevailing mood among civil rights activists, their family heritage counterparts are propelled by a sense of outrage at the spectrum of cultural change in contemporary Canada.

Neither economic nor political factors, contend family heritage activists, adequately account for the current 'abortion crisis.' Rather, they insist, liberalized abortion is the indisputable barometer of Canadian society's decline into moral viciousness. Thus, in language studiously avoided by civil rights activists, do they advertise the abortion issue. The 'slaughter of innocents' could be condoned only in a culture that is morally bankrupt and destined for possible extinction. And the chief force behind this cultural decline, they argue, is a baleful secularism which has neutralized traditional Christian social values and reduced them to common currency in a highly competitive market of life-styles and systems of legitimation.

Family heritage activists come closest to matching Kristin Luker's description of the prototypical anti-abortionist. Most (twenty-eight of the thirty-eight from the sample) are married women between the ages of thirty-five and fifty-five who have committed the greatest portion of their life resources to remaining at home to raise families. They fear that the newly voluntary status of motherhood, of which abortion is both symbol and partial cause, has undercut the role of nurturer in the home upon which is founded their identity and self-esteem. Accordingly, they find liberalized abortion appalling, not simply from a conviction of the intrinsic value of fetal life, but also because it seems to confer a legitimacy upon a life-style – one which treats motherhood as a contingent choice – that is in direct competition with their own.

Also under siege along with motherhood, according to family heritage women, is the *traditional* family, which they believe to be the linchpin of Western civilization. The family ideal to which they profess ardent attachment is centred upon the model wife-mother who takes employment outside the home only temporarily and for reasons of economic necessity and who is an emotional anchor for her husband and children. Groomed from early childhood to discover selfhood in a role of domestic service, they see feminism as an aberrant ideology which conspires to deny women the conjugal-maternal fulfilment for which they instinctively yearn. Between the lines of the feminist homily on equality, family heritage women claim, can be read a prescription for the social disfranchisement of stay-at-home mothers. Thus one woman says that 'Feminists preach reproductive freedom and abortion rights, but what they really want is to deny the majority of women the dignified choice of experiencing the joy of raising kids. This is the most important contribution anyone can make to society, especially today when the consensus is kids stand in the way of material happiness. Feminists just promote the anti-child bias of the times, but where would they or anyone be without women who sacrifice to bring kids up in loving homes? We're the future. The world's very confused, and the only place where genuine values are taught is in the home.'

In addition to an undertone of status-envy, this quotation conveys the belief of family heritage activists that the traditional family is the last line of defence against an influx of moral chaos into Canadian society. Their effort to reconstitute the bourgeois family as a bastion of normative order may thus be seen as a quest to circumscribe a 'safety zone,' a *nomic* domestic principality, that would serve as a refuge from the unsettling winds of modernity.[32] And precisely because liberalized abortion represents for them the dissolution of cherished family values, they conceive the anti-abortion campaign as utterly pivotal to this quest.[33]

Family heritage activists, then, link anti-abortion protest to a larger battle against the total breakdown of family, community, religion, and traditional morality in Canadian society. To the extent that they have influenced its dominant mood, the broader pro-life movement may profitably be viewed as a *countermovement*, a concept defined by Mottl as 'a conscious, collective, organized attempt to resist or to reverse social change.'[34] Though possessing considerably less political clout, family heritage activists share with neo-traditionalists in the United States (the so-called Moral Majority) the desire to thwart the cultural successes of secularism, feminism, and sexual permissiveness.[35]

The main adversaries in the current 'war over the family' in the United States, according to Peter and Brigitte Berger, are neo-traditionalists and the *knowledge class*, more commonly known as the New Class.[36] As the Bergers put it, the American *knowledge class* consists of intellectuals, or *quasi*-intellectuals, who derive their livelihood from the production, dissemination, and administration of symbolic knowledge and who populate the 'helping' professions of social work and psychiatry, the educational system, the media, and the vast welfare infrastructure. Besides having a strong vested interest in the expansion of the welfare bureaucracy, these people aspire to define and direct all spheres of cultural life in accordance with their stock of purported 'cultural wisdom.'[37] But the attempt to transfuse their values and cultural agenda into the bloodlines of American society has provoked a concerted opposition in the rise of neo-traditionalism. Neo-traditionalism represents a challenge to the power aspirations of the *knowledge class* as well as a rejection of the latter's presumed monopolization of value prescriptions for all facets of American society.

This class conflict, if it may be interpreted as such, has thus far made its appearance in Canada only in inchoate form, partly because of this country's historical lack of a vibrant populism, but mainly because evangelical Protestantism, which forms the social base for American neo-traditionalism, is not a potent constituency in Canadian politics.[38] Canadian family heritage activists, nevertheless, display a similar impulsion toward wresting cultural authority from the hands of professional moral entrepreneurs. They aspire to break free from the stranglehold of educators and therapeutic professionals and to reclaim some element of control over the formulation and inculcation of social values in Canada. Thus, a woman of conservative Protestant background insists that

> We represent grass roots Canadians who are sick and tired of having values which totally contradict what we believe in shoved down our throats by self-serving groups like the militant feminists, Planned Parenthood, homosexuals, and teachers who equate any form of positive morality with close-mindedness. These people only stand for a minority of Canadians, and eventually a lot more of us are going to rise against them and demand nothing less than an equal say in the future of this country. We're only beginning to shake Canadians out of their lethargy so they can see this country's headed down the road to destruction. We don't want to persecute anyone like lesbians, just make sure that the values this country was built on aren't swept into the garbage. These groups have all the power, and they've got the politicians totally intimidated. Now it's time we found the guts to fight for what we want. That's why the fight against the abortion clinic is the most important battle facing us. Because if this becomes accepted in Canada, then absolutely anything and everything will go.

Not surprisingly, in light of these sentiments, thirteen family heritage women from the sample are charter members of REAL Women of Canada, an organization founded in 1983 to undertake political lobbying on behalf of stay-at-home women. Although REAL Women is not formally part of the anti-abortion movement, its six stated objectives would be heartily endorsed by most family heritage activists:

1. To gain political recognition of the family as society's most vital organ.
2. To secure legislation which upholds the traditional Judeo-Christian view of marriage and family.
3. To win greater appreciation of women's role as educator and nurturer in the home.

4. To support programs of assistance for women who prefer to stay home and raise their children.
5. To secure equal opportunities in education and employment for women who must work outside of the home.
6. To support the right to life of all individuals from conception to death.[39]

The REAL Women agenda was expressed even more pointedly by Grace Petrasek, then president of the organization, in a call-to-arms prior to the 1984 federal election. 'These politicians *must* know that the feminists' agenda does not represent the grassroots of Canada. We do not want our politicians capitulating to the anti-family, anti-life ideology of pro-abortionists. They must know that there is a very strong pro-life voice that will not tolerate this pandering to a handful of extremist feminists.'[40]

As if locked in a time warp, the vision of the good society held by most family heritage activists centres upon the mythical middle-class white family of the 1950s and the Canada of past generations when Christian values held sway over the national consciousness.[41] This 'moral traditionalism'[42] is at the root of the ideological variance which has plagued the pro-life movement as a whole since the mid-1970s. The world-view championed by family heritage activists is one that precludes the life circumstances of most civil rights activists, many of whom are career women and several of these the primary financial supporters of their families.

The religiosity of family heritage activists is as conservative as their social views. Both Catholic and Protestant among them believe in a sovereign, transcendent God to whom all are called to submit, an inerrant Bible, the literal existence of a heaven and hell, and a demonic force active in the world personified as 'the devil.' The idea that humans might actively co-operate in God's design for creation, to the degree of exercising a greater control over their biological nature, is condemned by most as idolatrous. (Even though conservative Protestants do not uniformly eschew the use of artificial birth control, many among them have grown quite receptive to the anti-contraception position of their Catholic allies.) All family heritage activists cite religious teaching, and only secondarily scientific evidence, as their primary authority for the humanity of the fetus. They regard abortion as the ultimate Promethean blasphemy whereby mortals arrogate to themselves the power of meting life and death.

Most family heritage activists understand current social ferment to be a violation of God's hierarchically ordered plan of creation. Indeed, some interpret the 'abortion crisis' as a possible harbinger of Western civilization's eschatological judgment. This theme is expressed by a Protestant woman who is a regular picketer on Harbord Street:

> The legalized abortion holocaust proves beyond doubt that our society has fallen into barbarism. Sweeney was right when he noted the connection with the Nazis and abortion.[43] The abortion chambers are no different from the Nazi crematories. They both have the same results and stem from the same nihilism. There's no other way now – unless we can reverse this situation and return to a respect for life, we're doomed. We can learn this from a basic reading of history. The greatest nations have fallen into moral decay only to be wiped out. You can call it divine punishment if you want, it doesn't matter. This seems to be the course that we're headed along.

Comparison of the current abortion situation with the Jewish Holocaust is a favoured rhetorical tactic of both family heritage and Catholic Revivalist activists. As James Burtchaell has pointed out, Auschwitz is summoned up by anti-abortionists as a term of execration because nothing else quite so vividly captures their sense of rage and helplessness.[44] Though the Holocaust analogy has wide appeal in both the Canadian and American movements, and has been provocatively elaborated in William Brennan's *The Abortion Holocaust*,[45] it is not a comparison with which all anti-abortionists are comfortable. Besides questioning its historical appropriateness, some American activists think that it doesn't pack as much comparative punch as the slavery analogy, which links up suggestively with the equality, justice, and emancipation components of American 'civil religion.'[46] Thus, many American activists attempt to draw a parallel between the 1857 *Dred Scott* decision, when the Supreme Court decreed that a slave or a slave's child was not an American citizen, and the 1973 Supreme Court decision when Justice Blackmun ruled that 'meaningful humanhood' did not begin before birth.[47] In Canada, where there is no comparable history of slavery or readily recognizable tradition of civil religion, some civil rights activists oppose the Holocaust analogy on the grounds that it is tactless and may be resented by Canadian Jews. Family heritage activists are generally less concerned with nicety. Wanton killing, they argue, whether it occurs in the gas chamber or the womb, draws its justification from the same cultural sickness.

Protestant women of the family heritage type have generally had to overcome a greater resistance to activism than have their Catholic counterparts. Some of them belong to religious traditions which, though in tune with the theme of an impending apocalypse spawned by social anarchy and moral depravity, have historically been more inclined toward a fatalistic withdrawal from the dominant culture than toward engagement in political action. Moreover, unlike Catholic women, whose anti-abortionism is well-rehearsed and undergirded by a tightly knit social network, Protestant women have sometimes joined the protest at great personal cost, such as reaping the opprobrium of a home congregation or of a husband whose notion of female protocol has no place for marching placard-in-hand in downtown Toronto. An aggrieved social status and moral disapproval of abortion are, at most, *predisposing* conditions for undertaking pro-life activism; they do not by themselves explain why these particular Protestant women have decided to act on convictions which are likely shared by many others of related social status and cultural background.

A partial explanation for their activism is the sociologically unsatisfying one that certain people are by nature more readily given to political activism when values foundational to their 'symbolic universe' are threatened.[48] But there is more to it than that. The abortion issue is able, on both sides of the political fence, to evoke impassioned responses because it often resonates deeply felt and emotionally perduring experiences. Thus, many of the pro-choice women studied by Kristin Luker were motivated to political activism by the painful memory of their own or a close friend or relative's botched back-street abortion. Luker likewise discovered that personal hardship was responsible for 'bringing the issue home' to a high percentage of pro-life activists. 'A significant proportion of those who made the decision to become active in the pro-life cause did so because of an experience that convinced them that abortion was not simply an abstract, theoretical issue but something that was both personal and relevant. For an astounding one-third of the pro-life people we interviewed, the event that "brought the issue home" was a problem of parenthood: an inability to conceive, a miscarriage, a newborn child lost to congenital disease or defect, or an older child lost to childhood illness.'[49] A perception shared by many pro-life activists afflicted by parental tragedy, Luker notes, is 'the disparity between the loss of a deeply wished-for child and the seemingly casual ending of pregnancies in abortion.'[50] Such parental loss, when combined with the belief that embryos belong to a moral category similar to post-natal life, can be a potent precipitant for anti-abortion activism.

This study's availability sample likewise includes a striking proportion of subjects (thirty-seven of the aggregate sample of one hundred and eleven, and eight of the thirteen family heritage Protestants) who link their participation in the pro-life cause either to parental bereavement or to the experience of raising a defective child. Some of the women from the sample define such experiences as the threshold of discontent which brought them into the anti-abortion movement.

To this point, family heritage Protestants and Catholics have been discussed more or less in tandem. In concluding this section, however, it is important to say a few words specifically about the latter, particularly for the sake of distinguishing them from the *Revivalist Catholics* to be considered next. Family heritage Catholics (alternatively designated in this study as *Parish Catholics*) have for over a decade been the movement's most reliable resource. They are, in short, the bedrock Catholics who, with their parents and grandparents, have for generations been the mainstay of Catholicism in rural and small-town English Canada.

In terms of a generalized profile, family heritage or Parish Catholics are likely to be third- or fourth-generation Canadians, over thirty-five years of age, married with at least three children, modestly middle-class with a high school and possibly some college education, and residents of small cities or rural areas. Having fully internalized from childhood the 'sanctity of life' ethic, they view abortion as self-evidently wrong, and protest against it is as much a part of their taken-for-granted reality as raising children and believing in God. Recruited to the movement mainly through the parish-school network, these Catholics are uneasy about certain developments within the wider culture, particularly the diminished prestige of the traditional family, and within the church, particularly an apparent lowering of doctrinal rigour and spiritual discipline. Yet *unlike* Revivalist Catholics they have not translated their religious discontent into a full-fledged *ideology of crisis*. They attend mass weekly and confession monthly and, though nostalgic for certain elements of pre–Vatican II piety and ritual, have adapted without traumatic strain to the reformed church. While acquainted with his angularities and wishing he would dedicate more sermons to the subjects of abortion and contraception, they are both fond and respectful of their parish pastor. And while they disapprove of and do not themselves use artificial contraception, they have learned to turn a blind eye to the non-observance of *Humanae Vitae* by friends and relatives. Similarly, while disappointed that not all of their children are practising Catholics and that one or more of them have been sexually active prior to marriage, they are proud parents who claim to see the imprint of grace in each of their children. They are not in favour of women priests, but would meet the eventuality of female ordination without undue psychological maladjustment.

These are Catholics who are friendly toward Canada's system of mitigated capitalism, more confident perhaps in the economic wisdom of private capital than of state-sponsored programs. They find South African apartheid abhorrent, though they are inclined to regard it as somebody else's fight, are mystified about the current political strife in Latin America, and are instinctively suspicious of Canadian voices, especially within the church, which tout political views steeped in anti-Americanism. Believing that the church, through her infrastructure of charitable organizations, has historically shown concern for the poor and underprivileged, they do not understand the current fuss in the Canadian church over the 'discovery' of social justice.

Parish Catholic activists, then, are the simple, unglamorous faithful who seldom attract notice in the offices of either the institutional church or the public media. Their religious style is less intense, their anti-abortionism less dramatic, than is found in the Revivalist Catholics who constitute the pro-life movement's third activist type.

THE SHOCK TROOPS – REVIVALIST CATHOLIC ACTIVISTS

Perhaps the most striking aspect of the pro-life movement is the enmity with which many of its Catholic participants regard the institutional

Canadian church. These activists express anger toward the church hierarchy as well as contempt for the transformed face of Canadian Catholicism. Among their complaints are the Canadian church's apparent relaxation of Catholic sexual norms, particularly in the area of contraceptive practice, its involvement in ecumenism, which they think has diluted Catholic ethical and theological principles, and its seeming shift from a theocentric to an anthropocentric doctrinal emphasis. Indeed, the anti-abortion protest of these Catholics is umbilically connected to a *contracultural*[51] vision for Canadian Catholicism. They understand themselves to be a holy enclave destined to rescue the Canadian church from absorption in the melting pot of secularism. To their mind, mainstream Canadian Catholicism has lost its way and betrayed its past. Having sold its soul for cultural relevance, it would rather make peace with evil than stare it down. And worse, at least where abortion is concerned, it no longer even seems to know what evil is.[52]

These sentiments are recurrently expressed both in interviews and on the picket line by, significantly, the more bellicose of Catholic activists. Indeed, so unified are they in these beliefs that it seems appropriate to speak of them as a distinct subculture within Canadian Catholicism, one with roots extending deeper than anti-abortion protest. This subculture is designated in this study as *Revivalist Catholicism*. Its participants interpret social reality through the same ideological lens, are bound together by the same religious values, and share a common ideal of Catholic vocation.

By virtue of its inbred certitude, ascetic toughness, and claim to inviolable fidelity with the Catholic past, Revivalist Catholicism counts as one of the most significant, and perhaps the least understood, of factions within contemporary Canadian Catholicism. It is essentially a crisis response to the profound cultural transformations of modern society and corresponding upheaval in the Catholic church. The Revivalist subculture will be discussed in greater depth in the final chapter. What is of central interest at this juncture is the manner in which anti-abortion activism functions as a ritual medium for confirming the Revivalist self-identity, thereby binding these Catholics into a cohesive moral community. In anti-abortion protest, they have found a public liturgy which is ideally suited to their vision of a heroic, culturally separatist Catholicism.

Whereas the pro-life movement's civil rights wing has fallen into activist doldrums, Revivalist Catholics have snatched the anti-abortion torch with unsurpassed zeal. As the movement's most vigorous and indefatigable wing, Revivalists are primarily responsible for stocking and replenishing its picket lines and public demonstrations. It is Revivalists for the most part who participate in acts of civil disobedience and who 'witness' outside the private residences of abortion clinic employees. And given the graphic quality of 'public witness,' it is chiefly they who provide the raw material for distillation of popular impressions of the movement.

The anti-abortionism of Revivalist Catholics is predicated on an intriguing conjuncture of moral beliefs, social and political interests, and religious values. As is the case for civil rights and family heritage activists, it is grounded upon an ethical conviction of the humanity of the embryo. And similarly to the case for family heritage activists, it is partly motivated by concern for the future of traditional cultural mores. But beyond this, anti-abortion protest is regarded by Revivalists as a signature of faith, as that which sets them apart from modernizing tendencies of the larger Canadian church.

Anti-abortion activism, thus, serves for Revivalists as a rite of self-identification within a national church which they believe has assimilated the ethos of secularism. The breakdown of a confident consensus within Canadian Catholicism since Vatican II has, in their view, resulted in an obfuscation of all reliable lines of demarcation between *church* and *world*. No longer may Canadian Catholics be counted upon to share a basic agreement on religious education, sexual morality, family life, doctrine, or the meaning of the Mass. Theological pluralism, catechetical tentativeness, institutionalization of dissent on the Catholic college campus, widespread disregard of *Humanae Vitae*, unfettered liturgical experimentation, abandonment of clerical vocations, and the fall into desuetude of cherished devotions are seen by Revivalists as the bitter fruits of an unfiltered 'opening to the world.'

The anger of Revivalists is brought to boiling point by the apparent failure of the Canadian bishops, and of Canadian Catholics generally, to rally to the anti-abortion cause. If the destruction of life itself is insufficient to arouse Catholics to united action, Revivalists contend, then the Canadian church is shown as little other than a fossil, an empty shell inhabited by the spiritually insipid. Passivity in the face of abortion, they believe, is testimony to the church's capitulation to the values of secular society. The following remarks by a forty-seven-year-old woman capture this 'last-straw' mentality:

> They have impoverished our liturgies, turned them into slick variety shows with stupidly grinning hosts. The new theologians are fond of saying God is everywhere. This isn't quite true. They've forced him out of the Church. They've turned doctrine into pious platitudes, cultural truisms, that couldn't inspire anybody to reflection let alone to martyrdom. Sexual teaching, the Blessed Virgin, you name it, it's gotten to the point where the Church runs to the secular culture saying: 'Look, we're a little embarrassed about this stuff ourselves. It just doesn't seem to fit the modern mood. So if you can't ratify it for us, tell us and we'll change it to make it more acceptable to you.' What we're saying is they've excavated the Supernatural from the Church, but there's no way we're going to stand by while they desanctify human life as well. Abortion is the last line of defence. This is where we draw the line and say: 'These babies are created by God. They are sacred. Respect at least this. Have at least this much faith.'

The pro-life movement has historically held great appeal for Catholics disaffected with change in the post–Vatican II Canadian church. Not all Revivalist activists, however, are lifelong Catholics. Of the forty-two Revivalist subjects from the sample, twenty-four are either converts to Catholicism or Catholics who have returned to the church following a period of religious doubt. Interviews with these twenty-four subjects reveal a similar pattern: a personal life crisis or period of spiritual drifting was resolved by an actual conversion to Catholicism or a self-described 'faith awakening,' which was in turn followed shortly afterward by entry into anti-abortion activism. After either converting to or re-embracing Catholicism, these subjects were eager to consolidate their new-found faith commitment in some manner beyond the humdrum of normal parish life. Moreover, most were dismayed to discover that the church to which they had come for certainty was itself in the throes of doctrinal doubt and inner convulsion. Anti-abortionism thus provided for them both a means of self-consecration and a tangible focus for an invigorated religious energy. It also brought them into close contact with veteran Catholic activists who would indoctrinate them into the beliefs of Revivalism.

While Revivalists have come to pro-life activism by different paths, they share alike both a compressed conception of Catholic orthodoxy and the belief that they are a countervailing force against the descent of Canadian Catholicism into secularism. They conceive their activism as a defiant affirmation of both Transcendence and Mystery in the modern world. Secularism may have infected the spectrum of Canadian institutional life, including Canadian Catholicism, but what is invulnerable to disenchantment is *life itself*. It is through the creation of new human life, they believe, that God's power is most vividly revealed. To defend nascent life is also to defend the truth of its supernatural origin and, concomitantly, of Catholicism itself.

Anti-abortion protest is thus sacralized by Revivalists and elevated to a holy crusade. It is regarded as the beach-head upon which is waged a battle for the future of Western culture and for the soul of the Canadian Catholic church. This is a battle to which all Catholics are summoned but only a select few, the soldiers of orthodoxy, decide to join.

Of the forty-two Revivalist subjects represented by the sample, twenty-four are women, and of these twelve are married with at least two children, two are married and childless, two are unmarried and beyond child-bearing age, and the remaining eight are single and under thirty years of age. Only three of the married women work outside of the home, and all of the younger single women plan on marriage and full-time motherhood. Nine of the men are over thirty years of age and married with families, one is a sixty-five-year-old widower, and the remaining eight are under thirty and single. Significantly, all of these Catholics are lay, a fact which reflects the scarcity of priests and nuns in the Canadian pro-life movement.[53] Fifteen are either unemployed or underemployed and thus part of Canada's expanding underclass,[54] eight are university students, and the social location of the rest ranges from working class to comfortable middle class. They are all at least second-generation Canadians and, while ethnically mixed, twenty-two are of Irish descent. Almost all of them share the experience of having been raised in a large, closely knit family.

Perhaps the views of these Catholics on sexuality provide the best key to their religious world. Revivalists of all ages strongly disapprove of extra-marital sexual practice. They believe that sexual intercourse is a sacramental activity which harmonizes with God's design for creation only within marriage. And though they do not unanimously recommend its criminalization, all denounce homosexuality as an aberration of the modern age. Sexuality in their view is saturated with supernatural meaning and thus suffers distortion when detached from its sacramental matrix.

The stand taken by Revivalists on contraception exemplifies this supernaturalistic understanding of sexuality. Their opposition to artificial birth control is founded first of all on the Catholic natural law position that every sexual act should be open to procreation. They believe, furthermore, that contraception is the chief cause of the desacralization of Eros in modern society, a process which has alienated people from authentic love and turned sexual pleasure into an impersonal, objectified commodity. Contraception, they contend, interposes a psycho-spiritual barrier between couples which inhibits the growth of mutual intimacy and thus banalizes the most sublime medium of marital love. Moreover, they argue, the casualization and mechanization of sex brought about by widespread contraceptive usage is causally connected to increased abortion rates. Because the 'contraceptive mentality' divorces sexual pleasure from procreation, abortion is more readily accepted as a belated solution to unplanned and unwanted conceptions.[55]

With the exception of two unmarried women in their sixties, all Revivalists interviewed for this study have large families exceeding two children or at least the desire for and expectation of a large family. All believe that openness to children is a principal requirement of Catholic belonging. Implicit in this procreative disposition is the belief that family life, as a *nomos* of intimacy, attains sanctification mainly to the extent that it is freed from the utilitarian shackles of the workaday world and is oriented instead toward ultimate value. And the *conception* of new life, according to Revivalists, is an unparalleled manifestation of ultimacy as well as an opportunity for self-surrender before divine power.[56] The element of human control afforded by contraception is deemed blasphemous by Revivalists precisely because it is seen as a prophylactic against the sacred. Thus, they insist that all Catholics, as a testimony of faith and regardless of personal disagreement or consternation, are required to submit to the papal ban on artificial birth control.

Younger Revivalists subscribe equally to this rigorous sexual ethic.

All of the unmarried subjects from the sample profess that they are virgins and intend to remain so until marriage. The sexual scrupulosity of these young Catholics is not simply a case of prudery or of psychological fallout from an austere upbringing. During the interviewing process, most spoke candidly and without embarrassment of their sexual experiences, desires, and apprehensions. Their values here as elsewhere reflect a yearning for a disciplined Catholicism, a Catholicism which by the force of its rigour and surpassing influence upon daily existence might serve as an antidote to the moral and cognitive ambiguity endemic in modern society. Their concern to re-enchant sexuality, to enfold it with supernatural meaning, is an effort to reclaim this potent aspect of human experience under an all-embracing sacred canopy.[57] *Humanae Vitae* is valued so highly by them not just for its contracultural message, but also because it prescribes certain parameters and promises a divine terminus for Catholic sexual conduct.

This thirst for a disciplined, totalistic Catholicism is reflected as well by the concentrated devotionalism of Revivalists. All maintain a ritual schedule that includes daily mass (whenever possible), frequent confession, daily recitation of the rosary, and participation in such auxiliary rites as Perpetual Adoration and Benediction of the Blessed Sacrament. They are attached as well to other devotions which have receded in popularity since Vatican II, such as novenas and the veneration of saints.

In addition, Revivalist Catholics seek spiritual nourishment in a network of pious oases. Of those represented by the sample, several are members of Opus Dei. Indeed, with its strict ethic of lay sanctification, anti-worldly asceticism, and ultramontane enthusiasm, Opus Dei appears especially congenial to the Revivalist mentality. It is possible that the pro-life movement will be a recruiting ground for Opus Dei as the latter continues to make inroads into English Canada.[58] Also, five sample subjects are affiliated with the Cursillo Movement which, like Opus Dei, is geared toward the awakening of Catholic vocation and the cultivation of an ethic of total sanctification.

With the exception of an inflamed Marian piety (which functions in part as a counter-ideology to feminism), the religiosity of Revivalists is lacking in exotic curiosity. It is striking mainly by virtue of its disciplined intensity and thoroughgoing scope. In this vein, it is significant that none of the Revivalists from the sample is a participant in the charismatic renewal. Most Revivalists view neo-Pentecostalism, with its propensity toward private revelation and spiritual ecstasy, as suspiciously individualistic and antinomian. Similar to the solemn circumspection they display in matters of sexuality, the piety of these Catholics is controlled and Apollonian. They aspire to confine both sexual and religious experience within the safe boundaries of an established *nomos*.[59]

The attachment of Revivalist activists to traditional devotional practices should not in most cases be construed as a pious hangover from pre-conciliar Catholicism. A significant number of them are under thirty years of age and, accordingly, acquired their religious life-style after *aggiornamento* had given these practices an antiquarian stamp. Nor in most cases is their preoccupied piety a consequence of early socialization, a lingering effect of having been raised by fiercely devout parents. Some of them grew up in households where religion exercised a negligible influence, and some where parents and other significant others were Catholic more by habit than by conviction; still others are recent converts to Catholicism. It is profitable to regard the intense religiosity of most Revivalist activists as a piety-by-design, a quite deliberate self-envelopment within a devotional aura in order to shield against incursions of secularism into their lives. Secularization may be partly described as the process whereby religious belief and commitment is banished to a 'finite province of meaning' and thereafter made the subject of merely episodic observance.[60] The cultivation by Revivalists of an all-absorbing religiosity is part of their more general project for a *desecularized* church.[61] They have surcharged the total breadth of their lives with Catholicism and thereby indicated their refusal to negotiate the terms of their faith with the modern world.

Legalized abortion, Revivalists believe, manifests a terminal decadence within Canadian society which only divine intervention will redress. A similar conviction, likewise embellished by organismic metaphor and apocalyptic surmisal, has already been encountered among family heritage activists. And also like family heritage activists, Revivalists regard abortion as one link in a chain of societal ills which also includes feminism, homosexuality, sexual permissiveness, secularism, and the ravaged ideal of the traditional family.

Despite their ideological propinquity, however, Revivalist and family heritage activists disagree on several critical issues. A clear finding

distinction between Revivalists & family heritage

which emerged from the interview data is the almost unanimous opposition of Revivalists to capital punishment. State-sanctioned executions, they insist, are like abortion a form of 'selective killing' which under no circumstances should be allowed. (Interestingly, however, none of the Revivalists from the sample translates this 'sanctity of life' principle into an ethic of radical pacifism; they all, for example, subscribe to some variant of the 'just war' theory.) Family heritage activists tend to regard abortion and capital punishment as separate issues, and believe the state should reserve the right to inflict the death penalty upon criminals guilty of heinous offences. In addition, Revivalists have fewer moral qualms than family heritage activists about performing acts of civil disobedience in the line of abortion protest. Where human life is at stake, they insist, civil law must be subordinate to divine law.

More significant than these differing views on capital punishment and civil disobedience, however, is the belief of Revivalists that artificial birth control is the cultural progenitor of liberalized abortion. Family heritage activists are generally less certain that contraception bears an obvious relationship to abortion and, in any event, are reluctant to present the two as cognate issues. Revivalists are at present faced with a dilemma over how loudly to broadcast their stance on contraception. On the one hand, they recognize that it does not evoke consensus within the wider movement and could irreparably damage the movement's public reputation. Yet, on the other hand, convinced as they are of the inextricable connection between contraception and abortion, they worry that to remain silent on this may be an unforgivable deference to popular taste.

Revivalist activists describe their faith as the most momentous and enduring property of daily existence. They think of everyday life as a moral drama in which discrete decisions fashion the soul toward either corruption or virtue. Despite their suffusive piety, however, many of them express dissatisfaction with their level of holiness and depth of faith commitment. Younger Revivalists in particular are religious athletes driven toward a forever-retreating horizon of spiritual excellence. It is this compulsion for Catholic virtuosity which sustains their pro-life activism. They regard the abortion issue as the arena in which Catholics may best demonstrate heroic witness and world-transcending discipleship.

The ideological homogeneity among Revivalists is partly a consequence of their intensive involvement in the movement. As Stallings has shown, the degree of consensus within social movements generally seems to be highest among those members who are most active and who display the greatest level of commitment.[62] Revivalist Catholics practise pro-life activism as a total life-style, and regard other pursuits (with the exception of family life) as frivolous by comparison. Their involvement in the movement is not simply associational, or directed to the accomplishment of some discrete goal. Rather it is a communal enterprise that covers the breadth of their day-to-day existence.[63] Anti-abortionism is the consuming subject of conversation and prayer. It is the basis for making and sustaining friendships, which in turn provide an ironclad reference group for corroborating the pro-life world-view and reinforcing a common sense of vocation. Activism thus performs an expressive function, satisfying a need for companionship and providing a web of sympathetic relationships.[64] And for many Revivalists, it is also a conveyance for an accelerated spirituality beyond the banality of the local parish.

Civil rights activists have frequently complained that the religious gratifications of pro-life protest have been more important to Revivalists than the movement's goal of arresting, and possibly reversing, Canada's escalating abortion rate. It is true that the tactics preferred by Revivalists – civil disobedience, sloganeering, public demonstrations – are selected as much for their symbolic meaning as for their probable effectiveness. When praying the rosary and singing hymns on Harbord Street, for example, Revivalists seem to be primarily concerned with expressing their religious convictions and solidarity, sometimes without reference to anticipated results. In the terminology of social movement analysis, one may say that Revivalists display a greater proclivity for *expressive*, as contrasted to *instrumental*, behaviour. Some Revivalists frankly acknowledge that conspicuous and dramatic modes of protest serve activists' expressive needs without appreciably advancing their political goals.[65] Nevertheless, they insist that such behaviour is justified for two reasons. First, they believe that the present political situation is hopeless, and since the movement has no foreseeable chance of success, the most that can be done is to keep the pro-life cause alive in the public mind. And second, they claim that 'public witness' enhances activists' sense of solidarity and refuels their commitment to the pro-life cause.

'Public witness' is in fact a form of ceremonial behaviour that promotes a greater esprit de corps among these militant Catholics. As defined by Herbert Blumer, esprit de corps gives 'life, enthusiasm, and vigor to a movement' and is 'the sense which people have of being identified with one another in a common undertaking.'[66] Thus, the religiously ostentatious protest of which some in the movement disapprove is actually a collective ritual, a celebration of the contracultural asceticism which is the special calling of Revivalists.

As is customary for sacred crusaders, Revivalists regard their pro-life activism as providential. It is their duty, or *mission*, to perform God's will unstintingly and without compromise, leaving the final outcome to divine justice. The founding of Campaign Life in the late 1970s was an attempt by Revivalists to raise the pro-life movement from a political to a sacred plane, where it would be guided more by nobility of purpose and religious valour than by concern for mere historical consequence. Campaign Life has since continued to be the main organization representing Revivalists within the Canadian pro-life movement.

THE ACTIVIST FRINGE

While the activism of the subjects thus far considered is enmeshed with other political agenda and cultural commitments, it is motivated in large measure by a conviction of the humanity of the fetus. But any social movement may attract some individuals who participate for reasons clearly other than its primary objectives. This study's availability sample includes ten subjects whose involvement in the pro-life movement seems only remotely or quite indirectly related to the goal of winning legal protection for fetal life. The *activist fringe*, then, denotes those subjects who are *in* the movement, if measured by the time and energy they give to it, but who are not *of* it, in that their activism is only *incidentally* concerned with the legal and social status of unborn life. This residual category encompasses the following:

1 *Religious seekers.*[67] For three of the sample subjects anti-abortion protest appears to represent a way station on a circuitous, and perhaps perpetual, journey toward spiritual fulfilment. It is one episode in a career of religious experimentalism, of searching for a personal

symphony of inner meaning and outer direction. With its strong religious overtones and propensity for street drama, the pro-life movement strikes them as an appealing synthesis of piety and action. But their involvement proves transitory: once having 'experienced' anti-abortion protest and found it wanting, they soon embark on a different path in pursuit of their elusive goal. *Religious seekers* check in and out of the movement at a regular rate, and their activist life span rarely exceeds three months.

2 *Sexual therapeutics*. Three of the sample subjects, all single males under thirty-five years of age, appear to participate in anti-abortion protest primarily to resolve severe personal anxiety caused by previous sexual experiences. (Interviews with these men had an almost confessional quality.) All three are plagued by guilt and a fear of female sexual power. Their activism seems to be a penitential rite which is observed during times of psychological disequilibrium.

3 *Punitive puritans*. Most pro-lifers view abortion as an issue which transcends individual morality. The movement does include, however, a number of puritanical stragglers, people who look upon unmarried pregnant women as sexual sinners who should be forced to pay for their transgressions by completing their pregnancies. The availability sample includes four subjects, three women and one man, who consider unwanted pregnancy to be the penalty for private indiscretion. All four are single and over fifty years of age.

People ordinarily view issues through the lenses of more or less coherent world-views, which themselves are the product of socialization influences, value commitments, status aspirations, and class location. Accordingly, while at an analytic level discrete and autonomous, issues when filtered through these lenses are variously assorted into ideological packages. In the present context it has been possible to discriminate empirical types of anti-abortion activist by comparing the different arrangements and contents of these packages.

It should be emphasized that the elaboration of an activist typology has not been merely an academic exercise. The three empirical types discussed in this chapter are *not* scholarly fictions. Rather, they correspond to actual ideological groupings within the Canadian anti-abortion movement. In other words, they have been discovered, not created, by the author.

This chapter has sought to examine the reasons why activists have made personal sacrifices of time, energy, and resources for the pro-life movement. It has been governed by the assumption that ethical belief is a necessary but not sufficient condition for undertaking political activism of any kind. Virtually any cause can enlist the moral, and sometimes financial, support of sympathetic *publics*, but the cause registers at a qualitatively more urgent pitch for those specialized individuals who adopt it as a personal crusade. The next chapter furnishes a more intimate look at such individuals in the Canadian pro-life movement.

5

Varieties of Pro-Life Activism

As must be the case with any social enterprise that commands a high level of personal absorption, pro-life activism is neither undertaken randomly nor sustained in a social psychological vacuum. In other words, it is not merely fortuitous, a biographical fluke, that someone commits herself to anti-abortion protest, often at the expense of considerable personal resources such as time, energy, money, and social acclaim. As the preceding chapter sought to demonstrate, pro-life activists are not made from whole cloth. Anti-abortion protest is invested with a variety of values and meanings and the discrepancy among these has been the major source of disunity for the Canadian pro-life movement. If, as is assumed here, Weber is correct that social and psychological reality is infinitely complex and inexhaustible, it would be fruitless to isolate a single cause, or configuration of causes, as determinative of pro-life activism.[1] The widely varying life situations of activists defy unilineal categorization. Nevertheless, because pro-life advocates share intersubjective worlds and define meanings and goals in collaboration with particular reference groups, their motivations for activism can be expected to conform to or, better, to reflect recognizable ideological patterns. The delineation of empirical types of activism undertaken in the previous chapter was conducted with an attentiveness to such patterns.

This chapter, an enrichment of the previous one, shifts from the exposition of activist *types* to a consideration of actual *individuals* in the Canadian pro-life movement. By employing the Weberian method of *Verstehen*, or 'empathic understanding,' it attempts to analyse the pro-life activism of selected individuals from the viewpoint of their own *subjective* meanings, experiences, and values.[2] The following case studies, or, perhaps more accurately, phenomenological vignettes, are thus concerned mainly with those ideas and emotions which comprise the life experiences of activists and which in turn shed light on their decision to participate in anti-abortion protest.

This approach takes seriously the personal testimonies of the activists themselves, and assumes that their self-understandings are indispensable guides for coming to terms with the pro-life phenomenon. Such an approach may seem shallow to the psychoanalyst and critical theorist, who would prefer that closer attention be paid to the possibilities of unconscious motivation and wilful deception at play in the lives of these subjects. However, as Reinhard Bendix writes in defence of a similar life-history approach: 'If as analysts we ignore the manifest content of social life, we will end by likening the human condition to a puppet show in which each action is due to a pull on a string and each voice to the impersonator.'[3]

The following sample vignettes have been selected for presentation, not because their subjects are endowed with extraordinary qualities, but because individually they breathe life into the typology developed above and taken together they provide a panorama of the Canadian movement's multifaceted personality. They are necessarily compressed because of considerations of space, and thus do not offer as intensive a treatment of their subject-matter as would be possible were they longer.

Finally, it should be mentioned that the author has attempted, by occasional alteration of fact and the use of pseudonyms, to disguise the real-life identities of the subjects featured in these case studies.

CIVIL RIGHTS CASE STUDIES

Case Study One

JANICE. Single, thirty-eight years of age, and a nurse, Janice has been involved in anti-abortion protest for three years. Her parents, both teachers and of Anglo-Saxon, Protestant background, were divorced when Janice was five, and she was raised by her mother in Vancouver. Sceptical of established religious traditions, Janice is a self-styled believer who professes faith in an ineffable and omniscient being which oversees, without directly intervening in, earthly affairs.

Janice has been sexually active since the age of sixteen, though she describes her present life-style as voluntarily celibate. Her first unplanned pregnancy ten years ago resulted in an abortion after her boyfriend pleaded unreadiness to meet the responsibility of parenthood. She underwent a second abortion three years afterward in the wake of a collapsed relationship with another lover. Janice subsequently desired to complete a pregnancy, but her efforts to conceive, with a variety of men, have proved unsuccessful. She has been advised by medical experts that complications stemming from her second abortion have left her permanently infertile.

Janice regards herself and women of similar experience as victims of a culture which 'falsely assures that abortion is nothing but a routine medical procedure.' She argues, on the contrary, that abortion subjects women to 'a violent technological imperialism' and undermines their 'natural instincts for delivering and nurturing new life.' Janice claims that her abortions induced an emotional trauma from which she has yet to recover. Nevertheless, she credits her 'sorrow and remorse' with convincing her of the humanity of the fetus. 'My suffering has put me in touch with my genuine feelings and instincts for life. I don't need religion or biology to tell me what's growing in the womb is a real child. However hard it is to live with, my own pain says it all.'

Unlike most pro-life activists, Janice doubts the wisdom of fighting for laws against abortion. She believes that in the present cultural climate they would be unenforceable and, additionally, would give rise to a flourishing back-street abortion industry with attendant health risks to women. Instead, she is committed to a long-term program of educating women that abortion is an 'untold brutality against both themselves and their unborn children.' Janice's activism consists almost entirely of *counselling* women who feel similarly victimized by their experiences with abortion.

Janice considers herself to be an outsider in respect to the larger pro-life movement. She does not share the anti-feminist views held by the majority of activists, nor does she think it fruitful to found opposition to abortion upon religious dogma. 'I know I don't fit the general pro-life scheme of things. They talk about abortion as an offence against God and the family, but check me out. I don't have a family, and my religious beliefs certainly couldn't be described as traditional. People in the movement try to accept me as someone who has compassion for the unborn, and so we can work together. It'd be easier, though, if they didn't tie the issue up with so much other stuff.'

Case Study Two

ANN. An English teacher of Scottish descent in her early thirties, Ann is a long-time veteran of the anti-abortion campaign. Ann credits two events with jarring her from an earlier position of neutrality on abortion. When pregnant fifteen years ago as an unmarried undergraduate, she was showered with advice that she undergo an abortion. Ann was surprised both by how personally inviting this option seemed and by the incredulity of friends and family when she expressed reluctance to take it. Having what she calls 'an acquired mistrust of quick solutions,' Ann resolved to carry her pregnancy to term and 'to challenge those social conditions that militate against a respect for all forms of human life.'

Ann's anti-abortion sentiments were crystallized two years later when she first met an American pro-life activist who would exercise an abiding influence upon her.

> She's a black woman who was raised and still lives in a ghetto. She has seven kids fathered by four different men. It's just her life-style, she loves raising children. She's been deeply involved in civil rights and anti-war protest as well as pro-life, so we're not talking single-issue tunnel vision here. She believes that the pro-choice position is really an elitist white phenomenon indifferent to the concerns of poor black and Chicano women. She made me sensitive to an implicit strain of racism in the pro-choice philosophy. It's in part an attempt to solve a situation of poor blacks who are reproducing faster than the white race, often outside of the nuclear family structure, and who are seen as a welfare problem by white corporate America. The other thing is, why are pro-choice advocates so opposed to women making informed consent on abortion – to letting them know the basic facts of fetal development and possible costs to themselves? Social workers advised my friend to abort her last four pregnancies, but she refused. More than anything, listening to her yanked me off the political fence.

Ann describes herself as a 'pro-life feminist' and says that 'coming out of the closet'[4] with her anti-abortion views scandalized the circle of friends she knew while at university. Ann hopes that she and like-minded women in the pro-life movement will someday stimulate within feminism a reassessment of 'the regressive moral and cultural implications of abortion.' As a self-professed socialist, Ann believes that permissive abortion is causally related to liberal capitalism's exaltation of private property and the self-sufficient individual. A full-scale social revolution is required, she claims, in order to create a climate which is conducive to 'an inclusive respect for human life.'

Recently widowed and the sole supporter of three boys, Ann has experienced firsthand the hardship of raising children alone and with limited economic resources. She thus decries the insensitivity of some pro-lifers to the plight of young unmarried women who frequently 'suffer social marginalization by childbirth.' Many women who decide to complete their pregnancies, Ann observes, are destined to a life of welfare dependency on the lowest rung of the status ladder. She argues that the pro-life movement would enhance its credibility by working to change social structures that 'penalize and economically degrade women who have children.'

Raised an only child by agnostic parents, Ann spent most of her life unconnected to organized religion. Recently, however, she has converted to Catholicism and claims that her new-found faith is a source of comfort when prospects for success on the anti-abortion front appear bleakest. Nevertheless, Ann is disconcerted by the 'self-indulgent piety' of some Catholic activists.

> Wrapping the pro-life position in an appeal to divine authority is a sure recipe for rejection in our society. I'm only concerned with winning the issue, and so any small progress we can make is a worthy accomplishment. But for many of the Catholics it's an 'all-or-nothing' situation, and they accuse people like myself of having impure motives because we're prepared to work out compromise solutions so that fewer babies will be aborted. I sometimes think some of these 'Tridentine Catholics' are as much concerned with playing out a personal drama of salvation as they are with saving unborn children. The religious emphasis can be oppressive.

Besides lacking a balanced social critique and endorsing an obsolete world-view, Ann says, the larger pro-life movement has adopted an abrasive tone which is offensive to 'the conciliatory temper' of Canadian society. Mainly because of these reasons, Ann feels out of step with the existing movement and her activism is currently in hiatus.

Case Study Three

HENRY. A fifty-year-old humanities professor, Henry has been involved with the anti-abortion movement almost since its inception. Although a devout Catholic with a 'conservative theological leaning,' Henry claims to have been persuaded of the humanity of the fetus ultimately by 'factual evidence.' Indeed, he does not think that the traditional teaching of the church decisively resolves the moral questions related to abortion.

We have to be honest about this. The most relevant scriptural passages are those on the Immaculate Conception, but even these are rarely invoked by the movement. I believe that human life begins at conception, but this has little to do with my faith. It can be formulated as a syllogism: firstly, it's always wrong to intentionally kill an innocent person; and secondly, every human being is a person, that is, an individual who falls within the scope of justice. One can certainly hold these premises without being Catholic, though they are deeply imbedded in the Catholic tradition. The question of when life begins should be settled by scientific evidence. You almost have to wilfully blind yourself to the humanity of the unborn – just look at aborted fetuses beyond six to eight weeks gestation. But there is a grey area at an earlier stage. You're not able to simply point to a two-week embryo and say: 'Look – here's a little baby.' But the pro-choice position strikes me as surprisingly dualistic, with its bogus distinction between the person and the human being. Ironically, it's a denial of the goodness of matter.

Henry fears that the pro-life movement's mounting cultural conservatism will earn it an early reservation in a museum of extinct political causes. The vitriol of many anti-abortionists toward feminism, he argues, hurts the movement by alienating women whose 'undeniable sense of compassion and experiences of ghettoization could make them especially sensitive to the plight of the fetus.' Henry believes that feminism and the pro-life position are reconcilable and that, in any event, the movement would profit by entering conversation with all groups, regardless of their present stance on abortion. In addition, he regrets that many pro-life activists have intertwined the issues of abortion, contraception, and sexual morality. 'In trying to turn back the cultural clock, they're damaging the whole movement. Don't insist that people practice sexual chastity, simply try to convince them that abortion affronts their best instincts for justice.'

Though Henry finds much disagreeable about the movement's current ideological direction, he continues to participate, albeit with bated enthusiasm, in the ongoing protest against abortion. He is pessimistic of the movement's chances for even modest political success, and worries that 'the same cultural forces that lead people to baptize abortion will also lead us to destroy ourselves in a nuclear war. I hope not, but perhaps in fifty years we'll be talking about the pro-life movement in an age of post-nuclear devastation.'

Case Study Four

CHANDRA. The most difficult aspect of anti-abortion activism for Chandra, a twenty-six-year-old woman of East Indian heritage and a self-declared feminist, is her sense of remoteness from the pro-life movement's ideological centre. Because she lives with her boy-friend and does not plan in the foreseeable future to have children, Chandra is uncomfortable with the movement's idealization of middle-class family life and its censure of pre-marital sexuality. And though she does not use artificial birth control, believing Natural Family Planning (NFP) to be more conducive to physical intimacy, Chandra rejects the argument popular among many Catholic activists of a causal connection between contraception and abortion.

The patently 'Catholic style' of the larger movement, according to Chandra, underscores her anomalous activist status. As a non-Christian Chandra feels ostracized by the extroverted piety so often displayed on the Harbord Street picket line, yet she generously concedes its emotive value for her Catholic allies.

> They pray outside the clinic, sing hymns, say the rosary, sometimes even carry pictures of Mary. I find this upsetting, really exclusionary. There's no room in my beliefs for this. I wonder how many people who otherwise might be supportive are turned off. I mainly do counselling at the clinic – trying to persuade women to consider an alternative. This is very hard – sometimes I'm just told to 'fuck off.' Once I broke into tears and a woman who pickets

often said to me: 'Don't worry, Chandra. Jesus is with you.' But Jesus means nothing to me. They assume everybody has the same beliefs. But I try to be tolerant because they need their religion to carry on against the incredible abuse they take. People are always driving by and shouting, 'Go home, Catholic assholes!' If not for their faith they wouldn't be able to take this and maybe wouldn't be there to begin with.

Chandra has recently completed a graduate degree in Biology, but does not attribute her views on abortion to exposure to scientific information about the fetus. Nor, given the pro-choice convictions of her parents and older brother, were they acquired at home as a child. Chandra traces the roots of her activism to a 'very private and unconventional religious faith.' Raised in a non-religious household, she yearned as a young girl for a personal relationship with a god who might give her direction and comfort. Chandra developed a daily regimen of prayer through which she would seek divine guidance, and she learned to interpret subsequent events as confirmation that her supplications had been acknowledged. From these quasi-mystical encounters emerged the conviction that all forms of life possess a 'sacred life-force' and hence must be protected against exploitation or violence. When her best friend joined the movement in 1984, Chandra followed suit, seeing anti-abortion protest as a natural extension of her evolving spirituality.

Chandra is also involved in animal rights activism, and wishes that pro-lifers would expand their horizon and 'not put a greater premium on life because it's human.' Because of her philosophy of universal reverence for life, Chandra is nonplussed by terminological debates concerning the appropriateness of defining the fetus as a person. 'What does it matter? Everyone knows it's life. Killing of any kind is wrong because it's denying a life-force which is a gift from God.'

Much to the chagrin of her parents and boy-friend, Chandra was arrested in early 1986 for trespassing at the Morgentaler clinic. She claims to have felt subtle peer pressure to *authenticate* her pro-life commitment by participating in an act of civil disobedience. Though Chandra expresses willingness to undergo arrest again, she has reservations about engaging in forms of protest that create headlines without appreciably improving the legal status of the fetus. The ideological tensions experienced by Chandra have made her ambivalent about anti-abortion protest, and her continued involvement in the movement hinges upon the slender social support provided by like-minded young women 'of both feminist and pro-life persuasion.'

Case Study Five

RACHEL. For the past five years Rachel has been in an activist limbo, committed as ever to the goal of winning legal protection for the fetus but unable to work in a pro-life movement she believes has been overtaken by 'a reactionary spirit.' Rachel does not identify with the traditional family ideals which are extolled by the majority of anti-abortionists. She works full-time as a commercial artist while her husband, with virility intact, stays home with their three children. Far from subverting a supposed cosmic order, Rachel argues, such role flexibility can enrich the life experiences of couples and their children.

Rachel describes her initial involvement in anti-abortion protest in the early 1970s as 'a response of compassion to a whole segment of human life being written out of the human race.' Like most activists, she went through childhood without direct exposure to the abortion issue, but does remember as an adolescent feeling 'deeply distraught' when a close friend who became pregnant made a mysterious trip to Buffalo. And though she does not recall as a child ever hearing abortion mentioned at church, Rachel suspects that she absorbed 'almost by osmosis' an abhorrence of it through the Catholic schools in which she was educated as well as through the influence of her 'moderately devout' German-Canadian parents.

Rachel believes that her underlying motivation for pro-life activism may stem from the experience of helping to raise a younger sister suffering from Down's syndrome.

> This isn't very clear, but deep down I realized that Sheila's the kind of person who's a prime target for abortion. My two brothers and I loved her so much, and she gave bundles in return. But in society's eyes she'd be unwanted for not conforming to some idea of perfection. Maybe my beliefs on abortion percolated through my love for Sheila. She taught me that life has unspeakable value, regardless of how difficult it is, and so abortion is a supreme injustice. This was never fully conscious, more of an intuitive response as a human being. I know I never looked to the teachings of the Church to justify my stance.

While she describes herself as 'a reluctantly addicted Catholic,' Rachel expresses consternation that many Catholic activists seem to espouse 'a fossilized, authoritarian faith' which is inimical to pluralism within both the church and the wider society. She characterizes the movement's militant Catholics as 'Tridentine,' and complains that they have 'mixed the pro-life cause into a hateful stew' which is inedible to most Canadians. Especially disquieting to Rachel is their frequent invective against feminists and homosexuals. 'The whole point is to fight discrimination of any kind, and they undercut this by defending the unborn but then attacking other groups.' Rachel also thinks it would be a 'tragic mistake' for the movement's militant Catholics to politicize their opposition to artificial contraception. 'It's this kind of unthinking submission to Church teaching that makes the movement a laughing-stock. We use NFP, but only because we believe it's a more personal form of family planning. It has nothing to do with religious obedience.'

Despite her uneasiness with its 'belligerent mood,' Rachel feels inescapably bound to the pro-life movement. The 'injustice of abortion,' she says, outweighs her personal disagreements with movement strategy. Rachel's involvement in anti-abortion protest, for several years in a state of dormancy, has recently recrudesced following the loss of an infant. 'It's intimate events like this that refuel your energy and reconfirm your commitment to pro-life. Birthing is such a powerful experience, and losing my baby, it just further impressed on me how sacred and terribly valuable life is. So here I am again. I cringe at the confrontational tactics of Campaign Life, but right now they're the only show in town.'

FAMILY HERITAGE CASE STUDIES

Case Study One

ALICE. Alice, twenty-five years old and the only child of a husband-wife evangelistic team, perceives her pro-life activism as a rite of passage from the ingrown and socially complacent piety of her upbringing to a more politicized spirituality. Describing her husband and herself as 'very Lord-conscious people' who 'wait on God each morning by reading Scripture,' Alice defines their shared activism as 'a very special way of walking with Christ to do justice.' Anti-abortion protest, she claims, is the mission of 'social responsibility' to which Protestant evangelicals are called today.

Alice has never personally known anyone who underwent an abortion, and only became aware of the issue in late adolescence. She believes the 'wrongness of abortion' should be obvious to Christians who 'are confronted with the Scriptural truth that all life is an inalienable gift from God' and to all people generally who recognize 'the democratic principle that society cannot define any one class – slaves, Jews, the handicapped, old people, the unborn – as unfit for life and disposable.' Faced daily by media coverage of the Harbord Street pickets, and living near the clinic, Alice in early 1985 began to read pro-life literature in order better to prepare herself for activism. Shortly afterward she and her husband 'prayerfully decided' to join the movement.

Alice's anti-abortionism is an abrupt departure from an upbringing which stressed the virtue of compliance with public authority. The climax thus far of Alice's activism was her participation in a sit-in at the Ontario premier's office, and she relates that her parents were appalled that 'I, always a straight kid and real conformist, would risk going to jail for something I believe in.' Alice claims that political protest is ill-suited to her 'placid temperament' but, nevertheless, a spiritual challenge she must meet head-on.

When Luke and I went to the picket line, our anti-abortion commitment became a desire of the heart instead of an abstraction. But I still have to fight against just wanting to stay home. I feel shattered seeing women coming out of the clinic after their abortions, and the heckling we take is also very hard on me. The sit-in was the turning point. I'd been brought up to bow before authority, but now for the first time I realize these politicians don't deserve my respect. This was my first ever challenge of authority, and I was prepared to get arrested and deal with the stigma of that. But they had locked the bathroom in the Premier's office, and I had to go so bad I couldn't hold it any longer, and so finally I had to leave. But this proved I'm no longer afraid to stand up and be counted. Now we're planning on fighting against apartheid, too, because the crimes against black people are horrible. It's like abortion, something has to be done, but sometimes I don't know exactly what to do.

Alice believes, however, that there exist divinely established limits to the defiance of authority. Thus, she condemns feminism, with its quest for reproductive freedom and doctrine of gender equality, as a 'rebellion against God's irrevocable plan for creation.' It is likely not accidental that Alice's entry into activism has coincided with her first pregnancy. She cherishes the prospects of motherhood, and feels personally assaulted by the feminist contention that pregnancy should be fully discretionary and terminable. Although she has a university degree and her husband is unemployed, Alice intends to remain at home as a full-time wife and mother. 'I've always wanted to be a housewife, and now that we're going to have kids, the most valuable work I can do is staying home with them.'

Alice acknowledges several areas of tension protesting alongside Roman Catholics. Though she practises NFP, 'using condoms as a back-up,' she disagrees with the wholesale rejection of artificial contraception by militant Catholic activists. Nor does she share their stance of opposition to capital punishment. Despite these differences, however, Alice professes admiration for her Catholic allies. 'I know people make fun of them, but I truly believe they're motivated out of love and would die for their convictions. I'm scared about the thought of dying for the cause. I haven't prayed it through whether I'd be able to give my life for these children. I have to take these things in stages.'

Case Study Two

MARJORIE. Twenty-five years ago Marjorie discontinued a promising career as a researcher in order to raise a family. Now that her four children are adults, she would like to resume her professional work, but is daunted by the retraining necessary to raise her level of competence to current professional standards. Marjorie has been involved in anti-abortion protest for five years, and recently became a member of REAL Women of Canada. She describes her activism as primarily 'a defence of marriage, family, and women's right to be full-time wives and mothers.' Marjorie regards feminism as an elitist, anti-family collusion that is remote from the values and experiences of the vast majority of Canadian women. She also believes that feminists, by their campaign for liberalized abortion, have helped to validate a prejudice against children in contemporary Western culture. The enemy for Marjorie is clearly defined, and she insists that any anti-abortionist who seeks a rapprochement with feminism is guilty of either naïvety or intellectual dishonesty.

Marjorie's anti-feminism seems to be mixed with a heavy dose of status resentment. Having many years ago suspended her own career aspirations in order to fulfil a traditional wife-mother role, she is distraught that this role appears to be tottering on the brink of cultural obsolescence. If pregnancy is made a strictly voluntary undertaking, thereby permitting women to pursue careers and sexual pleasure unencumbered by the demands of raising children, then full-time motherhood is reduced to a contingent life-style in competition with other life-styles of equal, and perhaps greater, claim to social legitimacy. The cultural advances of feminism, in Marjorie's mind, have undercut the values to which she surrendered her professional talents and have thus depreciated her as a person.

> Where would society be without women who sacrifice personal ambition for the sake of raising children and creating good citizens? I chose to be a mother with all the joys and tribulations that go with it, and it's a life most women would gladly choose. But now we're a despised lot and the feminists say we're parasitical because we're not in the executive board room. Whose kids will support them in their old age? So who's the parasite? I could have succeeded in my field, but I chose to be an expert at motherhood. I'm for freedom of choice – for women to be able to freely choose motherhood without being socially downgraded.

The third and middle child of Dutch-Canadian immigrants, Marjorie claims to have imbibed a 'sanctity-of-life philosophy' in the thickly religious atmosphere of her Calvinist upbringing. She traces her earliest activist stirrings to a 1979 television program, aired shortly after her eldest daughter's second miscarriage, in which pro-choice advocates lamented the difficulties faced by many women in procuring abortions. 'This was unimaginably offensive. Here I am consoling my grief-stricken daughter, and these people are speaking of the unborn as blobs of dispensable tissue. To me it was the denial of the existence of another human being. I bet even feminists hold baby showers, but they're trying to say we didn't lose a baby. This really clinched it for me.' The humanity of the fetus, Marjorie argues, is known foremost by the testimony 'of countless generations before this one which saw pregnancy as a sacred, life-giving event.'

As is the case for many middle-aged women in the movement, then, Marjorie's activism is partly a political avenue for defending a beleaguered life-style to which she has been dedicated since early adulthood. And this is a life-style which has sheltered and distanced her from the complex of factors that bring many women face-to-face with the dilemma of childbirth or abortion. Her home life – economically and emotionally – is apparently secure, and she is acquainted only by hearsay with the stress experienced by some women when an unplanned pregnancy intrudes upon social circumstances already stretched to the limit. Thus, she dismisses as 'left-lib gibberish' the argument of civil rights activists that abortion feeds off a basic structural disorder in Western society. For Marjorie the 'abortion crisis' is essentially moral, and it will be resolved only through a rehabilitation of traditional values of chastity, monogamy, and family solidarity.

Case Study Three

EVELYN. Evelyn embarked upon anti-abortion activism six years ago after a friend from her suburban Catholic parish gave her an article on the fetal diagnostic procedure known as amniocentesis. The article, Evelyn recalls, enthusiastically endorsed amniocentesis as a eugenic tool for weeding out defective fetuses and thus improving the hereditary qualities of the human race. Reading this, Evelyn says she felt as if there was 'some demonic force wrenching my heart.' At the time she was still mourning the loss of her eldest son, John, who had died at the age of nineteen after a life of suffering from a severe congenital disease. She saw the article as symptomatic of a general cultural bias that would deny the human worth and identity of her son and other handicapped people.

Evelyn's distress was compounded by remarks of acquaintances that the death of John was a 'blessing in disguise,' that it was preferable to a life of prolonged suffering and diminished human capacities, and that it had freed her of the burden of his daily care. Such comments, meant to be consolatory, offended Evelyn's ingrained Catholic belief that human life, regardless of its social utility or esthetic appeal, is 'a sacred continuum from conception until death.' The distinction between the 'normal' and 'less-than-normal,' Evelyn reasoned, is invidious and reflects a growing tendency of the dominant culture to divest of their humanity those who fail to measure up to assumed ideals of personhood.

Convinced that the time had arrived personally to defend 'the sacredness of voiceless treasures like John,' Evelyn and her husband visited their local pro-life office. There they were told that their concerns were well-grounded, that legalized abortion is in fact 'the thin edge of the wedge' for a systematic program of positive eugenics. When abortions are justified on the basis of fetal abnormality, they were told, it is but a short distance to the social legitimation of infanticide, with flawed post-natal specimens targeted as a disposable class.

Evelyn left the pro-life office believing that Canadian society had indeed sunk to a 'mean utilitarianism.' Further reflection over the next several weeks convinced her that the dilapidated condition of the 'traditional family' was the factor most responsible for 'a widespread cultural selfishness' that causes people to value only what does not stand in the way of personal gratification. Without the lifelong security and comfort provided by a loving home, she thought, individuals are cast upon trackless paths where egocentricity is learned as an art of self-survival. What social factors, Evelyn asked, were responsible for weakening the family and thereby disconnecting people from a sense of communal obligation? First of all, she reasoned, the 'dechristianization' of the family in modern society has separated it from its spiritual roots and thus turned it from a sacred institution into a contractual association that can be renegotiated or dissolved at will. And secondly, with the advent of feminism the dignity of motherhood itself has been tarnished, thereby lowering the social incentive for women to commit themselves to a role that invariably demands self-sacrifice. This 'crisis of the family,' Evelyn insists, is the larger context within which the abortion issue must be addressed.

I think this family-centred analysis is what the majority of us in the movement hold to. There are some pro-lifers who pigeon-hole us as reactionaries because we're concerned with the family, but I don't agree with them. Anyways, they sure haven't come up with a better alternative explanation of the abortion mentality. What I'm mainly trying to do is show the connection between abortion and the family. I discuss it in my parish and with friends, usually without much concrete success, but I'm patient. I feel this is more my role right now, not barging in on the clinic and getting arrested like the radicals do.

Case Study Four

MARIE. I couldn't believe it was me. Suddenly a whole gang of people poured into the street and sat on the road. I guess I got swept up into the emotion, because before I realized it, I had done the same thing. I have no idea where all the mounted police came from, but in no time at all I was being picked up and was brought to a paddy wagon. They charged me, fingerprinted me, and to top it off, it was even on the news. Jean rode home on the subway with me that night saying it was crazy for a forty-two-year-old grandmother to make such a spectacle of herself in front of the whole city. I laughed along with her, but I felt really good. I probably wouldn't let it happen again, but for the first time I felt as if I'd actually done something for what I believe in. My husband and the boys weren't too thrilled, but both of my daughters phoned me up the same night to say, 'Mom, we're really proud of what you did.'

Marie's uncharacteristic behaviour on Harbord Street in February 1985 may have been stimulated by the emotion of the occasion, but it also reflected a deeper anger she had been harbouring for almost a decade. When her fourth child was born nine years ago, Marie recalls, most friends and acquaintances responded with an aloofness that made her feel as if she had exceeded her culturally entitled allotment of children. People who had congratulated her for previous births seemed barely able to acknowledge this one. When pregnant again three years later, Marie says, she was made to feel like a social deviant. 'It was unbelievable. When the pregnancy was confirmed I was ecstatic. I was working part-time and wanted to share the news with everyone in the office. Do you want to know the typical response? "Well, I guess that's the last thing you need. What are you going to do about it?" It was the same with my own family. I became Catholic when we married, and my mother always blamed this on me having babies. She wanted me to abort every one but the first two. It made me feel like a misfit. No one could accept that we wanted a big family.'

It was only in 1982 when she met Jean at a parents' night in the local Catholic school, Marie says, that she began to regain her self-respect. Also a mother of five, Jean had for years been an active pro-lifer. She told Marie that many other women were likewise treated like social outcasts for having large families, and that some of them had found common cause in the pro-life movement. Marie claims that she had always assumed abortion to be wrong, but only after talking with Jean did she begin to think that the pro-choice ethic may be related to a cultural prejudice against women such as herself.

Joining the pro-life movement was an act of self-assertion for Marie. 'Of course I cared about children being lost, but I was also telling society to stop putting us down for having babies.' With Jean as her guide, Marie has since undertaken volunteer work in most aspects of the movement's operation. Most recently, she has begun a discussion and support group with other stay-at-home mothers in her Catholic parish. Marie's immersion in movement activities has its ironic side. As is the case for many of her cohorts, her heavy volunteer workload some weeks takes her away from the home almost as much as would a full-time job. 'My husband's a truck driver, and now that I'm fully involved in this, he's learned to fend for himself at home. Some nights I get back and supper's made, the dishes are done, and he's got the boys doing their homework.'

REVIVALIST CATHOLIC CASE STUDIES

Case Study One

ANDREW. Andrew is a thirty-three-year-old artist who lives alone in a basement apartment in Toronto's east end. He was raised with two sisters in rural Manitoba where his father worked as an insurance broker and his mother as an accountant. As an adolescent Andrew fostered a 'spirituality of nature,' and he would spend long hours at prayer while alone in the woods. He grew steadily disillusioned with the Anglicanism of his parents, which appeared to him to be little other than a pious dessert for their business appetites. At the age of nineteen he severed his own ties with Anglicanism when his parents, with the moral approval of their resident clergyman, arranged an abortion for his younger sister. Andrew claims that his repugnance of abortion was rooted in his reverence for the 'natural life cycle' and belief in God as the exclusive author of all life. He regarded abortion as 'an ultimate act of environmental desecration,' and believed that it could be condoned only by a society that had lost both communion with nature and its primordial instinct for conserving life.

After moving to Toronto and graduating from art college, Andrew for several years led a hermit's existence, working, meditating, and sleeping in his studio. At the age of thirty-one he finally found his 'spiritual niche' and converted to Roman Catholicism. Andrew's conversion seemed to him like 'a miraculous jolt of spiritual energy,' and he attempted to atone for lost time by immersing himself in Catholic culture. Daily mass, weekly confession, monthly retreats, meditation with the rosary, Benedictions, and veneration of the saints instilled in him a sense of oneness with the Catholic past. In addition, Andrew developed a special reverence for Pope John Paul II, whom he describes as 'the world's most heroic champion of human dignity and truth.'

About a year after his conversion, however, Andrew became troubled that his faith seemed to be confined to a 'devotional cradle.' 'I believed the Canadian bishops when they said faith must change the world, and it struck me that all these masses didn't mean a damn thing unless I became active in the struggles of the world.' Andrew's opportunity for activism knocked in early 1985 when he watched the televised arrest of several anti-abortion protesters on Harbord Street. He claims to have felt an irresistible calling to joint the protest, and immediately left his studio for the picket line. Anti-abortion activism in the months ahead would provide a channel for Andrew's burgeoning spirituality and also a sense of shared purpose with like-minded young Catholics. 'This has filled a void in my life by giving me true fulfilment and companionship. It has deepened my faith and brought friendship with profoundly committed Catholics. We believe that faith must be alive to suffering, especially if its cries are stifled by the deafness of our culture. Most Catholics, and I have to say bishops and priests too, have sold out. They're afraid to meet this challenge. When I'm on the picket line, I know I'm with the true church.'

Anti-abortionism thus satisfied Andrew's yearning for religious fellowship and for an enhanced Catholic self-identity. It appeared to him to be transparently righteous, laden with spiritual challenge, and thus ideally attuned to his quest for a specifically Catholic vocation. It furthermore represented a fateful crossroad on his personal journey of salvation. 'In a very real sense I'm doing this to save my soul; there is no other work as urgent for Catholics today.'

Despite his strong religious investment in anti-abortion activism, Andrew thinks that displays of piety should be restrained during public protest. He is concerned that the movement seems to have attracted a number of 'kooks and crackpots' whose zeal at times threatens to spill into unbridled 'fanaticism.'

In a sense it's like art. We're all making a statement about who we are as Catholics. But it's hard to control some of the people we get on the line. It makes us all look bad when you've got wild-eyed guys standing up on snowbanks praying the rosary. There's one guy who used to be a biker. Now he claims to have redemption through Mary. He'll come up to some of our young women protesters and say things like, 'You know, our Mother Mary is very unhappy that your dress is so tight. Very immodest of you.' Then he'll break into some chant. The media loves the guy, but we just wish he'd tone down his act.

Like most of his compeers, Andrew believes that artificial contraception and pre-marital sex are absolutely forbidden to Catholics. He dates several women from the movement but is determined to remain a virgin until marriage. 'I've never had a sexual relationship, and I know this sounds ridiculous in our society, but I see this as an important aspect of my faith commitment.'

In 1985 Andrew was arrested for trespassing at the Morgentaler clinic. He believes that the time may soon arrive for even more drastic forms of protest.

It's meaningless if it doesn't change anything. We feel like stooges just standing there with our signs knowing what's going on inside. If you knew a child was in a house being abused, wouldn't you be justified in breaking in and stopping it? Or would you give priority to laws protecting private property? It's time we took tougher action. If I could be sure there was no one hurt, I'd be prepared to bomb the abortuary and go to jail. You know, we're not sincere in this if we're always tabulating personal costs to ourselves. Martyrdom is what some Catholics might be called to in this struggle. I'd hope to meet it bravely. I'm already into the protest all the way. I don't even see my family anymore, because they're pro-choice and the arguments were too bitter. We have to accept the consequences of our commitment.

Case Study Two

KEVIN. Kevin, twenty years old and a third-generation Irish-Canadian, has belonged to the pro-life movement for almost a year. His father is a civil servant and his mother has devoted most of her adult years to raising nine children. Unlike some of his compeers, Kevin has not undergone a moral conversion to an anti-abortion stance. His parents and older siblings have been long-time supporters of the pro-life cause and Kevin recalls family discussions on abortion even when he was a young boy.

Kevin thinks that the convergence of several factors caused him to translate his 'natural and unquestioned' disapproval of abortion into political activism. First, after his mother suffered a miscarriage in 1984, Kevin says, his family openly mourned 'this lost child who was already part of our lives.' This incident reinforced Kevin's belief that intra-uterine life is 'fully human,' and he says that he 'prays to this little baby every day, knowing that he or she is in heaven.' On the heels of this family tragedy occurred the concentrated week of protest outside the Morgentaler clinic in February 1985. The intensive media coverage of the protest magnified for Kevin the importance of the abortion issue, and he decided that 'it was now or never for all good women and men to put themselves on the line for the unborn.' And finally, Kevin had for several years been dissatisfied with a 'merely private piety' and had been searching for some way to make his faith politically incarnate. Anti-abortion activism seemed to fit the bill perfectly. 'I had grown up and knew it was my turn to show leadership and the importance of a relevant faith.'

As is the case with all younger Revivalists, Kevin's piety is capacious and all-absorbing. He attends mass daily, confession weekly, and Perpetual Adoration (during which he remains kneeling a full hour) as frequently as possible. Kevin works as a warehouse labourer, and spends his lunch hours at prayer in the privacy of his car. He has retained his boyhood attachment to Mary, and prays the Hail Mary at intervals throughout each day. In addition to being strictly regimented, Kevin's piety is characteristically prosaic. He has never experienced a revelation or vision, and is unsympathetic toward Catholics, such as charismatics and devotees of exotic Marian cults, who seek to supplement established Catholic doctrine with extra-curricular afflatus. By unwavering obedience to the Roman Magisterium, Kevin aspires to align his will in total conformity with what he understands to be an unchanging basilica of Catholic tradition. The subject of artificial contraception provides, as it does for all Revivalists, the touchstone of Kevin's piety. The church through *Humanae Vitae* has spoken, and those who fail to heed her words show themselves as deserters from the faith. Kevin also believes that contraception is the gateway to abortion, and that the pro-life movement must, even at the expense of greater public opprobrium, assert its opposition to 'non-procreative' sex.

Kevin believes that the abortion issue has brought into the open a life-and-death struggle between 'pro-life' and 'cultural' Catholics for control of the Canadian church. With Pope John Paul II as their champion and *Humanae Vitae* their crest, he says, 'pro-life' Catholics aspire to rescue the church from cultural subservience. 'The battle lines are drawn, and *Humanae Vitae* is the distinguishing mark between the two armies. There are many cultural Catholics who are disloyal to *Humanae Vitae* and yet still claiming membership in the Church. They've already distanced themselves from the source of Catholic wisdom. It's not accidental that we don't see them protesting abortion.'

Kevin blames the Canadian bishops for what he describes as the church's 'assimilation into the wider pagan society.' The bishops, he contends, have been craven standard-bearers of public opinion rather than staunch defenders of the faith. Instead of appeasing the majority of churchgoers who do not want to hear the hard line on contraception and abortion, Kevin insists, the Canadian bishops should demonstrate their allegiance to Rome by threatening nonconforming Catholics with excommunication. The 'vapid support' given by the bishops to the pro-life cause, Kevin asserts, is damning proof of their cowardice. 'They've had their opportunities to speak out, but they come across so timidly. By fudging on contraception, they've diluted the force of *Humanae Vitae* and helped to make abortion more acceptable. They're not at one with the pope, and a house divided against itself can't stand. What I hope is that the turmoil over abortion will call the church to her true self. It's far better that we be a small church of true believers than a huge mass of name-only Catholics. You know, in a sense, I'm an activist because I'm doing the job the bishops don't have the guts to do themselves.'

Kevin has yet to engage in civil disobedience, but claims that he would welcome getting arrested as 'a badge of distinction, much like

Solzhenitsyn in the Gulag.' He argues that 'divine law' supersedes laws of the state and therefore must be the guiding beacon for anti-abortionists. 'The attorney-general can legislate where I can park my car, but we can dispense with his law where human lives are at stake.' That Kevin's activism is linked organically with his conception of Catholic vocation is made vivid when he discusses the possibility of personal martyrdom. He believes that pro-life Catholics must spiritually gird themselves for a reign of persecution and, like martyrs of the primitive church, be prepared to offer the ultimate sacrifice for their beliefs. 'I'd hope to hold true to my faith if I was called to this. Martyrdom would be a big honour – putting my life on the line for a child's right to live.'

Kevin thinks that liberal capitalism, with its promotion of individualism and competitiveness, is the chief catalyst behind the escalating abortion rate. Thus, despite his unhappiness with certain aspects of their moral leadership, he is pleased that the Canadian bishops have criticized Canada's dominant political and economic structures.[5] He agrees with the bishops that lay Catholics must overcome political complacency and become active in projects of social change. But, he insists, an *authentic* vocation to social justice must begin with the campaign against abortion. 'I'm a socialist, and I'm quite impressed with the bishops' challenge of capitalism. It's long overdue. But their priorities are confused. Abortion is the pollution of the whole of society. You can't wipe up the floor while the tap is running. The bishops speak out against unemployment boldly, but what they have to say about abortion is vintage "don't ruffle any feathers" stuff. I much prefer Pope John Paul II's approach – he covers all the issues, economic injustice and abortion. This is the kind of guts and conviction I admire.'

Case Study Three

ELLEN. Ellen, twenty-six years old and single, works as a special educator with mentally handicapped children. She is the third of seven children in a fourth-generation Irish-Canadian family. Her father is a pharmacist and her mother a part-time music teacher. Ellen regards her anti-abortion activism as a culmination of 'coming-to-terms' with the meaning and consequences of her Catholic self-identity. The event which Ellen believes indirectly led her to activism was the breakup several years ago of an engagement to a man she still professes to love.

Ellen says that her relationship with Paul ended mainly because he 'couldn't live up to' her ideals of marriage and family life. Whereas Paul wanted 'the perfect Yuppie family of one or two kids and lots of money,' Ellen believed it would be a violation of her 'Catholic principles' to enter a marriage in which the number of children would be limited by contraception. 'So it came down to deciding between a man I truly loved and fidelity to my faith. I went through a lot of emotional stress, but I had to ask: What does my faith mean if it's so easily compromised?'

Ellen claims that this experience rekindled her 'passion for the church.' For the first time in her adult life, she had stood up and affirmed at considerable cost her allegiance to Catholic sexual and family ideals and, in the process, had personalized the religious tradition of her upbringing. 'It was in a sense like a conversion because I felt as if I had truly adopted Catholicism instead of merely inheriting it.' Besides resolving her religious self-identity, this experience stimulated in Ellen a desire to put her aroused faith to concrete service. Given her lifelong belief that unborn life is human and hence sacred, as well as the eruption of publicity surrounding the Morgentaler clinic, anti-abortion activism presented for Ellen a tailor-made vocation.

Like other younger Revivalists, Ellen believes that increased social acceptance of abortion is a corollary of the individualism that has been promoted at the institutional level in the name of free enterprise, a free market, and economic competition. By consecrating the rights of the solitary individual, she argues, the dominant liberal society has alienated people from family and the natural impulses of community. Liberalized abortion, according to Ellen, benumbs people to the 'unfathomable mystery of life' and to the importance of corporate responsibility. She believes that small egalitarian groups, such as the Madonna House community founded by Catherine de Hueck Doherty and Jean Vanier's Daybreak communities, represent a yeast which will hopefully bring the larger society to a rediscovery of its communal roots. Ellen likewise understands the anti-abortion movement to be a countervailing force against the 'impersonality of mass society.'

I see this as a wonderful opportunity to express what's good about life. You don't have to be Catholic to see that we've failed as a society if we think that killing is the answer. Dorothy Day and Catherine de Hueck are two of my heroines. They believed in collective responsibility and never gave up on the weak and helpless. This system glorifies individuals at the expense of the most vulnerable. The pro-choice stand is accepting the ultimate in victimization. There's a lot of social problems that have to be solved with poor mothers, but once a baby is conceived, you can't solve the problem by killing the baby. God knows what He's doing.

As the lives of many younger Revivalists would attest, political beliefs are not always a window into a person's religious world. In striking contrast to Ellen's political nonconformity is her exacting adherence to an authoritarian, hierarchical conception of Catholicism. She insists that established Catholic tradition is the holy compass by which Catholics must navigate, ignoring it at the risk of falling into the blankness of unbelief. In typically Revivalist fashion, Ellen expresses ambivalence toward the Second Vatican Council. While conceding that Vatican II was 'inspired and pastorally necessary,' she laments that it seems to have given rise to a 'Catholic crisis of authority.' She claims that 'love and freedom' have been emphasized in the post-conciliar church at the expense of obedience and institutional loyalty. 'It's not like I yearn for the church of the 1940s, but we've swung too far to the opposite extreme. There needs to be a better balance.'

Ellen's theological stringency is complemented by a reverential, morally prescriptive attitude toward human sexuality. Though she regularly dates movement men, Ellen is a virgin and plans to await marriage for a complete sexual relationship. Her views here are anchored to the natural law doctrine that sex is designed primarily to bring into existence another human life.[6] The transcendent purpose of sexual experience, contends Ellen, is truncated whenever procreation is not intended.

The sexual puritanism of young Revivalists such as Ellen is not merely a legalistic conformity to traditional Catholic teaching. Rather, as mentioned in Chapter Four, it is a central aspect of their project for a disciplined, Apollonian faith. In an age of widespread challenge to traditional parameters of sexual conduct, they aspire to circumscribe Eros within limits thought to be fixed by supernatural design. As Ellen expresses it: 'I oppose all forms of contraception, and not just because of a rule imposed by the church. It's a decision based on my faith. But there is a real beauty in the rationale of *Humanae Vitae*, because it reflects God's intention for us. I'm committed to virginity until I marry, though I always have to deal with temptation. I'm a very sexual person. A celibate life wouldn't be feasible for me. I'd love to get married and have ten kids. It'd be a big disappointment if I didn't. Your sexuality isn't something to be played with. It has to be under control because it's a sacred expression.'

Because her anti-abortion activism is surcharged with religious meaning, Ellen claims that her continued involvement in the movement does not hinge upon political success or failure. 'Whatever happens in the political arena, I'll still be there. I witness a lot to people who work at the clinic, trying to convince them to stop what they're doing. Usually they just tell me to "Fuck off." One of the clinic doctors got so annoyed with me, he said to a cop, "Who'd want to sleep with this bitch?" I can afford to laugh these insults off. It's standing up against murder and at the same time saying you're not afraid to be a Catholic.'

Case Study Four

ROBERT. Anti-abortion activism has become a dominant way of life for Robert, a forty-four-year-old father of five and third-generation English-Canadian. Robert is a public relations officer in a large corporation and has been warned by his employers that he will lose his job unless he curtails his activism. Undeterred, he remains a regular fixture on the Harbord Street picket line and has been imprisoned twice for performing civil disobedience at the clinic. Robert is one of several Catholics from the sample whose involvement in the cause extends well beyond the customary repertoire of protest activities. He and his wife have opened their home to women with troubled pregnancies, have set up an 'employment network' for disadvantaged young mothers, and have adopted two severely handicapped children.

Robert believes that anti-abortionists must be prepared to sacrifice everything for the cause. He is part of a growing minority within the movement who refuse to rule out violence as a strategy of last resort. 'We shouldn't shed false tears. If an abortuary is blown up and no one is hurt ... I've been in a couple of candlelight demonstrations against American policies in Central America, and I could never condemn the Sandinistas for using violence to defend their people. I just pray for God to work His will through me, even if it means martyrdom. I'll go to jail indefinitely if it means saving one life. They can fire me from my job. There's an old saying about the company owning your soul. Well, they don't own mine.'

Robert links his involvement in anti-abortion protest to an intense religious experience which he says gave his life a new tonality and clarity of direction. After the death of his younger brother several years ago, Robert says, he underwent a prolonged period of spiritual drift during which his faith seemed opaquely impersonal. He overcame this ennui by attending a Cursillo retreat, which is designed as a concentrated encounter session for laymen seeking an aroused sense of Catholic vocation.[7] Although the subject of abortion was not explicitly addressed at the retreat, Robert claims that the experience drew him to a more intimate appreciation of the 'sanctity of life' ethic taught by the church. 'It wasn't so much a conversion as a powerful deepening of faith. After that I looked at abortion and knew I was called to commit myself to stopping it.'

Cursillo retreats have been a stepping-stone to anti-abortion protest for four other male Revivalists from the sample, all of whom display a level of commitment to the cause comparable to that of Robert. While not quite on a par with the radical alteration of identity which commonly figures in the classical conversion experience,[8] the Cursillo retreat produced in these men a sensation of having shifted to a higher, more purposive plane of existence. It was like a spiritual strop which sharpened their Catholic sensitivities, and they emerged from the retreat bristling with a religious energy which threatened to dissipate if not channelled into some recognizably vocational stream.

Besides serving to consolidate a newly-affirmed Catholicity, anti-abortionism has become for these men the pulse of their daily lives. Work schedules are manipulated, leisure activities rationed, and family life adjusted so that regular stints on the protest treadmill may be accommodated. All of them conceive their activism as a mission of evangelization not only to the wider society but also and especially to Canadian Catholics themselves. For they are convinced that the Canadian church is a renegade institution which has lost the will to preach what is discordant to the secular ear. Robert expresses this point with clarity.

More than anger, I feel great sadness that the bishops, and Canadian Catholics in general, haven't given a powerful witness against abortion. Because they're afraid to swim against the stream, they haven't been able to speak forcefully on it. The bishops probably realize that a vigorous witness against abortion and contraception would empty their churches. This creates real tension for me. I still feel loyalty to them, and don't want to give scandal to the church by publicly defiling them ... This is the most important apostolic action of our time. When we're on the picket line we're testifying our faith, not just to an unbelieving society but to an unbelieving church. Most Catholics aren't awakened to the issue. And so it's very hard. Most Catholics just wish we'd go away. The coldness and annoyance is written all over their faces when we speak with them.

Case Study Five

PAULA. A third-generation Polish-Canadian, Paula is forty-six years old and the mother of three teenagers. Prior to joining the pro-life movement two years ago, Paula relates, she lived in a twilight zone where all relationships seemed unnervingly out of focus. Her marriage was without spark, both her parents were seriously ill, and she felt spiritually unfulfilled just attending Sunday mass. She and her husband decided on a trial separation, and Paula took a part-time job and moved into her younger sister's downtown apartment. Her sister had recently experienced a 'spiritual rebirth,' and she encouraged Paula to 'turn her troubles over to the Lord' and to dedicate herself to the church.

After two months' absence Paula returned home, reconciled with her husband, and began a daily routine of prayer. Her feelings of angst and isolation, however, soon reappeared, and Paula worried that her faith was in danger of 'slipping away.' Paula tried to make friends at her local parish, but the Catholicism of those she met in the Sunday pew seemed to her passive and unabsorbed. Paula's sister once again entered the picture, this time with a copy of *Abortion: The Silent Holocaust* by Fr John Powell, a book popular in pro-life circles.[9] Reading it convinced Paula that anti-abortionism was the vocation she had been seeking. 'Once again I feared I was losing my beliefs. My husband and myself were getting trapped again in materialism. We were neglecting the only basis for keeping our marriage together. This book knocked us both off our horses, it radically changed the direction of our lives. We were just unaware of the scope of abortion. And then everything seemed to come together. We joined the movement and have spent so much time working with really committed Catholics who share our faith and love for the Church. This is our life now.'

A cardinal belief of Revivalist activists, and one shared fully by Paula, is that a de facto schism between 'pro-life' and 'cultural' Catholics is at present unfolding in the Canadian church. Paula asserts that the majority of self-declared Catholics in Canada have opted for a generic brand of Catholicism which is scarcely distinguishable from the surrounding secular culture. Even the Canadian bishops, she laments, have wilted under the pressure of secularism. Paula regards anti-abortion protest as a rite of purification which will reconstitute Canadian Catholicism as a remnant of the truly faithful.

> We desperately need shepherds, but the bishops are not acting as shepherds. There's so much confusion within the church – most people don't know what it means to be a Catholic. I have suffered so much despondency over this. People are losing their faith in droves, and the unborn are being massacred. Abortion is so simple – it's the killing of innocent souls and denying created humans the right to grow in knowledge of God. The bishops don't seem to care, maybe they need to be sensitized to what's happening. It's amazing, the more we get involved with this, the more you can see the schism between pro-life Catholics and the apostates, including most priests, nuns, and bishops. It'll soon become a matter of public knowledge. The secularizers will leave and form a church independent of Rome, leaving devout pro-lifers as a tiny minority in the faith.

Although a relative newcomer to the movement, Paula has learned her lessons well from veteran Revivalist activists whom she meets regularly on the Harbord Street picket line. The various statements on abortion issued by the Canadian Catholic bishops, she thus contends, are pale, ineffectual discourses guaranteed to offend or to challenge no one. Rather than speaking the unvarnished truth on abortion and contraception, she says, the bishops have taken the path of least resistance in their pursuit of social relevance. The abortion issue in particular, according to Paula, represents an ecumenical roadblock which the bishops would prefer to sidestep. But worst of all, Paula claims, the bishops are afraid to preach what their own flock does not want to hear.

The bishops are political animals, and they realize their authority is on shaky ground. They know in their hearts they should take a stronger stance against contraception and abortion, but if they did the churches would empty. The people don't want moral direction from the bishops, thinking the bishops are poking their noses in their private lives. They'd say, 'Mind your own business or we'll take our business elsewhere. We've been liberated from a religion that makes demands on us.' And the Protestant churches would accuse the bishops of trying to return the church to the Dark Ages. But true shepherds of the church should say, 'Who gives a damn if we're made a laughing-stock? This isn't a popularity contest. It's our job to teach the truth in a clear, undiluted way.' So what does it matter if there's a stampede out of the churches or if their progressive friends forget their phone numbers? The church isn't run by polls. It's based on supernatural truth.

Case Study Six

BERNARD. Bernard is one of only three sample subjects who claim to have at one time held the pro-choice position. A third-generation Irish-Canadian, father of four, and a salesman, Bernard tells how he once visited an anti-abortion display at the Canadian National Exhibition and accused the exhibitors of promoting fascism by seeking to force women to complete unwanted pregnancies. The turning point, according to Bernard, occurred during a period of acute personal depression brought about by the loss of a child several hours after birth. After meeting weekly for over a year with a psychiatrist and still failing to climb out of his depression, Bernard decided to return to the Catholicism of his youth. He had not been to mass for ten years ever since undergoing a 'crisis of faith' while in his early thirties.

At his parish Bernard developed a close friendship with a man who was a prominent anti-abortionist, and shortly afterward joined the pro-life movement himself. Anti-abortion activism, he says, helped to compensate for the loss of his child and also stoked his rekindled faith commitment.

I flipped out when my kid died. I could only handle the grief when I went back to church. You know, I was an altar boy from age ten till twenty, and I served mass almost every day for ten years. I only missed thirty-five days. I was damn proud of it and still am. It's hard to explain why I just dropped out of the church. I think it's because I realized I was a Catholic out of a fear of divine punishment – a fear of going to Hell – and I finally grew up and saw that this was a wrong motivation. So I said, 'Bullshit – that's it, I'll live my own life,' and I became one of the main rats in the rat race. But since I dedicated myself to pro-life work five years ago, I haven't missed a single day of mass. And now I go out of love and thanksgiving.

Bernard's entry into activism exemplifies a pattern which may be discerned in the lives of many Revivalist Catholics. This familiar pattern begins with emotional turbulence occasioned by marital troubles, personal tragedy, or general life-style dissatisfaction. Then follows a spiritual stock-taking and subsequently either a re-embracement of or conversion to Catholicism. The pattern culminates in pro-life activism. This sequence suggests that anti-abortionism serves for these subjects as a means of certifying a freshly determined Catholicism.

There is an additional dimension to this pattern which Bernard's case helps to make vivid. Like many Revivalists, Bernard acquired his religious disposition at a time when the church breathed into the most intimate regions of life: marriage, family, sexuality. The church to which he returned after a prolonged absence, however, appeared to him disconcertingly different from that of his boyhood memories. Not only did it seem to have at most a partial and tenuous hold on the lives of its members, but it appeared unprepared to receive the absolute commitment which he yearned to offer. It was in the pro-life movement that Bernard discovered a sanctuary of unabridged and impassioned faith. And once fully immersed in the movement, he could only see the church outside as otiose and indifferent.

In typically Revivalist fashion, Bernard accords anti-abortion activism redemptive significance. Mainstream Canadian Catholicism, he contends, is wracked by unbelief and compromise, and therefore incapable of confronting the demons of the modern age. It is Catholics on the front line of the abortion battle, he insists, who are called to usher the church into a new dawn. The pro-life movement, according to Bernard, is the prototype of the new church which will come into existence following the present period of purification. This revitalized church, he says, will be shorn of secular embellishment. It will be robust and defiant, a social outcast, and composed only of those 'true believers,' numbering perhaps only several thousand, who yield total obedience to Rome.

What you see here is the remnant. The phoenix will rise from people like this. The church is alive and well here. I think the church will be stripped to its bare bones and will be made up of only the true believers who'll put their lives on the line for the faith. That's a big part of this movement – a renewal of the church at the grassroots by dedicated Catholics. John Paul II is the key. Those not in step with the drum major will fall by the wayside. Many of these will be priests and bishops. Many of us are here because we see this as a battle between good and evil. The evil is a total selfishness in our society – a total inward-looking, look-after-me-and-screw-everybody-else attitude. Most Canadian Catholics are so wimpish and gutless, they're geniuses at debating the pros and cons, anything to use as an excuse for not getting involved ... This is a campaign of faith – we're fighting a new kind of paganism that's infiltrated the church. Deepening our faith and prayer is the only way we can hope to succeed. If we tie our chariot to the state and count just on political intervention to stop abortion, we're doomed to disappointment and failure.

6

Revivalist Catholics, Social Justice Catholics, and the Politics of Ecumenism

The investigation thus far has focused on the broader Canadian pro-life movement, with special attention paid to its evolving fortunes in Toronto. As stated at the very outset, however, this study is not solely an exercise in social movement analysis. More especially, it is concerned with the ideological tensions which the abortion issue poses for Canadian Catholicism. In this and the following chapter, the discussion shifts to this narrower Catholic focus.

Much of the groundwork for this specifically Catholic discussion has already been laid. Previous chapters have highlighted the discord between the pro-life movement and the institutional church, as well as the emergence within the movement of a spirit of radical Catholic sectarianism. In the present chapter, it is argued that Revivalist Catholics are one of two bitterly opposed factions competing for ideological ascendancy within the Canadian church. Whereas Revivalists have established their identity through pro-life activism, their nemeses, designated here alternatively as Progressive or Social Justice Catholics, have been conspicuously absent on the anti-abortion front. Ironically, therefore, the abortion issue has helped both to widen and to solidify this basic ideological dichotomy within Canadian Catholicism.

THE PRO-LIFE MOVEMENT AND CANADIAN CATHOLICISM: AN OVERVIEW

By the 1980s the pro-life movement had become a fulcrum of disunity for the Canadian Catholic church. In addition to operating at cross-purposes with the church hierarchy, it was clear that it had come to represent a version of Catholicism antipathetic to liberalism within the wider society *and* the Canadian church. Most Catholics drawn to anti-abortion protest, especially since the downfall of the Coalition, have been proponents of a world-view that on most theological and cultural counts may be characterized as dogmatically conservative. And Catholics uncomfortable with this world-view have systematically dissociated themselves from the movement, many of them experiencing second thoughts about the desirability or feasibility of criminalizing abortion if not about the morality of abortion itself. Indeed, it is impossible to overstate the extent to which the pro-life movement has been converted in less than two decades from a vehicle of consensus to one of fundamental dissension for the Canadian church.

Like an irresistible magnet, the movement has pulled into itself Catholics who speak the same religious language, partake of the same rites, and affirm the same values. It is Revivalist Catholics, above all others, who have embraced the anti-abortion cause as an apostolic 'call-to-arms,' thereby making it their privileged preserve and self-identifying 'ritual of goodness.' Catholic anti-abortionists today constitute a distinct society within the Canadian church, and the abortion issue has risen as a metaphorical wall of division between Catholics of radically opposed faith commitments.

The pro-life movement has thus been turned into a theological compass which gives clear indications of where Canadian Catholics stand on matters of belief, devotion, and sexual morality. By 1986 one could safely infer that most Catholic pro-lifers regard John Paul II as the saviour of a crisis-ridden church, that they adhere reverentially to *Humanae Vitae* and view it as a prerequisite of Catholic belonging, and that Marian piety ranks high on their devotional hierarchy. One could also assume, just as confidently, that those Catholics unsympathetic to the pro-life movement are, to varying degrees, in league with the movement of modernization within the church which is described below as Social Justice, or Progressive, Catholicism. Thus abortion, the very issue which is popularly supposed to evoke consensus among Catholics, provides the line of fracture for a widening ideological bifurcation within the Canadian church.

Revivalists do not, of course, constitute an exclusive Catholic presence within the pro-life movement. Catholics of various shades of liberalism remain attached to the cause, but since 1980 their numbers have declined precipitously and their activist profile has steadily receded. Catholics of the civil rights type, for example, continue to give the movement liberal injections, but these are not enough to alter its dominant mood. The movement also continues to draw support from the Catholic parish-school nexus. While Parish, or family heritage, Catholics do not fully share the Revivalist critique of mainstream Canadian Catholicism, it none the less strikes a responsive chord among many of them. Parish Catholic activists are particularly perplexed by the relative silence of the Canadian bishops on the anti-abortion front, as well as the apparent desertion of the pro-life cause by the vast majority of priests and nuns. They are thus increasingly receptive to the Revivalist contention that stewardship of the faith has been passed by default to an enclave of Catholic laity.

Indeed, the disestablishment of the movement – its almost total severance from the official church – is perhaps the most intriguing aspect of the Canadian pro-life saga. Although the movement from its outset was lay-initiated and completely independent of the Canadian Catholic hierarchy, most bishops encouraged its lay development and were, frankly, relieved to pass the anti-abortion ball to the Alliance and Coalition. The unofficial co-operation of the bishops, however, ceased abruptly when the movement, under the militant leadership of Campaign Life, took a more choleric and confrontational direction. Since the late 1970s the movement has been informally excommunicated from the graces of the Canadian hierarchy, and the attitude of most prelates toward it has been one of studied avoidance.[1]

In order to understand the basic cleavage which the abortion issue represents for Canadian Catholicism, it is necessary to describe briefly the new theological and political trend which has recently engaged the imagination of many Canadian Catholics and against which anti-abortion Catholics are largely, and adamantly, opposed.

THE NEW SOCIAL TEACHING OF THE CANADIAN BISHOPS

In the decade following Vatican II the absorbing concern of most Catholic intellectuals, in Canada and elsewhere, was one of fundamental theology: how could contemporary Christians continue to make sense of their faith in an advanced age of secularism, liberalism, and pluralism?[2] In the 1970s and 1980s this question has been upstaged by a different, more pastorally urgent one: what is the mission to which the Catholic community is called in the modern world? For many Catholics the answer to this latter question, and by implication to the former as well, has been found in social involvement and, more particularly, in the adoption of what is frequently termed a *transformative* social ethic.

The contemporary movement of Progressive, or Social Justice, Catholicism is committed to reconceptualizing the meaning of Catholic vocation and virtue. Social Justice Catholics regard a privatized and other-worldly piety as constrictive and, if only by its remoteness from concrete political struggles, as an ideological defence of existing societal arrangements. They argue that the traditional Catholic emphases of personal conversion and moral perfection are inadequate in the face of world-wide poverty and oppression.[3] Instead, the church is called to become a vehicle of political emancipation and the conversion of unjust social structures and cultural attitudes.

Not only are Social Justice and Revivalist Catholics the most bitter of foes in the contemporary Canadian church, but the abortion issue has become the chief totem symbolizing their mutual enmity. Before analysing the conflict between these two groups, and the role played in it by the abortion issue, it is first necessary to discuss the new social teaching of the Canadian bishops. This teaching has placed the bishops in the forefront of Progressive, or Social Justice, Catholicism in Canada. It is also a teaching which curiously, and much to the chagrin of Revivalists, seems to omit consideration of abortion.

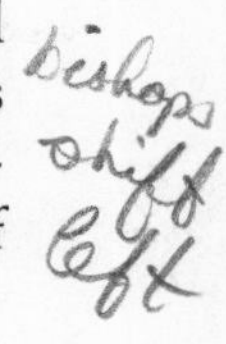

As Gregory Baum has observed, the social teaching of the Canadian bishops has undergone a noticeable 'shift to the left' during the past decade and a half.[4] The emerging social theory of the bishops, Baum writes, has been undergirded by two ethical principles, namely, 'the preferential option for the poor' and 'the value and dignity of labour.'[5] This recent 'shift to the left' can be better understood within the context of the evolving social ethic of the universal Catholic *ecclesia*.

For over half a century, dating from the 1891 publication of Leo XIII's *Rerum Novarum*, Catholic social teaching consisted of a synthesis of ideals which may be described as corporatist and paternalistic. This teaching regarded society as an organism which was sustained by shared values, co-operation, and submission to duly established authority. Justice in this organic order was conceived as the attainment and maintenance of a proper balance of both rights and responsibilities among society's various classes. Government was expected to intervene in the social order only to protect the poor against exploitation or to forestall some serious communal rupture. Both hierarchy and private property were taken to be permanent features of society. This social teaching opposed both collectivism and an untrammelled economic liberalism, and advocated a reformist course of improving the social welfare, a course which would defend both the rights of workers to justice and the value of private property as the linchpin of social harmony.[6]

In the 1960s this corporatist social doctrine was abandoned by theologians and grass roots Catholics in Latin America who perceived its inapplicability to the hideous squalor and inequality in their countries. They adopted instead a conflictual approach which focused upon the structural pathology of a trans-national capitalism geared exclusively to the maximization of profits while condemning entire populations, especially in the third world, to economic dependency and poverty. Christians everywhere, they insisted, are compelled to challenge these structures of domination and to enter into solidarity with poor and oppressed peoples. The substance of this liberationist, or political, perspective was endorsed by the Latin American bishops at Medellín (1968) and Puebla (1979).[7]

The impact of this innovative social teaching, which drew attention to the *sinfulness* of existing political systems and economic structures, was not confined to Latin America. It exerted a profound influence upon subsequent statements from the Vatican dealing with the nature and demands of Christian commitment in the modern world. In his 1971 letter *Octogesima Adveniens*, Pope Paul VI cautiously conceded the value of Marxism as a diagnostic tool for overcoming social injustice, though he reiterated the church's opposition to Marxism understood as a totalistic and materialistic *Gestalt* and as a theory of class conflict.[8] Also in 1971, at the Second Synod of Bishops, this liberationist perspective was given deepened expression through the enunciation of an ethical principle – the preferential option for the poor – which would later be defined more explicitly in the documents of the Puebla Conference (1979). In their 1971 document *Justitia in Mundo*, the bishops asserted the importance of a new 'praxis' for the worldwide Catholic community, a faith orientation of solidarity with the struggles for justice of poor and marginalized peoples. And more recently, in his 1981 encyclical *Laborem Exercens*, Pope John Paul II taught that responsible discipleship in the modern era requires a political witness on behalf of workers and the poor.[9]

The Canadian bishops have endorsed and contributed to this developing social ethic. In a speech given to the 1971 Synod of Bishops, Cardinal Flahiff, then archbishop of Winnipeg, urged an expanded understanding of sin which would include those social structures that cause oppression and called on Catholics to participate in the promotion of gospel values in the political arena.[10] In the intervening fifteen years, the Canadian bishops have issued several social justice statements which criticize Canada's economic system and recommend a program of action for socially concerned Catholics. Common themes of these statements are that the Canadian economy produces a maldistribution of wealth, increases the gap between rich and poor, permits valuable resources to be monopolized by selfish elites, and results in expanding corporate profits at the expense of massive and dehumanizing unemployment.[11]

By the mid-1970s this new structural understanding of sin and political sense of vocation had found a home in what may loosely be termed a 'movement' for social justice in the Canadian church. In *From Words To Action* (1976) the bishops saluted this 'significant minority' for their affirmation that the struggle for justice is 'integral to bringing the Gospel to the world.'[12] In the same pastoral letter the bishops proposed several guidelines to facilitate a 'prophetic' critique of the existing social order: Canadian Catholics should study the Bible to discover the social implications of the Christian message, develop allegiance with the victims of injustice, inquire into the causes of oppression, and engage in direct political action to reconstitute Canadian society according to Christian ideals.[13]

In their 1977 Labour Day Statement, *A Society to be Transformed*, the Canadian bishops repudiated the ideological foundations of both doctrinaire Marxism and laissez-faire capitalism. They argued that neither the former, which tends to reduce individuals to an economic function and to absorb individual freedoms into a collectivist order, nor the latter, which extols as supreme values the pursuit of self-interest, competition, and an unbridled market, affords a satisfactory solution to the Catholic quest for justice.[14] What the bishops advocated instead was that Catholics discover, through a praxis of critical engagement with poor people in Canada and elsewhere, an alternative economic order that is conducive to justice and in which all may participate. Significantly, the bishops in this 1977 statement attempted to remove the taboo against socialism that had long been a feature of Catholic social thought in Canada.[15] While cautioning against the 'grave dangers' of a materialistic and conflict-centred interpretation of history, they affirmed socialism as an acceptable option for Canadian Catholics. Moreover, they argued that a 'Marxist analysis,' if employed circumspectly, might help to 'free present-day society of its idols' and to 'identify certain injustices and structures of exploitation.'[16]

In *A Society to be Transformed* the bishops also emphasized that Catholics should adopt vocations of social justice and 'commit their lives to the task of creating a more just social order.'[17] Bringing the gospel message into the political arena, they insisted, is central to the church's mission and thus a moral imperative for all Catholics. If Catholic faith is to be authentic, they said, it must transcend the narrow sphere of private devotion and focus on the conversion of secular institutions to gospel principles of love, peace, and equality: 'God wills that the Gospel should transform not just our personal and private life but also all social and public behaviour, that is, the attitudes, customs, laws and structures of the world in which we live.'[18]

In their 1980 social message, *Unemployment: The Human Cost*, the bishops urged that Canada's economic system be replaced by one better able to 'serve the basic needs required by all people for a more fully human life.'[19] But their most damning indictment of the Canadian economy awaited the release, on New Year's Day 1983, of the pastoral letter entitled *Ethical Reflections on the Economic Crisis*.[20] Here the bishops inveighed against the objective immorality of a system that is geared toward the protection of capital at the expense of heightened unemployment and the corresponding degradation of thousands of ordinary Canadians. What is required, they insisted, is a new social imagination, one that would resolve the present 'structural crisis of capitalism' by providing for workers and the unemployed equal participation in the planning and organization of industrial production.[21] The prevailing economic system, they contended, is tailored to satisfy the greed of self-serving power elites while the majority of Canadians suffer a diminished dignity and a growing sense of alienation and powerlessness. The bishops argued that increasing unemployment reveals a deepening moral disorder in Canadian society. The dominant economic model which governs the country, they said, is oriented toward the perpetuation of inequality and social division. Accordingly, the bishops condemned 'monetarism,' the anti-inflationary policy which countenances higher levels of unemployment in order to restrict price increases, as detrimental to the rights of workers and to Canada's social integrity. Taking their cue from John Paul II's 1981 encyclical *Laborem Exercens*, the bishops called for critical public discussion, informed by the principle of 'the priority of labour over capital,' on how best to reshape and humanize the Canadian economy.

It is beyond the scope of this study to assess, from a specifically economic point of view, the validity of the bishops' economic critique.[22] Nor is it important for present purposes to determine to what extent these various social justice statements correspond to the personal views of individual bishops. *Ethical Reflections*, for example, the most widely publicized of these episcopal statements, was authorized by the Social Affairs Commission of the Canadian Conference of Catholic Bishops, and at least one leading prelate registered his public dissent against it, claiming that it did not necessarily represent the opinions of the entire community of Canadian bishops.[23] Nevertheless, despite possible misgivings of individual bishops, these statements convey the impression, both within the broader community and particularly within the Canadian church, that the bishops have established a new tonality for Canadian Catholic social ethics.

First, and as mentioned above, the substance of these various statements bespeaks an undeniable 'shift to the left' in the thinking of the Canadian bishops. In claiming that the economic recession of the early 1980s was 'symptomatic of a much larger structural crisis in the international system of capitalism,'[24] and in pointing out the stratified nature of Canadian society by contrasting the interests of owners and workers, rich and poor, the bishops employed a language that could be construed as Marxist in origin. As Gregory Baum has pointed out, however, though the bishops' social teaching has evolved through critical dialogue with Marxist ideas, its primary inspiration has been the liberationist perspective developed in Latin America and endorsed, at least in its essentials, in the social encyclicals of Pope John Paul II. While the bishops are highly critical of capitalism, they oppose as well a centralized communist economy which would preclude the participation of workers and local communities in determining the allocation of capital and profits.[25] What the 'shift to the left' means, then, is that the bishops have encouraged Canadian Catholics to create an alternative society, one characterized by the decentralization of ownership and the democratization of economic power. As such, they have explicitly aligned their authority to an ideology of social change.

Second, and again noted by Baum, the bishops have begun to define the mission of Canadian Catholicism 'in terms that include both salvation and earthly liberation.'[26] In other words, they have attempted to conceptualize sin and redemption in broadly, though not exclusively, social and political language. In thus recommending a conversion to an exteriorized piety, the bishops are in step with a cross-national trend within Catholicism of advertising a 'politicized gospel' as the blueprint for a newly relevant church.[27]

There is nothing about this renascent social gospel that could be construed as inherently prejudicial to the anti-abortion cause. Indeed, the emphasis it accords political activism would seem to be highly congenial to Revivalist Catholics, who arguably are the most politicized of groups within the Canadian church. And yet, by a curious conjuncture of circumstances, many Revivalists have denounced the new social ethic as a pernicious corruption of the true faith and have defined themselves in diametrical opposition to the 'movement' of social justice it has inspired. And, conversely, most Social Justice Catholics are contemptuous of the pro-life movement, seeing it as a regressive social and political force without redeeming value. Indeed, the mutual repugnance felt by Social Justice and Revivalist Catholics provides the most graphic demonstration of how the basic ideological alignments within contemporary Canadian Catholicism have crystallized around the abortion issue.

REVIVALIST CATHOLICS AND SOCIAL JUSTICE CATHOLICS

While the new social teaching of the bishops has been accorded a mixed reception within the Canadian church, it has been earnestly embraced by a growing number of people who collectively comprise what may be termed a 'movement for social justice' within Canadian Catholicism. These Catholics (for descriptive purposes they are alternatively named here *Progressive* or *Social Justice* Catholics) have addressed a complex of issues that includes women's rights within and outside the church, aboriginal Canadian rights, peace and disarmament, nuclear energy, environmentalism, poverty and unemployment, racism, neo-colonial exploitation in Latin America, and regional economic disparities within Canada. Social Justice, or Progressive, Catholics uniformly advocate the replacement of Canada's present political and economic system with some version, variously conceived, of democratic socialism. Just as significant as their political views is what Progressives call their 'vision' of the church. In contrast to Revivalists, who conceive themselves as defenders of an ancient yet beleaguered orthodoxy, Progressives regard themselves as a Catholic avant-garde charged with the responsibility of advancing the process of modernization within the church that was ostensibly set in motion by the Second Vatican Council. Thus, they prefer a church that would have a democratized authority structure; that would give women access to the ordained ministry; that would accommodate a greater range of doctrinal, liturgical, and ethical pluralism; and, above all, that would be broadly ecumenical.[28]

Progressive Catholicism is as much a religious mentality – a way of thinking about church and world – as it is an organized movement for change. As the favoured religious orientation of Catholic intellectuals, it has emerged as the elite orthodoxy of Canadian Catholicism. Its symbols, language, and presuppositions have been adopted by many religious orders, academics, and chancery officials. To the extent that it has become institutionalized wisdom in the Catholic academy and the Catholic liberal media, Social Justice Catholicism in Canada has lost much of its radical tincture and has settled into a familiar domesticity. As is the case with any orthodoxy, adherence to it often involves little more than sending out the correct signals, learning the appropriate terminology, and displaying good intentions. Despite its rhetoric of radical political engagement – to which only a virtuoso minority are personally committed – it has largely become a viewpoint that may be subscribed to without the forfeiture of middle-class comforts, career opportunities, or social standing. Indeed, mastery of its conceptual framework and stylized discourse affords one a password of sorts into the ranks of Canadian Catholic professional life.

Although most Social Justice Catholics have not recanted the traditional Catholic teaching against abortion, they have generally avoided political entanglement with the issue and have maintained a fashionable distance from the Canadian pro-life movement. To the extent that it has been dropped from the progressivist agenda of Social Justice Catholics, the abortion issue has become the symbolic point of division between Catholics of contrasting theological stripes. This has not, of course, always been the case. When reforms to Canada's abortion law were first proposed in the 1960s, Canadian Catholics from across the theological spectrum spoke with a common, demonstrative voice in defence of the church's traditional teaching.[29]

It is not always clear by what process a political stance comes to be seen as either progressive or reactionary. There seems to be nothing about anti-abortionism per se that would preclude its attractiveness for Social Justice Catholics. In his discussion of the American pro-life movement, for example, James Kelly argues that the 'sanctity of life' ethic bespeaks a radical egalitarianism which is in direct conflict with the principle of meritocracy upon which liberal capitalism is largely based. 'There is a clear universalism in the right to life movement's objection to all abortions, whether by welfare parents, minorities, or white women and pro-life objections to government funding of abortion includes foreign population aid even to countries commonly identified as ideological foes of American interests, such as China. On nationalist premises anything that reduces the population size of a potential enemy is a political good. Right to life activists place principle before national security or national affluence.'[30]

The egalitarian implications of the anti-abortion ethic would seem to accord with the political ideals that are preached by Social Justice Catholics. Moreover, anti-abortionism could feasibly be integrated into a radical critique of Western society's penchant for sexual consumerism, its exaltation of technology and individualism at the expense of intimacy and communal responsibility, and its preference for the violent 'quick-fix' to addressing problems that are perhaps the result of its own internal contradictions and structured inequalities. Although some Social Justice Catholics acknowledge these broader ramifications,[31] even they discuss the abortion issue with an embarrassed reticence, carefully disowning any connection with the pro-life movement itself.

Interviews conducted by the author with twenty-five Social Justice

Catholics reveal the reasons for this discomfort with, and avoidance of, the anti-abortion movement.[32] Four of the sample subjects support the pro-choice contention that decisions pertaining to abortion should reside exclusively with pregnant women and that unrestricted access to abortion is essential for women's self-determination. All four argue that the moral value of the unborn child is always subordinate to the right of women freely to control their reproduction. All of the remaining twenty-one subjects profess personal, and vehement, opposition to abortion. While claiming respect for the moral autonomy of women, they argue that the right to abort is far from absolute and should not, except under extreme circumstances, override the right to life of the fetus.

Despite their opposition in principle to abortion, only several of these latter subjects admit to even a modest sympathy with the pro-life movement. When asked to explain this, fourteen of them offered the opinion that abortion primarily involves questions of personal or private morality and thus has no legitimate place as a public issue in the political arena.[33] So pervasive is this view among Social Justice Catholics that it warrants separate analysis.

First of all, this supposed dichotomy of *private* morality and *public* issues is sociologically untenable. Ever since Durkheim demonstrated that suicide, ostensibly the most private and socially secluded of acts, is subject to identifiable social pressures, it is naïve to think that any area of human conduct can be understood merely by reference to the individual subject.[34] Besides being sociologically invalid, the belief that certain zones of behaviour are intrinsically *private* and thus unsuitable for the political arena ignores the social processes by which issues are constructed.

Smoking, to take one contemporary example, has recently in Canada been redefined as a public health issue instead of a matter of personal taste. The demand for smoke-free work and recreational environments, as well as government legislation banning smoking in public places, would not have occurred without medical evidence of the potentially harmful effects of inhaling second-hand smoke. But this did not by itself *create* smoking as a public issue. What was necessary was that this evidence be appropriated and given a specific political interpretation by pressure groups such as anti-smoking lobbies and opinion-making elites in the medical profession and the media.

And furthermore, the anti-smoking crusade could not have gained public legitimacy without a cultural climate that was receptive to its message and goals. In this context, it is significant that the crusade has been most successful in English Canada, while in Quebec it has largely been given the cold shoulder. Arguably, the anti-smoking movement has been energized by the same cultural impulses that once made temperance the quintessential public issue for Protestant Canada. The relative impotency of the anti-smoking lobby in Quebec, despite the fact that French Canadians have access to the same medical data regarding the deleterious effects of second-hand smoke, shows that the politicization of smoking is a cultural fabrication, not a metaphysical inevitability. Is it not possible, to return to the temperance analogy, that the *privatization* of alcohol consumption in contemporary Canada has a great deal to do with the political demoralization of Protestantism and very little with anything inherent in the question of drinking itself? The recent politicization of pornography provides another illustration of the manner in which something ostensibly private is given new meaning as a public issue in which the whole of society has a vital stake.

While the distinction between *private* moral concerns and *public* issues does not have sociological validity, it can perform an ideological function for privileged social groups who do not want their private sins redefined as public crimes. Wife battery, for example, has historically been treated as an internal domestic affair and even at times tolerated as a form of male social control and emotional catharsis. Only when feminism successfully challenged some of the cultural assumptions which consigned women to a chattel status did domestic violence surface as a public issue.[35] Child abuse has similarly been reconstructed as a political issue after a long history of being understood as a strictly private, familial matter.

The point is that the cultural conditions which allow certain concerns to be designated as private and others as public are subject to fluctuation. What is today a matter of personal choice – such as owning an automobile – may very well in the future be transformed into a question of public controversy, providing that environmental protection agencies gain more political clout and the cultural assumptions underlying consumerism are more effectively exposed. And conversely, as the question of temperance shows, yesterday's political crusade may very well be recast as tomorrow's private business.

The abortion question perhaps best of all illuminates the sliding boundaries that condition the perception of an issue as either private or public. James Mohr has shown that the medical profession in nineteenth-century America was primarily responsible for mobilizing public sentiment against abortion and raising it to the level of a criminal offence.[36] And yet in the 1950s and 1960s when, paradoxically, far more scientific information about the fetus was available, the same medical profession was in the forefront of efforts to make abortion a purely private matter concerning only the pregnant woman and her physician. The reappraisal of abortion was entirely the consequence of altered political circumstances and cultural pressures, and had nothing to do with the ontological status of abortion itself. And because history is a mistress of surprises, it is entirely possible that the pendulum will swing once again and abortion will be rediscovered as a worthy political issue by cultural elites.

Issues are socially constructed, they do not fall from the sky. Why then do Social Justice Catholics, especially those who reject the pro-choice position, avoid political involvement with the question of abortion? Four of the sample subjects argue that abortion is *private* in the sense that it could never be effectively legislated against. Much like the question of contraception, they say, any attempt to criminalize abortion would lead to widespread contempt of the law, prolonged bitterness, and worst of all, strife between Canada's Christian churches.[37] Thus, one man, who was part of the 1968 bishops' delegation which appeared before the parliamentary committee reviewing the abortion law, says:

I find abortion-on-demand just as abhorrent as the pro-lifers do, but there's one big difference between us. They take the jump from saying something's morally wrong to saying we should make a law against it. But good morality can sometimes be very bad, very pernicious law. How can they make that jump? They're very naive. I was disappointed with the way the 1969 law turned out, but there's no way I would support, either then or now, a law that simply illegalized abortion. This law would be a mockery. It would be unenforceable, would just drive abortions underground and so wouldn't save that many human lives, would endanger the health of women, would create tremendous animosity against Canadian Catholicism, and, finally, would pretty well wipe out the very good practical ecumenism we've developed with the Protestant churches.

A principal reason why eleven of the sample subjects have taken a hands-off approach to the pro-life cause is that the anti-abortion position is closely associated in their minds with the traditional Catholic preoccupation with sexual sin and private virtue. Too often in the past, they argue, has this preoccupation stultified personal psychological growth and diverted the energy of the church into a socially detached pietism.[38] Moreover, the idealization of procreation implicit in the anti-abortionism of many Catholic activists too closely reminds them of the highly biological view of sexuality to which Catholic ethical teaching has historically been allied. Social Justice Catholics are uncomfortable with the model of sexuality represented by *Humanae Vitae*, and some of them worry that the crusade against abortion is at bottom an attack against contraception and non-procreative sexual expression in general.[39] Thus, a Progressive nun chastises Catholic pro-lifers for sexual 'up-tightness.' 'I'd be more comfortable with these people if I thought their sexuality wasn't coming from the Dark Ages. They still think that every time you screw you're supposed to make a baby. We're committed to exploring alternative, more creative conceptions of sexuality, a sexuality that is liberating and self-expressive, not just a biological function.'

There are other reasons why Social Justice Catholics prefer to steer clear of the abortion controversy. Although most of them are uncomfortable with the pro-choice orthodoxy of established feminism, they believe that the Women's Movement is an authentic, if somewhat flawed, movement of emancipation to which they owe support and solidarity. As members of a church which is frequently accused of insensitivity to women, they are self-consciously protective of their own feminist credentials. Thus, they worry that a criticism of the pro-choice doctrine would be construed as a betrayal of the cause of women's liberation itself. Some of them claim on this score to be struck by the fundamental ambiguity of the pro-life position: it can be, and has been, put to the service of either a radical social critique or a reactionary, anti-feminist ideology. Most Social Justice Catholics think that the Canadian pro-life movement has fallen prey to the latter tendency and that, accordingly, involvement with it would be tantamount to 'guilt by association.'

The pro-life movement's right-wing reputation, which is partly deserved but not completely justified, has also discouraged Social Justice Catholics from joining the anti-abortion protest. Several, for example, recall their repulsion upon learning that a Canadian brigade of Tradition, Family, and Property – an ultra-conservative, anti-communist vigilante organization of Brazilian origin – had made an appearance on the Harbord Street picket line.[40] Indeed, as the following remarks by a prominent Canadian theologian reveal, some Social Justice Catholics believe that anti-abortionism is largely a pretext for forwarding a right-wing political vision: 'I don't think these people really care about babies or human life. Were they so concerned about Jewish babies being killed, or the oppression of French Canada, or the horror of South Africa? Are they really concerned with dignity and justice? Do they oppose the taking of life in war? I think we have to adopt a hermeneutic of suspicion when looking at them. Basically they're fascists simply intent on controlling people's lives. I'm appalled that you would even consider doing a study of them.'

Not only are anti-abortionists hypocritical, claim Social Justice Catholics, they are also 'single-issue' fanatics who have isolated and devoted themselves to one social problem without placing it in a larger context of social liberation. By abstracting abortion from other issues such as discrimination against women and racial minorities, economic injustice, violation of human rights in the third and fourth worlds, and peace and disarmament, they contend, anti-abortionists betray themselves as both socially unenlightened and less than sincere in their professed concern for human equality. In this vein, one Social Justice woman asserts that 'Pro-life means a whole lot more than being against abortion. I don't see these people on the peace marches or protesting against American intrusion in Latin America. We don't see them fighting racism. I'll take them seriously when they show a wider concern for justice. Right now they come across as mean-spirited and petty.'

To what extent do these accusations have a basis in reality? While it is true that the anti-abortion movement has displayed a seemingly inborn penchant for extreme political conservatism, this is an ideological liaison with which some pro-life activists are also uncomfortable.

Furthermore, the charge of crypto-racism implied in one of the foregoing quotations is not supported by the empirical evidence. The author interviewed no anti-abortion activist who placed a greater premium on healthy white children than on children of other racial backgrounds or disabled children. On the contrary, at least several Revivalist activists have adopted non-white children.

Moreover, it is not true that anti-abortion activists wear ideological blinders which blacken out every issue but abortion. Rather most are concerned with a different set of issues than are Social Justice Catholics: the generational continuity of the family,[41] public morality, euthanasia, abortion, and infanticide. Anti-abortionists, furthermore, resent the idea that they should have to prove their sincerity by becoming active in other causes.[42] The following comments by one Revivalist summarizes their feelings on this matter:

> I work my butt off fifty hours a week, I've got six kids, my wife's been sick for over a year. I spend as much time as I can protesting abortion because we're talking about life and death here. Human life. Isn't this important enough? But the trendy liberal Catholics tell me I'm not genuinely pro-life because I'm not involved in all their battles. What do they want me to do? Quit my job, leave my family, turn my back on abortion, and spend all my time on their peace and justice causes, and then maybe they'll say: 'Hey, after all, you know, maybe you are sincere. How about that?' It's like they've got guilty consciences about not fighting abortion, so they have to run us down. But why should we be defensive? Maybe it's time they proved themselves to us.

There are additional reasons why Social Justice Catholics in general avoid, and in some cases anathematize, the pro-life movement. One of these is related to the processes of theological self-identification and boundary construction. Revivalist and Social Justice Catholics occupy separate, mutually exclusive religious worlds which are symbolically demarcated by the pro-life movement. Revivalists in the movement subscribe to a traditional institutional model of the church, with heavy emphasis given its pyramidal authority structure, sacramental discipline, and system of dogmatic control. In contrast, Social Justice Catholics are adherents of the more flexible, dynamic, and democratic ecclesiology that was discussed briefly earlier in this chapter.[43] In addition to espousing a doctrinal liberalism and latitudinarian sexual ethic, they advocate a transformation of the Catholic authority structure, such that the power now concentrated in the Roman Curia and national episcopal conferences would be diffused throughout the community of believers.

To the increasing extent that Revivalists have become a major force in the Canadian pro-life movement, Social Justice Catholics perceive the movement as the embodiment of a style of Catholicism which is the antithesis of their own. Although most disapprove of abortion, all Social Justice Catholics are careful to maintain a hygienic distance from the pro-life movement, not just because they disagree with its social conservatism, but more profoundly because it too closely reminds them of an authority-bound, anti-worldly Catholicism which they find repellent and which they wish to exorcise from the Canadian church. But as much as they desire to avoid contamination by the movement, the abortion issue is something that will not leave Social Justice Catholics alone. It is like a ghost prowling in the subconscious, every so often rearing its head, taunting and conjuring feelings of guilt. As a Progressive nun says:

> The ironic thing is that it's on abortion that we and the Tridentine – can I call them that? – Catholic pro-lifers can agree. There are a few of us who are pro-choice, but there's a real consensus with us that abortion is a terrible injustice. And it's true – we haven't made it our issue. It's dominated by the Tridentines. And we really are two totally different camps. It's not that we hate them – though I'm quite sure they hate us – it's just that they have invested the issue with so much emotional and theological baggage it makes us squirm. They give pro-life a bad name. And yet I think some of us have a secret admiration for their courage and determination, even though if they got control of the church they'd have us all excommunicated. Speaking for myself – and I know others in the same boat – I do sometimes feel guilty when I think about abortion, about our commitment to justice, and realize that these people, who are so different from us, seem to be the only people doing anything about it. I don't think we share any part of the same religious vocabulary. Abortion's the only bridge connecting us, but we don't know how to cross it and they don't want to cross it.

The awkwardness of the abortion issue for Social Justice Catholics is reflected in the way it is treated, and sometimes ignored, in their publications. The bi-weekly *Catholic New Times*, the main literary and informational depository of Progressive Catholicism in Canada, has given occasional coverage to the ongoing Harbord Street protests and has also addressed the question of abortion in several editorials. The customary approach of *New Times* is to treat the issue in a sweetly reasoned manner, interpreting it as a subsidiary theme in a larger context of structural disorder in Canadian society and as a complex problem which defies simplistic solution.[44] Perhaps more telling is the total absence of any reference to the abortion issue in such works as *Solidarity: Christian Social Teaching and Canadian Society* and *Political and Social Rights and Human Dignity*.[45] And in *Getting Started on Social Analysis in Canada* by Michael Czerny and Jamie Swift, an influential book within Progressive Catholic circles, the authors do not say anything on the subject beyond the following: 'When it comes to the very important issue of abortion, Canadians disagree strongly. Even among the Christian churches of Canada, there is profound disagreement. Similarly, the authors of *Getting Started* could not agree on a common approach to this issue. It has therefore been deliberately omitted.'[46] If abortion is not quite an unmentionable issue for Social Justice Catholics, it is clearly the one that causes them the most hesitation.

There is no reason to think that the Canadian bishops ever intended to exclude the abortion issue from their new social teaching. Indeed, they complemented their celebrated 1983 economic critique, *Ethical Reflections on the Economic Crisis*, with a hard-hitting statement against abortion which was released in late summer of the same year. In *Ethical Reflections on Respect for Life*, the bishops characterized abortion as a 'radical anti-life position' and 'a direct attack upon the most defenceless.' 'When we have intervened in areas such as peace and disarmament, the economic crisis or capital punishment, one sole motive moved us: to serve human life in all its forms and at all the successive stages of its evolution ... When, in the name of "quality of life," individual freedom, egocentric well-being and the fear of a changed lifestyle become idols to which we sacrifice even human life, particularly that of the unborn child, we must cry out a very resolute no.'[47] The bishops similarly spoke against abortion in 1986. In *To Love and Serve Life*, they wrote: 'We thank and encourage all those who are already doing so much to serve and safeguard human life from the moment of conception. We salute in particular those whose untiring efforts are marked by a combination of determination, tenderness, and sensitivity. For, it is not by violent efforts that life can be saved from violence.'[48]

In both of these statements the bishops implicitly acknowledged their preference for a 'seamless garment' pro-life ethic, one which would integrate anti-abortionism into a wide-scale critique of Canadian institutional and cultural life. It was such an integrative approach that Bishop Remi De Roo, the chief episcopal architect of the new social teaching, had in mind when he spelled out the following agenda for socially concerned Canadian Catholics: 'Defending human life (especially the "economically unproductive" lives of the unborn, the aged, the chronically ill and unemployed), proclaiming the equal rights of all women and men to our resources, and critiquing capital and technology according to the needs of the whole human person – female and male.'[49]

With the exception, however, of the aforementioned statements, the occasional pastoral letter on abortion by provincial episcopal conferences,[50] as well as guarded references to the issue in Remi De Roo's *Cries of Victims – Voice of God*,[51] the abortion issue has effectively been edited out of the bishops' social teaching. In 1979 Ottawa staff members of the Episcopal Commission for Social Affairs prepared an educational guide to the new social teaching for distribution in Canadian Catholic parishes. Entitled *Witness to Justice: A Society to be Transformed – Working Instruments*, this one-hundred-and-twenty-four page document does not include a single reference to the abortion issue.[52] Also in 1979, the Canadian Catholic Organization for Development and Peace published a booklet entitled *Witness to Justice*. This booklet, again intended for distribution in Catholic parishes, contains four episcopal statements, none of which deals with the subject of abortion.[53] More recently, Fr E.F. Sheridan of the Jesuit Centre for Social Faith and Justice compiled a catalogue of episcopal statements under the title of *Do Justice!: The Social Teaching of the Canadian Catholic Bishops*. Not one of the fifty-nine statements in this four-hundred-and-seventy-page book is on the subject of abortion.[54] The Canadian Jesuit journal *Compass*, which is devoted to propagating the new critical Catholic social teaching, had not as late as 1987 included an article on abortion.[55]

This de-emphasis, if not outright suppression, of the bishops' teaching against abortion reflects the general discomfiture of Social Justice Catholics with both the issue itself and the anti-abortion movement. An even more decisive reason, however, is that abortion constitutes the major ecumenical taboo for Progressive Catholicism in Canada.

ABORTION AND THE ECUMENICAL CONSENSUS

It is worth noting that in none of their economic critiques do the Canadian bishops spell out as scrupulously as they did in their statements in the late 1960s on contraception and abortion the distinction between the religious and temporal spheres and the corresponding provinces of responsibility to be exercised, respectively, by clergy and laity. Rather, they seem to take for granted, and unapologetically so, both their own public authority and the political relevancy of Canadian Catholicism. As a consequence, the economic statements of the bishops communicate a boldness and resoluteness that were absent in their earlier presentations on contraception, abortion, and divorce. And yet, surprisingly, the reception accorded *Ethical Reflections on the Economic Crisis*, the episcopal statement which has generated the greatest public reaction, was generally favourable, and in some places, even enthusiastic. The doctrine of church-state separation, which had earlier been invoked so frequently in the news media in order to truncate the bishops' involvement in the abortion debate, was this time scarcely even mentioned. Quite in contrast, many commentators expressed gratitude that the bishops had lent their religious voice to the economic and political problems facing Canadian society.[56]

To the extent that the bishops were criticized, at least in English Canada,[57] it was mainly on the basis that they had perhaps exceeded their competency by proposing specific solutions to the problem of unemployment.[58] But the negative reaction even on this point was moderate at most, and limited mainly to leaders of the Canadian business community.[59] Virtually no one, at least in the Toronto media, challenged the right of the bishops to offer, under the auspices of their religious authority, practical guidance to the formulation of Canadian economic policy.

Even more telling was the panegyrical response given *Ethical Reflections* by the leaders of Canada's major Protestant denominations. Ted Scott, primate of the Anglican Church; Clarke MacDonald, moderator of the United Church; and Wayne Smith, moderator of the Presbyterian Church, all made public declarations in the press of their total support for the Catholic bishops. Thus, for example, Reverend Smith proclaimed that 'Presbyterians should find no difficulty in identifying with the principles that underlie the Catholic bishops' statement ... We are directed by Christ to listen to the voices of the poor and the powerless in our midst. We as Christians are called to struggle for economic justice and participate in building a new society ...'[60]

The argument that bedevilled the bishops during the debate in the 1960s over reform of Canada's abortion law – namely, that the *private* convictions of particular religions should exercise no *public* influence in a pluralistic society – seemed to have been momentarily forgotten. This is especially noteworthy in view of the expressly Catholic mentality reflected by *Ethical Reflections*. The bishops made no effort to disguise the statement's indebtedness to Pope John Paul II's *Laborem Exercens* nor, apparently, to temper its pontificating tone. Nor did Canada's Protestant leaders in their responses to it hesitate to employ a frankly Christian language of approval. For all intents and purposes, it was as if the Canadian cultural mosaic had been eclipsed by a modernized, and decidedly unpluralistic, rendition of 'His Dominion,' a nation restored to Christian values and political ideals. The concern expressed so often throughout the course of the 1960s abortion debate, that non-Christians (and especially non-Catholics) as well as unbelievers be spared the burden of religious beliefs held by particular churches, seemed this time somehow disposable.

Why are the Canadian bishops culturally *entitled* to speak on economic matters but not on abortion? Although this question cannot be discussed fully here, it is possible to make several significant observations.

Over the past decade and a half a consistent pattern has developed, whereby the principle of Canadian church-state separation is suspended for certain issues that satisfy certain criteria. The first and most decisive criterion is that the issues bear an *ecumenical consensus*, foremost among the respective leaderships of the United, Presbyterian, Anglican, Lutheran, and Roman Catholic churches, secondarily with those of the Reformed and Baptist traditions, and only tangentially and by way of ecumenical bonus with Canada's non-Christian faiths.[61] The second criterion, concomitantly, is that the issues must not wear a distinctively Catholic label. And lastly, they must suit the requirements of the *progressive liberalism* to which Canada's major Christian churches are variously committed.

What qualifies as progressive liberalism is not at every point clear, and the ecumenical consensus is therefore a product of ongoing reality negotiation. Thus, the major churches have unanimously opposed the legalization of Sunday shopping ostensibly on the ground that workers deserve a guaranteed weekly respite, not, at least explicitly, because they wanted to salvage a traditional religious meaning for Sunday as the Lord's Day.[62] Likewise, they have denounced pornography and advocated limited state censorship, again not presumably out of a puritanical religious motive, but for the sake of correcting the negative images of women and sexuality to which pornography is thought to give rise.[63] In both cases, the churches seemed untroubled by the suppression of individual liberties that would potentially follow for Canadians (for example, non-Christians, non-believers, hedonists) who may not share their views.

The progressive liberalism of the ecumenical consensus is undergirded, if only in a quite fuzzy sense, by the principle of compassion for the underdog. Thus, over the past several years the churches have spoken out loudly and in unison on a plethora of other issues such as capital punishment, free trade, nuclear disarmament, American political involvement in Central America, Canada's immigration and refugee policies, the rights of native Canadians, discrimination against women and ethnic minorities, and apartheid.[64] In all of these cases, they have attempted to sway public opinion and influence governmental policy by virtue of their institutional *religious* authority.

This is not to suggest that the churches have thereby violated any supposed protocol governing church-state relations, but rather that this is a question to which they have been entirely oblivious. In this vein the style of discourse adopted by the churches is perhaps revealing. In many of their public interventions, they have employed a focus of analysis and a terminology that is unabashedly Christian. Thus, Canadian legislators are insistently encouraged to evaluate economic priorities according to 'Gospel values' and to develop an immigration policy that is faithful to 'Christ's call for compassion and identification with the oppressed.' Taken collectively, the various public statements issued by the churches assume the appearance of a counter-secularization strategy, only with the emphasis now placed on political rather than on personal virtue. Furthermore, the churches tend to speak with the presumption of privileged insight and morality: despite their rhetoric of multiculturalism, they seem not to doubt that the heritage of Canada's religious history is weighted heavily on their side.[65]

The progressive liberalism or, perhaps better, *post-millennial orthodoxy* that undergirds this ecumenical consensus is implicitly accepted as well in most of the Canadian news media. While individual commentators will occasionally take exception with one or more of the churches' political proposals, the criticism is almost always substantive and very seldom aimed at the idea of the churches taking a public role. In other words, whereas the Catholic bishops *interfere* on the abortion question, they and their Protestant counterparts engage in constructive politics on other issues. The established news media themselves retain perhaps a residue of post-millennial optimism that causes them to sympathize for the most part with the churches' political endeavours. Thus, very rarely are the churches accused of trespassing any presumed boundary between church and state or of attempting to transform Canadian society into a benevolent theocracy.

Considering this state of affairs, *screen of separation* is the metaphor which perhaps best characterizes the current interrelationship between Canadian religious and political culture. It is deemed culturally acceptable for the churches to press their viewpoints in the political arena provided that these viewpoints have been filtered through and baptized by the *ecumenical consensus*.

Abortion is the issue with the greatest potential for jeopardizing this delicate modus vivendi. Thus, when the Catholic hierarchy in the 1960s seemed poised to lobby the federal government against liberalization of Canada's abortion law and when, more recently, Cardinal Carter rallied the troops against the Toronto Morgentaler clinic, there were cries of indignation and accusations of foul play from the media and, even more vociferously, from Protestant leaders. In trying to press a particularly Catholic viewpoint on the subject of abortion, the bishops were charged with fostering community division along religious lines, with infringing on the rights and freedoms of non-Catholic Canadians, and with submitting a secular state to unpardonable, hierocratic coercion.

In addition to the heavy Catholic investment in the issue, what makes abortion an unfit subject for the bishops' political involvement, their critics have claimed, is that it concerns questions of merely private morality, which in a pluralistic society must not be raised to the normative political level. The distinction between private moral concerns and public issues was introduced in the earlier discussion on Social Justice Catholics. In this context as well it seems arbitrary at best and for the most part conceptually empty. On what grounds, for example, do pornography and gambling qualify as public issues while abortion does not? And yet the politics of masturbation has been canonized by the Canadian ecumenical consensus as something worthy of its devout attention. And though mainstream Protestants seem resigned at present to restricting their fulminations against race-tracks and lotteries to the Sunday pulpit, it is entirely possible that these matters might be included in a future theocratic agenda. If all parties to the ecumenical consensus were of one mind with the Catholic bishops on the subject of abortion, it is not unlikely that it too would be defined by them as a public issue.

The point here, of course, is *not* that Catholic opposition to abortion should be welcomed into the political arena, nor that the churches should withdraw from the political arena on other issues. It is simply to understand the terms by which the political involvement of the churches is tacitly negotiated. Indeed, there are sociological grounds for defending the politicization of questions such as pornography. As C. Wright Mills has argued, no aspect of human existence is an exclusive, private island, unconditioned by the wider society and devoid of public impact.[66] The pictures people look at and the books they read for sexual arousal, even the day of the week on which these pictures and books are purchased, *do* in fact intersect with larger social realities. In this sense, no ostensibly private activity is culturally innocent. Thus, it is understandable that the churches would be concerned with issues such as pornography and Sunday shopping. Anti-abortionism is different mainly because it fails to meet the requirements of the ecumenical consensus: progressive liberalism and inter-denominational agreement. Anti-abortionism, in short, is *too* Catholic.

It is significant that the anti-abortionism of a Protestant fundamentalist such as Rev Ken Campbell does not arouse a comparable outrage among Canada's cultural elites. Unlike Roman Catholicism, fundamentalism resides on the fringes of Canada's cultural landscape, far beyond the reach of the progressive liberalism by which the ecumenical consensus defines itself. The activism of Ken Campbell, as the following remarks by a United Church academic reveal, is thus dismissed as the inconsequential raving of a cultural neanderthal: 'The religiosity of the Ken Campbells and their ilk is terminally stupid. Canadians aren't interested in what the loony-tunes say. The point is the Catholic bishops aren't generally seen as loony-tunes, and so they have to exercise a greater public responsibility and restraint. When Cardinal Carter gets into the act, what he's doing is damning every opinion on abortion that's different from the official Catholic one. Imagine what this means for Canadian pluralism, for ecumenism, and for democratic processes. It's like you either submit to the Catholic yoke on abortion or else.'

Indeed, the dynamic of mutual exchange underlying the ecumenical consensus is based upon balancing the impressive public authority of the Catholic bishops with the apparently diminished influence of the country's mainstream Protestant churches. The discrepancy in the respective public profiles of Catholicism and mainstream Protestantism was amply demonstrated by the massive volume of media attention accorded *Ethical Reflections*, the bishops' 1983 statement on the economy. It is extremely unlikely that a comparable statement from one of Canada's Protestant churches would generate a cognate reaction or be similarly massaged by the media for weeks after its release.

There appear to be three factors which account for the apparently higher prestige enjoyed by the Catholic bishops. First, in terms of sheer religious demography, Catholicism has been confirmed as Canada's leading denomination. According to the 1981 census, the Canadian population of 24,083,494 contained 11,402,605 Catholics and 9,914,580 Protestants.[67] These numbers are put into comparative perspective by George Gallup, Jr, who notes that 'Roman Catholics outnumber Protestants five to four in Canada, while Protestants outnumber Catholics two to one in the United States.'[68] The nineteenth-century proclamation of Canada as a 'Protestant Dominion'[69] no longer inspires the national imagination, but rather has been reduced to a faint and rather embarrassing echo. Furthermore, as *ethnic churches* of the very white and fairly comfortable, the major Protestant denominations have become defensive concerning their apparent loss of national relevance.[70] Reginald Bibby observes that 'over the century, in relation to the nation's population, all the major Protestant denominations have experienced a pronounced decline in membership. United Church membership, for example, comprised 6% of Canadians in 1946, about 5% by 1966, and only some 3% by 1986.'[71] Quite in contrast, Roman Catholicism, which today represents 47 per cent of the Canadian population,[72] has been a favourite landing place for new Canadians, and thus embodies the ethnic and class variety typical of the wider society.

The second factor concerns the higher level of authority which, at least theoretically, is invested in statements issued by the Canadian Catholic bishops. Although these statements ordinarily are drafted by the church's Ottawa bureaucracy, their approval by the bishops gives them a quasi-dogmatic, normative status and, accordingly, implies that they *should* bear a practical consequence for the lives of Canadian Catholics. Official political discourses from the main Protestant bodies tend, in comparison, to convey an ephemeral, non-obligatory quality. Conclusions achieved by Protestant committee are not nearly so arresting, it seems, as the same conclusions proclaimed by episcopal mandate.

Thirdly, the public stature of the Canadian bishops is enhanced simply by virtue of Catholicism's international intrigue. Besides giving the bishops an enduring spotlight on Canada's religious stage, Vatican II made vivid for many Canadians the key role played by the local church in the more extensive drama of a universal *ecclesia* undergoing the throes of change.[73] Similarly, there is nothing in Canadian Protestantism's repertoire to rival the publicity of a papal visit to Canada[74] or the spectacle of bishops preparing for a Roman Synod.[75] Accordingly, political and economic statements from the Catholic bishops possess an intrinsic fascination that similarly inclined ones from the Protestant bodies cannot hope to match. They seem to cast a longer shadow into the theological trends and controversies of Western Europe, Latin America, Poland, and Asia.

Because Canadian Catholicism wields a greater public presence than do any of the main Protestant churches, the ecumenical consensus is maintained by negotiating the appearance of *moral equity* between its various partners. In taking public stands on issues that have already received an ecumenical imprimatur – unemployment, capital punishment, peace, and disarmament – the Catholic bishops are assured a favourable response from their Protestant counterparts, who in turn are provided with an opportunity to publicize their own principles of peace, justice, and progressivism.

As the issue with the greatest capacity to scuttle the ecumenical consensus, abortion requires a special code of etiquette, one based upon the art of mutual concession. Thus, the liberal Protestant churches produce documents filled with hand-wringing about the tragic necessity of abortion in situations of distress, while some of the authors of these documents privately confide befuddlement, and annoyance, about the fuss made by Catholics over the issue in the first place. And the Catholic bishops for their part, no doubt sensitive to the insecurities of the Protestant leaders in this post-Protestant era, voluntarily restrict their references to abortion to the occasional pious sermon, which invariably includes a petition to 'all Christians and people of goodwill to co-operate in common projects which promote life and justice.' The Protestant churches graciously recognize the ecumenical bind in which the abortion issue ensnares the bishops, and are thus prepared to tolerate these pious sermons so long as they do not become too much of a distraction or threaten practical political consequences. The churches will even be willing to discuss abortion at an official ecumenical level, if only to let it be known that they don't deem the issue insignificant.[76]

Special circumstances, however, periodically expose the fragility of this arrangement and, in the process, put a temporary end to all politeness. Thus, when Cardinal Carter became directly involved in the February 1985 protests against the Toronto Morgentaler clinic, he was guilty of attacking the ecumenical consensus at its most vulnerable point and of violating its most serious taboo. Carter's sin was not political involvement itself – his episcopal predecessor had, after all, been widely praised for helping to organize a grape boycott in support of Cesar Chavez – but rather his *choice* of political involvement. In calling his flock to the anti-abortion picket line, Carter betrayed a complete disregard for the implicitly understood rules of the game. He was both exploiting the numerical advantage enjoyed by Catholicism and aligning his moral authority to the very issue that most obviously lies outside of the ecumenical gamut. Carter shortly afterward repented of his indiscretion and tried to repair this breach in the ecumenical consensus by reaching an agreement with Ian Scott and Norma Scarborough to limit the number of picketers outside the clinic.

But the crisis into which Carter's action plummeted the ecumenical consensus was still in evidence two months later as the Ontario Liberal government prepared to pass legislation that would extend public funding of Catholic schools to Grade Thirteen. The historical status of the Ontario Separate School system is a hornet's nest which cannot be examined here.[77] Nevertheless, it is difficult to appreciate the rancorous opposition of mainline Protestant church leaders to the funding decision apart from the events of February 1985. Lewis Garnsworthy, Anglican archbishop of Toronto, and Clarke MacDonald, a former United Church moderator, had led the opposition to the proposed funding legislation when it was first announced by former Premier William Davis in June 1984. The ostensible grounds of their opposition were that the decision had been taken without benefit of full public debate and was thus undemocratic, that its implementation would endanger public education in Ontario, and that it violated the principle of church-state separation by conferring privileged treatment to a particular denomination.

The second and third of these complaints may have some justification, but the first, that the funding decision was undemocratic, cannot withstand the test of closer scrutiny. When first announced by Premier Davis, the funding proposal carried the overwhelming support of all three parties in the Ontario Legislature. But even beyond this, it is ironic that Garnsworthy would accuse those politicians supportive of the legislation of insensitivity to public opinion. When the federal Parliament prepared to vote in 1987 on a bill that would reinstate capital punishment in Canada, Garnsworthy's church was among those which petitioned politicians to ignore the overriding popular sentiment in favour of reinstatement and to vote entirely according to conscience.[78] When something, as in this case abolitionism, fits the agenda of the ecumenical consensus, considerations of theocratic righteousness take priority over the popular will.

Thus, when Garnsworthy lambasted the funding decision (Bill 30) as a 'Nazi dictatorial decree,'[79] it seems likely that a more primordial issue was also at stake. The funding decision, compounded shortly thereafter by Carter's intervention at the Morgentaler clinic, had resurrected the traditional Protestant dread of Roman Catholic cultural hegemony. These two events had in combination raised anew the spectre of Catholic domination, the menace against which Ontario Protestants had sought common solace as long ago as the Victorian period,[80] and which suddenly seemed one ominous stage closer to realization. Though at least one media commentator smelled the odour of anti-Catholicism in their opposition to Bill 30,[81] Garnsworthy and his allies persistently denied that they were motivated by bigotry. If indeed bigotry, it was likely coloured more by fear than by maliciousness. For in the aftermath of February 1985, with the ecumenical consensus battered and rendered temporarily dysfunctional, there was no longer anything to cushion the horror of being devoured by the Catholic leviathan.

The ecumenical consensus, then, is the modus vivendi by which denominational equilibrium is maintained, a sense of common moral importance is accomplished, and the cultural ambitions of Catholicism restrained. Moreover, the ecumenical consensus has developed since the early 1970s its own infrastructure of inter-church committees and task forces which collectively are the main sinews of its ongoing identity. As Archbishops Gilles Ouellet of Rimouski and Joseph MacNeil of Edmonton have stated: 'When we Canadian bishops face a social problem we feel we must deal with, our first question is whether we handle it alone or go inter-church. Inevitably we go inter-church.'[82] Among the coalitions and task forces of the ecumenical consensus are the following: GATT-Fly, Inter-church Project on Population, Inter-church Committee on World Development Education, Inter-church Committee for the Promotion of Justice in Canada (PLURA), Inter-church Fund for International Development, Task Force on the Churches and Corporate Responsibility, Project North, Inter-church Committee on Human Rights in Latin America, Project Ploughshares, Inter-church Committee for Refugees, Inter-church Coalition on Africa, and the Canada Asia Working Group.[83]

Parties to the ecumenical consensus are fond of describing these various committees as grass roots Christian organizations. More accurately, they are composed for the most part of denominational professionals, many of whom are ordained or else lay seminary graduates. A high percentage of Social Justice Catholics, who stock the Catholic side of these organizations, are members of religious orders.

These Catholics are accustomed to working in close collaboration with like-minded Protestants and have no desire to jeopardize this relationship, nor the ideology of social change to which it is directed, by introducing the subject of abortion. Thus, a Progressive Catholic woman says:

All of these issues we're working on ecumenically and making tremendous progress. We're concerned with a whole different spirituality, a vision of a transformed global order. It just wouldn't be worth the damage it would bring to start talking about abortion again. In a sense we've graduated beyond it, but in a different sense it's in the back of our minds and something we're totally against. Maybe it's one compromise we've had to make in order to bring the churches together in a common quest for justice. I suppose I'm saying this quest shouldn't be endangered by bringing up something as unwelcome and divisive as abortion. And anyways, we feel much closer to our ecumenical justice contacts than we do to the pro-life movement. Catholic pro-lifers don't have the same vision.

The other main vehicle of the bishops' new social teaching, in addition to these inter-church structures, is a network of Social Action offices which has arisen in dioceses throughout the country. Like the inter-church organizations, these Social Action offices are staffed primarily by clergy, religious professionals, and theologically trained laity who regard themselves as a progressive force for change on the Canadian politico-religious landscape. And here too the abortion issue is a taboo subject.

There is no room, then, in the ecumenical consensus for the abortion issue. The bishops no more enjoy being cast as cultural cretins than anyone else, which in the present historical period is the likely consequence of aligning oneself with the anti-abortion movement. It is highly likely as well that they derive a high measure of personal gratification from the ecumenical consensus. They have captivated the media with their economic critiques, have won the approval and sometimes praise of their denominational counterparts, and have come to enjoy a hitherto unprecedented reputation for compassion. It would be difficult to sacrifice all of this for the sake of taking a harder and more visible stand against abortion.

THE UNRECOGNIZED RADICALS: REVIVALIST CATHOLICS AND THE NEW SOCIAL TEACHING

While Revivalists in general do not deny the importance of the social dimension of the gospel, they mistrust the motivation of both Social Justice Catholics and the new social teaching of the Canadian bishops. In the Revivalist view, faith in political transformation has, for many Progressive Catholics, displaced faith in a transcendent God and everlasting life. As they see it, the Catholic avant-garde, having presided over the relativization of Catholic dogma and morality, now attempts to salvage a sense of the absolute in the political arena by adopting the agenda of pragmatic benevolence. They regard the bishops' call for a politicized gospel as a thin camouflage for a religious institution, grown spiritually otiose, seeking to gain relevance in terms more readily agreeable to the secularist disposition of the wider society.

In addition to decrying the new social teaching as a 'counterfeit of faith,'[84] Revivalists like to point out that Social Justice Catholics are drawn to 'fashionable' causes such as feminism, disarmament, and the re-allocation of economic resources, while displaying a snobbish aloofness to the issue of abortion. They wonder how Bishop De Roo can claim a prophetic role for the Canadian church – 'independent and courageous enough to question the current definitions and truths of a culture'[85] – when mainstream Catholicism has for all intents and purposes given up the fight against abortion. According to Revivalists, the relative silence of the Canadian church on abortion is damning evidence that it has become acquiescent, not prophetic, before the dominant secular culture. And lastly, Revivalists accuse Social Justice Catholics of selective indignation, of shielding their eyes from injustices perpetrated by left-wing regimes and reserving their outrage for Western capitalism. Social Justice Catholics, Revivalists say, identify structures as either sinful or graced according to a revisionary Marxist theory of the world.

Does a conscious or unconscious right-wing political vision lurk behind this Revivalist contempt for Social Justice Catholicism? Considering that Social Justice Catholics advocate socialism and endorse a neo-Marxian social analysis (though not as a rule Marxism as a guiding mythos), and that many Revivalists express affection for free enterprise capitalism, it is reasonable to suspect that there is an ideological basis to this disdain for the new social gospel. Because most Revivalists are at best modestly middle-class, it is improbable that this animus toward Social Justice Catholicism is based primarily on vested economic interest. More likely, it has to do with the fact that many of them were socialized into the 'cold-war' mentality of the 1950s and 1960s and, like most Catholics of that generation, internalized a view of socialism as the nemesis of religious truth and of capitalism as a sacral order that may be tinkered with but not fundamentally altered. In this vein, most grass roots Revivalists over the age of forty, despite an otherwise voracious appetite for Vatican *pronunciamentos*, are astoundingly unversed in papal social teaching, particularly concerning the reappraisal of socialism undertaken by the Catholic hierarchy since Paul VI's *Octogesima Adveniens*.[86] Socialism still conjures up for them images of godlessness, materialism, and social decay. Typical in this regard are the following comments by a man in his late forties: 'The bishops have taken a terrible track with their economic statements. Sure, capitalism isn't perfect, but think of the alternatives. They're flirting with socialism, which has always been hostile to Catholicism. Look at the reception the Pope received in Nicaragua at the hands of the Sandinistas. The bishops and the so-called progressive Catholics have had a crisis of faith, and now they want to guarantee their salvation in a political utopia. There's no utopia, though, outside of heaven.'

This dread of socialism among older Revivalists is fraught with irony. First of all, it shows that the ultramontanism of Revivalists, indeed, as ultramontanism always seems to be, is selective and qualified. Whereas the sexual and family ethic espoused by the pope is celebrated,[87] little attention is paid to his critical social teaching on economics, politics, and nuclear armaments. For some, notably the Revivalist rank and file, this partly reflects an ignorance of the church's evolving social doctrine. But where the intellectual leaders of Revivalism are concerned, most of whom are familiar and quite surprisingly in sympathy with the scope of Vatican social thought from Leo XIII's *Rerum Novarum* (1891) to John Paul II's *Laborem Exercens* (1981), it bespeaks an ingrained habit of measuring Catholic orthopraxy almost exclusively according to criteria of individual morality.[88]

And second, the ardent attachment of many Revivalists to free enterprise capitalism does not square with their equally ardent opposition to moral individualism. The former has historically been a strong inducement for the latter. For all of their groaning over the moral libertinism which has swept across Western society,[89] one would expect them to be more favourably disposed toward socialism, which in its centralized Marxist-Leninist guise has tended to lean toward a puritanical sexual ethic. As the most obvious example, although abortions are rife in the Soviet Union (as is the case generally for the Warsaw Pact nations), homosexuality is illegal and AIDS is officially ascribed to the moral degeneracy and sexual perversity of the bourgeois West. This is the Soviet equivalent of attributing AIDS to the wrath of God.

As already suggested, the aversion of older Revivalists toward the new social gospel is partly a matter of psychological inertia, and thus reflects a disinclination to embrace a way of thinking which departs significantly from what may have been habitual since early childhood. In the case of some older Revivalists, however, there is an additional factor at work. The underbelly of popular Catholicism on the far right of the politico-theological spectrum is a mélange of heterodox Marian apparitions, secret prophecy, and doomsday reckoning. A common strand through all of this is the theory that holds all change in post-conciliar Catholicism to be a sinister Communist plot to destroy the church.[90] While none of the older Revivalists from the sample completely swallow this 'Communist conspiracy' theory, it is nevertheless a peripheral element of their religious culture and thus something to be nibbled at whenever they are confronted by disquieting developments within the church.

That there does not exist a natural affinity between Revivalism and a right-wing political doctrine, however, is attested by the enmity with which many Revivalists thirty years of age and younger regard liberal capitalism. Indeed, as Colin Francome has observed, religious opposition to abortion in the Western world has not infrequently been linked to a radical critique of the dominant society.[91] Many second-generation Revivalists believe that liberalized abortion has been promoted by elitist, inegalitarian impulses inherent in capitalism and, additionally, that the pro-choice ethic is the apotheosis of nineteenth-century liberalism with its exaltation of the individual, private property, and technology.[92] Much like their counterparts in the American movement, these young

Catholics are of unsettled social standing, contemptuous of the existing social order, and mainly products of a blue-collar (and in the present context) Irish-Canadian Catholicism.

Unlike their American counterparts, who have tended to form separate pro-life groups independent of the larger movement,[93] these young Canadian Catholic militants have thus far been content to work within Campaign Life. Although several profess unhappiness with the right-wing political views of the Campaign Life leadership, they are comfortable with the organization's militant Catholic spirituality as well as its uncompromising stance on the abortion issue. Nevertheless, it is possible that these political differences will become an internal source of conflict for the Canadian movement in the years ahead.

One would at first glance expect these young Revivalists to be friendlier toward Social Justice Catholicism than their older compeers. Indeed, they are sympathetic toward the economic and political critiques of the Canadian bishops and, additionally, are excited by the prospect of Canadian Catholicism riding the crest of a resurgent social awareness. Despite this apparent congruence of political views, however, the paths of Social Justice Catholics and young Revivalists rarely intersect. The latter express both frustration and disappointment that the abortion issue seems not to have warranted the attention given by Social Justice Catholics to other issues. Because they regard liberalized abortion as a quintessential expression of liberal capitalism, they insist that the pro-life cause must be the cornerstone of a fully Catholic vocation to social change. Thus, a young Revivalist woman says:

> The anti-abortion position is the most radical Catholicism because it calls for a total conversion away from killing. That's why I'm upset with Catholics who march for peace and justice but are too snobbish and embarrassed to fight against abortion. Abortion feeds off the mentality which condones militarism, racism and war. Justice begins in the womb. When you kill unborn babies anything goes and we're all diminished. Violence against the most defenceless paves the way for violence against other innocent people. It seems that these Catholics have lost something of their faith not to make pro-life their top priority – the faith which sees every child as an incarnation of God's love. I've even tried to attend some social justice rallies against nuclear arms, but it's too monstrous a contradiction to see some banners that read: 'Pro-Choicers for Peace.' And I'm no reactionary. I despise capitalism. Abortion

is the logical outcome of its principles of survival of the fittest and placing the individual over the family. So we feel like an island in the church. The social justice Catholics have sold out to the liberal culture and we're the unrecognized radicals.

Younger Revivalists believe that Progressive, or Social Justice, Catholicism, with its proclivity for theological liberalism and ethical pluralism, is itself a product of a consumer-oriented, capitalist culture. Like their older compeers, they take their religion in heavy dogmatic doses and believe that the genuine faith is open neither to multiple interpretation nor to a gradation of commitment. By appearing to soften Catholic requirements of doctrinal belief and ethical conduct, they insist, Progressives have attenuated the transcendent dimension of the faith and thereby turned it into a commodity that can be purchased piecemeal by religious consumers. The anti-abortion position, younger Revivalists contend, is a fundamental contradiction of conventional wisdom in modern society. To defend this position, they say, requires a piety which is equally a contradiction of the times, not one tailored to suit the agnostic temper of contemporary culture.

The political generation gap among Revivalists, however, evaporates on the subject of feminism. All regardless of age and social standing view the Women's Movement with undisguised loathing, and link it to the breakdown of family, community, and traditional morality in Western society. And the slow impress of feminism within the church is regarded by them as a lethal aberration which, if left unchecked, will further subvert sacred order and tradition. One does not read far into virtually any Revivalist publication from the past five years before hearing alarm bells warning of the feminist infiltration of the church.[94]

TWO SOLITUDES

Discrepant norms and definitions of a religious organization give rise to conflictual claims over who most faithfully stands for the religion's authentic tradition. What is at stake in the conflict between Revivalist and Social Justice Catholics is largely the exercise of religious power, the question of what group, using what criteria, will authorize the identity and future course of Canadian Catholicism. And what gives this conflict a particularly poignant edge is that no group in the Canadian church takes its Catholicism more seriously than do either Revivalist or Progressive Catholics.

Yet, ironically, despite their mutual antagonism, Revivalist and Social Justice Catholics display some surprising similarities. Both subscribe to an objectivist morality wherein certain actions are seen as intrinsically good and others as intrinsically evil. Moreover, both conceive their respective definitions of Catholicism in heroic and elitist terms. Whereas Revivalists regard themselves as a holy leaven called to rescue the Canadian church from spiritual lassitude, Social Justice Catholics regard themselves as a vanguard called to lead the wider church into political enlightenment and righteousness. Both, although in quite different ways, represent projects of counter-secularization: Revivalists aspire to purge the church of worldly contamination while Progressives seek to convert the world to a politicized version of the Christian gospel.

This chapter has demonstrated the symbolic importance of the pro-life movement to a fundamental ideological conflict within Canadian Catholicism. Revivalist Catholics have been given the spotlight because they are utterly central to this conflict. It must be remembered, however, that the sum of the Canadian pro-life movement is considerably larger than its Revivalist component. Most civil rights activists, for example, including those who are themselves Catholic, are either somewhat bewildered spectators or strangers altogether to the antagonism between Revivalist and Social Justice Catholics described in this chapter.

By this point, then, the variegated character of the Canadian pro-life movement may be assumed as well-established. As indicated earlier, however, this study is foremost a contribution to the sociology of Roman Catholicism. It seems fitting, therefore, to narrow the focus further by dedicating the final chapter to a more sustained and systematic discussion of Revivalist Catholicism. For not only are Revivalists the most militant faction within the pro-life movement, they are also a vital, and perhaps revolutionary, force within Canadian Catholicism itself.

7

Revivalist Catholicism, Pro-Life Activism, and Pursuit of the Sacred

Preceding chapters have explored the circuitous route taken by the pro-life movement (principally in Toronto) in its metamorphosis from a movement of political reform to one of religious crusade. Although the movement retains to the present a healthy measure of pluralism which is mainly due to the influence of civil rights and family heritage activists, its dominant tone is now set by Revivalist Catholics whose anti-abortionism is symbiotically connected to a contracultural piety. In pro-life activism Revivalists have discovered a public ritual ideally suited to their enterprise for a culturally separatist Catholicism.

Perhaps the most significant research discovery of this study is that Revivalist Catholics constitute a distinctive and increasingly self-enclosed subculture within the Canadian church. This subculture is grounded in an ideology of opposition to the ferment of change within the broader society and, more important, within Canadian Catholicism itself. Anti-abortion protest is in fact only Revivalism's most visible and public expression.

Chapters Four and Five provided an initial reconnaissance into the Revivalist subculture and thereby introduced some of the religious ideals and practices of its adherents. The first part of the present chapter is a further exploration of Revivalist Catholicism for the purpose of drawing a preliminary map of its basic theological and sociological terrain. The second part examines more closely the organic link, or what Weber would call 'elective affinity,'[1] between pro-life activism and the anti-worldly asceticism of Revivalism.

First, a word of clarification. Although the accents may vary, the subculture identified here as Revivalist Catholicism is likely to be found in most countries where Catholicism is confronted by the challenge of fashioning a new modus vivendi with the modern world. There exists, for example, a flourishing Revivalist subculture in the United States which has been patently influential in the intellectual formation of Canadian Revivalism. Because the ideological topography of Revivalism is consistent on both sides of the forty-ninth parallel, the following discussion is based on a content analysis of both Canadian and American Revivalist literature.[2]

NAMING THE SUBCULTURE

The Catholics designated in this study as *Revivalist* are probably vaguely familiar to many North Americans. They are the Catholics who appear to be refugees from a former era when choices were simpler and fewer, truth was guaranteed, and the path to salvation was certain if difficult. They seem to inhabit the sombre regions of the church, denouncing every theological and liturgical innovation as reckless iconoclasm and smelling the odour of heresy at every juncture of church and society. They, furthermore, appear anxious to immunize the church against democracy, feminism, and all else that counts as enlightenment in contemporary Western culture. In addition, as this study has shown, they above all others are the Catholics in the trenches of anti-abortion protest. Known mainly by reputation, these Catholics represent an abidingly disgruntled subculture within North American Catholicism, and yet have not been given the attention by scholars of religion that their influence would seem to warrant.

Revivalist Catholicism has been the name given to this subculture throughout this study because it seems the best of available alternatives. *Conservative* Catholicism, the standard designation in both the popular media and scholarly literature,[3] suffers from a generic blandness and fails to convey anything of the missionary zeal and ideology of crisis that are germane to the world-view of these Catholics. In addition, they themselves reject the adjective *conservative* because it implies an admissible pluralism in Catholic modes of belief and conduct, something which is offensive to their univocal conception of Catholicism. As they see it, Catholicism is an either-or proposition: one is either completely loyal to the Roman Magisterium, and hence *orthodox*, or else deviant and *heterodox*. But *orthodox* and *neo-orthodox*, their own preferred self-designations, are evaluative theological terms and thus ill-suited to present analytical purposes. And while it has some descriptive merit, *traditionalist* likewise bears a normative connotation and, besides, carries the risk of confusing these Catholics with the separatist Traditionalist movement, with which most of them have little sympathy. Catholic *fundamentalism*, while suggestive, is apt to be construed as a term of opprobrium and to invite facile comparison with so-called movements in the Protestant and Islamic worlds.[4] *Ultramontanist* Catholicism is enticing but, unfortunately, focused somewhat too narrowly.

Revivalist Catholicism circumvents these conceptual pitfalls and, additionally, packs a greater descriptive clout than do any of the aforementioned options. The term *revivalistic* is borrowed from the anthropology of social movements. In his epochal study of native American ghost dance religion, James Mooney employed it to characterize movements of protest that aspire to overcome social stress by restituting customs and values from a past Golden Age.[5] Wallace includes *revivalistic* movements in his general class of *revitalization* movements, which he defines as 'deliberate, conscious, organized efforts by members of a society to create a more satisfying culture.'[6] Revitalization movements, according to Wallace, occur when social collectivities experience high levels of stress and feel disillusionment with the prevailing cultural gestalt.[7] They are, in other words, recurrent responses throughout human history to conditions of social disaffection and psychological disorientation. As a particular type of revitalization movement, writes Wallace, the *revivalistic* movement professes to resolve structural and psychological strain by *reviving* 'a traditional culture now fallen into desuetude.'[8]

Revivalistic movements historically have arisen under circumstances of enforced acculturation, and have thus represented efforts by segments of aboriginal populations to reverse European domination by recrudescing elements of an eclipsed indigenous culture. But the concept may also be applied, mutatis mutandis, to describe efforts by people in a milieu of first world cultural conflict to redress collective anxiety by embracing an apparently lost or endangered tradition. The world-view of those Catholics under consideration here is founded upon twin convictions:

1 North American culture has relapsed into a state of moral viciousness and institutional anarchy, and this is a state into which mainstream Catholicism has been largely absorbed.
2 The *authentic* church in North America is an enclave of stalwart believers in fidelity to an ancient and unchanging Catholic tradition and at war against the neo-paganism of the wider society.

Revivalist Catholicism thus communicates at a purely descriptive, analytic level the contracultural and traditionalist flavour of this worldview.

According to the perception of Revivalists, the church's doctrinal and ethical certitudes, luxuriant ritualism, imperial government, and supernaturalist ethos have been successively downgraded. These elements had served for many Catholics as the signposts of a religious culture that was a sacred *realissimum*, an eternal citadel protected against the contingencies of human meanings and social change. It was within this symbolic universe that they were able to locate, with the ease born of inherited repetition, the report of ultimacy which set them apart as a believing community from the unconvinced and unconverted. But this enchanted canopy has been sundered, as pluralism, a mitigated situation ethics, and a catechesis which invokes the primacy of experience as its point of departure have become the common backdrop – in the pew, confessional, and seminary – for the daily performance of Catholic life. Whereas many North American Catholics have made a relatively painless adjustment to the resculptured church, Revivalists believe that mainstream Catholicism has been vanquished by or, at the very least, forced into an unholy syncretism with an alien culture, and that its redemption hinges upon a retrieval of the Catholic past. While Vatican II promised the fresh air of a 'second spring'[9] for the church, Revivalists inhale only the smoke of destruction.

REVIVALIST CATHOLICISM AND TRADITIONALISM

Strangely, in an era of resurgent fundamentalism, and an attendant fusion of religious and political ideals, Catholic Revivalism has almost entirely escaped the notice of sociologists of religion.[10] While it shares with the quasi-schismatic Traditionalist movement a tendency toward theological rigidity and ethical rigorism, as well as the belief that the poison of modernity has infected the bloodstream of the church, Revivalism differs from its more extremist cousin on several counts. First, as Dinges has pointed out, Traditionalism is promoted by priests who yearn for a restoration of pre-conciliar clerical elitism.[11] Quite in contrast, Revivalism is mainly a response of dissatisfied laity to recent convulsion in the Catholic universe. For from endorsing the Traditionalist ideal of a magisterial, inscrutable clergy standing above a passive flock, Revivalists defend their religious militancy by invoking the Second Vatican Council's teaching on the vocation of the laity.[12] Revivalism, thus, much more readily qualifies as a species of popular religiosity.[13]

Second, despite energetic recruiting, Traditionalism remains a closed-circuited phenomenon, cannibalized by paranoia and exerting a very limited claim on anyone under the age of forty. Thus, Traditionalism in North America is little other than a refuge for chronically disaffected antiquarians who have 'sullenly drawn up the walls against all reform.'[14] But while uncomfortable with Traditionalism's repudiation of Vatican II and the church hierarchy, many North American Catholics feel homeless in the post-conciliar church. They desire a re-enchantment of Catholicism, a restoration of liturgical, ethical, and doctrinal certitudes, and a strict definition of the boundaries between *church* and *world*. These are the Catholics who comprise the popular basis for Revivalist Catholicism, and it appears to be an expanding basis which includes a surprising number of young people under the age of thirty.[15]

And what is the attitude of Revivalists to the vernacularized liturgy, the *casus belli* of Traditionalists? Unlike their schismatic cousins, Revivalists do not dispute the doctrinal validity of the *Novus Ordo*. They do believe, however, that the modern mass no longer provides the sinews of Catholic identity, and many of them retain an emotional and esthetical affection for the Latin rite. Liturgical reform in general, they contend, has fostered a decline of beauty and a loss of mystery in Catholic worship.[16]

The Second Vatican Council is the Achilles' heel of the Revivalist world-view. While claiming to accept Vatican II, and merely to protest what they consider its erroneous outgrowth, Revivalists nonetheless are hard-pressed to describe what difference the council should have made for the life of the church. Herein lies the basic and perhaps unresolvable dilemma of Revivalists: outright disavowal of Vatican II would cast them as schismatics and, furthermore, would put a pall on their theory of an unbroken, inspired Catholic tradition; yet because they believe that the council unleashed a Pandora's box of woes on the church, they seem sometimes to regret that it ever occurred. In attempting to balance this tightrope act – claiming acceptance of Vatican II while rejecting most of the developments subsequent to it – Revivalist critics argue that a liberal elite within the church has manipulated the council documents and given them an unjustifiably adventurous interpretation.[17] Careful analysis of the conciliar documents, Revivalists contend, shows that Vatican II was a revolutionary event only in the imaginations of Catholic liberals. The council Fathers wanted at most to wipe clean the stained glass windows of the church, they certainly never intended to smash them. Thus James Hitchcock, the dean of American Revivalism, concedes that pre-conciliar Catholicism was marred by legalism, formalism, and clericalism and thus was in need of renewal, but he rejects as spurious the Progressive view that the council was both harbinger and charter for a transformed church.[18] The tragedy for Hitchcock, then, is not that Vatican II transpired, but that so many Catholics have been duped into believing the liberal interpretation of it.

Revivalists favour a cautious, reconstructionist interpretation of Vatican II, one that emphasizes its continuity with Trent on a seamless road of Catholic tradition. They argue that the council's singular purpose was to revivify the spiritual vitality of Catholics and to purge the church of secular contamination. Thus, the *authentic* renewal intended by John XXIII is said to be comparable to landmark reforms of religious orders, such as the Reform of Cluny in the Benedictine Order or that of St Bernardine in the Franciscan, which aspired to return monastic life to the strict rule of its founders and to restore as a highest priority among monks the pursuit of personal sanctity.[19] *Reform* thusly conceived is directed not so much toward change as to the recapitulation of an earlier, pristine state. Vatican II likewise, insist Revivalists, was meant to re-inculcate the traditional vocation to holiness, and to bring the laity more fully into the lifestream of the faith, without in any way softening the radical antagonism between church and *saeculum*.[20]

THE SMOKE OF SATAN WITHIN THE TEMPLE OF GOD[21]

You see the trouble we are in: Jerusalem is in ruins, its gates have been burnt down. Come, let us rebuild the walls of Jerusalem and suffer this indignity no longer. (Nehemiah 2:17)

This passage, which serves as the epigraph for *Fidelity* magazine, encapsulates the siege mentality of Revivalists. With her barricades trampled, the church is reduced to obsequiousness before the spirits of a re-paganized world. Because contemporary Catholicism appears to many Revivalists as a foreign religion, it is fair to suggest that they are suffering an acute case of culture shock. Most Revivalist literature, in fact, is meant as a form of shock therapy. It is a high-voltage jeremiad of rebellious nuns, wayward bishops, apathetic priests, and dishevelled liturgies designed to rouse the faithful to spiritual combat. Its most striking feature, apart from alarmism, is a penchant for ad hominem attack. The Revivalist imagination interprets everything in terms of a dualistic drama of light versus darkness. And in spiritual warfare, where everyone is aligned on the side of either angels or demons, there is no point in sparing feelings or reputations, in passing over scandal, or in deferring to qualms of civility. The enemy must be exposed and brought to judgment.

The graphic exposé is the literary genre to which most Revivalist literature conforms. Thus, the indignant reader is brought face-to-face with nuns participating in pagan goddess ceremonial, theologians defying the Vatican condemnation of non-celibate homosexuality, and bishops shrugging their shoulders at the latest disfigurement of Catholic liturgy. As a *lamentation of crisis*, Revivalist literature revolves about three interrelated themes: contemporary Catholicism is confronted by 1) a loss of sacred identity; 2) a collapse of moral norms; and 3) a disintegration of authority. As the author has written elsewhere on these three cardinal themes of Revivalist literature, discussion of them here is deliberately condensed and programmatic.[22]

1. Crisis of Sacred Identity

During the past twenty-five years a new theological agenda has emerged and won ascendency within the Catholic world. The basic tenor of this 'new theology' can be expressed in capsule form.[23] After Vatican II Progressive theologians were convinced that renewal should not be restricted to an updating of time-worn thought structures, merely to pouring new wine into old bottles. They believed that the demythologization of scripture and the dehellenization of dogma were required to prevent faith in the twentieth century from becoming an anachronism. The church's traditional understanding of truth, which stressed the conformity of the intellect to a deposit of revelation encoded in dogma, tended in their view to reduce Catholicism to a skeleton of frigid concepts, thus emptying faith of its experiential vitality. The Counter-Reformation mentality reflected by this *extrinsicism*, they contended, was a strait-jacket that inhibited an awareness of the role of the supernatural in the creation of personal and social life. The new theology's task, then, was to crack open this scholastic shell and to reinterpret divine revelation as an immanent power, a dynamic symbolic language, that discloses the gracious presence and infinite possibilities hidden in human life. Rather than a passive submission to a deposit of dogmatic truth, faith in this new perspective is understood as a dynamic agency for transforming consciousness and transcending cultural limitations. The question of the historical facticity of central biblical narratives – such as the exodus-covenant experience of Israel and the resurrection – become in this view quite secondary. Instead, what is crucial is the ongoing recasting of these *stories* and *symbols* for the sake of illuminating the meaning of sin and redemption in the historical present.

Revivalist critics consider the new theology to be a deformation of the Catholic message. By their emphasis on the pragmatic role of faith as a matrix for historical change and the creation of meaning, Progressives are accused of reducing God to a derivative construct, contingent upon the vagaries of subjective feeling and cultural fashion. Such a development, Revivalists insist, is a mockery of the church's great conversion stories, in which individuals felt compelled by encounter with a sublime, transcendent reality fundamentally to alter their lives.[24] The immanentism extolled by Progressives is said to trivialize the *sensus supranaturalis*, turning God into a fuzzy, historicized inkling incapable of commanding that commitment-unto-death exemplified by saints and martyrs. It seems to Revivalists that the North American church has deserted the God of Abraham, Isaac, and Jacob and converted to the Feuerbachian god, that projection onto the cosmos of humanity's deepest aspirations and unrealized possibilities. In attempting to make faith relevant, Revivalists moan, Progressives have debased it to a weepy sentimentality or, at best, a sociological hypothesis and, accordingly, have removed any compelling reason for becoming or, for that matter, remaining a Catholic.[25] A Catholicism of merely anthropocentric virtue, which conceives the divine-human relationship horizontally and which elasticizes the categories of heresy and orthodoxy, is one that has yielded to the secular *Zeitgeist*.

2. Crisis of Moral Norms

The dismay of Revivalists over what they see as an unfiltered *opening to the world* has its basis in an aversion toward almost all aspects of contemporary Western culture. The society to which reformers in the 1960s and 1970s looked for imprints of the sacred was itself in a state of ferment. Authority in every guise, as well as traditional life-style constraints, role expectations, and patterns of stratification, had become subject to challenge. All cultural reality appeared to be endlessly malleable and negotiable. Whereas many Catholic reformers saw these 'signs of the times' as the birth pangs of a new epiphany, Revivalists saw them as danger signals of a dissolute society.[26] To the Revivalist mind this was the worst time possible for the church to shed her protective covering and enter dialogue with the world. The fallout from *aggiornamento* – a depleted priesthood, feminist nuns, an upheaval in Catholic sexual morality, doctrinal tentativeness – only served to confirm that the chaos of the larger society was being duplicated within the church. This cultural pessimism is above all else the hallmark of the Revivalist mentality.

The affluent West, contend Revivalists, is preoccupied with therapeutic well-being and a vision of interminable personal comfort. They believe that most North American Catholics, under the spell of the dominant culture, desire to win liberation from previously imposed obligations, from self-sacrifice and ascetic demands, and from all institutional constraints. What they crave, in the words of James Hitchcock, is a church which will function as 'a warm matrix within which and from out of which individuals have unlimited freedom of action, without the danger that membership in the Church will make inconvenient demands on them.'[27] The clearest barometer by which to measure the acquiescence of the North American church to the reigning consensus of *therapeutic* culture, Revivalists argue, is the collapse of Catholic sexual norms.[28] The emergence of gay rights groups within the church, increasing evidence of homosexual conduct among priests, an institutionalized defiance of *Humanae Vitae*, and a general passivity among Catholics toward the 'abortion epidemic' indicate to Revivalists that the moral sights of the North American church have been lowered to the permissive level of the wider society.[29] Revivalists claim that new approaches in Catholic moral theology, which emphasize the relational, temporal, and teleological context of decision-making, tend toward the elimination of a sphere of actions that are 'objectively wrong' and thus turn sin into a matter of purely subjective interpretation.[30] Accordingly, the power of the church to 'bind and loose,' to pronounce judgment on what is true and false about human experience, is undermined.

3. *Crisis of Authority*

Revivalists are not satisfied to interpret the shifting climate within North American Catholicism as a self-adjustment of the church to processes of pluralization and secularization within the wider society. Rather, the church's present troubles are so severe that a more personal agency of calamity must be identified. Thus, Revivalists invoke a conspiracy theory: liberal theologians and diocesan bureaucrats, no longer themselves in possession of supernatural faith, have assumed the role of 'second magisterium' and are determined to convert the church to the characteristic values and thought modes of secular humanism.[31] In the Revivalist view, the authority structure of the church, historically aligned in vertical descent from pope to bishops, and then from clergy to laity, has undergone a major gravity shift, with power now increasingly concentrated in the hands of a 'new class' of religious professionals.[32] This 'revolt of middle management,' according to Revivalists, has brought into the open a confrontation of forces struggling for control of the church. On the one hand are dissident theologians, liberal catechists and liturgists, as well as compliant bishops who would redefine the basic postulates of Catholicism and make the church a mere adjunct to the world; on the other are stalwart believers who have thrown down the gauntlet against any further erosion of Catholic distinctiveness.[33]

By invoking a false 'spirit of Vatican II' to justify their revolutionary intent, argues the Canadian Revivalist Anne Roche, the Progressive elite has subverted Catholic order and discipline and opened the floodgates to rampant dissent.

The Council left Catholic doctrine untouched, even went to great lengths to reiterate it ... Nevertheless, the Second Vatican Council was the unwitting vehicle of a second Protestant reformation. Again, from within the ranks of the Church's theologians, there is an assault on papal authority, on the Church's claim to interpret the Scriptures authoritatively and teach infallibly, and on Catholic laws governing human behaviour, especially in marriage ... There are thus *two* Second Vatican Councils to be considered – the one that under the guidance of the Holy Ghost actually took place, and which any reader who cares to devote himself to a perusal of its documents can identify; and the second Council of the popular imagination, the creation of the reformers' propaganda, the one that was supposed to have changed everything Catholic, and which sent forth 'the spirit of Vatican II' ... It suffices ... to note the presence in the Church since the Council of a vigorous, protestant dissenting group of influential professionals, theologians lay and clerical, teachers and religious superiors, nuns and priests.[34]

But it is the North American bishops, according to Revivalists, who bear ultimate blame for the collapse of Catholic battlements before the forces of secular humanism. Rather than reassuming control of the 'runaway church,'[35] they say, the bishops have been seduced into doubt over the very validity of their own ecclesiastical power. 'The *contemporary disdain for all authority*,' observes Monsignor Kelly, 'has made bishops nervous about the use of authority in the Church.' Unless the bishops recover their nerve and demonstrate a resolve to impose penalties for wilful disobedience, Kelly argues, the church is certain to suffer further institutional atrophy.[36] The bishops have become too timid and defensive, Revivalists bemoan, to withstand the 'neo-Modernist heresy' which has been ushered into the church by the Progressive elite.[37] Their role, according to Hitchcock, has been reduced to 'merely one of ratifying whatever [their] bureaucracies do and defending them from the criticisms of irate lay people.'[38] Anne Roche is quite clear about the shortcomings of the North American hierarchy: '[If] the bishops still believe that the Church is the repository of truth, it is their particular duty to defend her. The hierarchy as a group has stopped doing that. Individual bishops are valiant, but most seem to have succumbed to a sense of inevitable doom. [The Progressive elite] have so far been fortunate in a hierarchy that lacks both the will and the guts to throw them out ... The prospects are not strong that the hierarchy will soon act to restore the teaching of orthodoxy to the faithful.'[39]

The impact of this fifth column of Progressive Catholics, Revivalists lament, has been devastating. It has ransacked the church of her supernatural heritage, subordinated doctrine to personal experience, preached a form of religious pluralism which negates the special status of Catholicism in salvation history, and, summarily, made the church a mirror image of secular culture. But as is the case with all revolutions, Revivalists assert, this one required a 'triggering incident,'[40] something that would avail as a critical point of attack. This, they claim, was provided by Paul VI's 1968 ban against artificial contraception.

The contraception issue, Revivalists claim, has been used by Catholic Progressives as a battering ram to flatten the church's system of authority.[41] Indeed, it would be hard to overstate the significance of *Humanae Vitae* as a dividing line between Revivalists and Progressives. For the former, *Humanae Vitae* is most obviously an acid test of obedience to Rome. But it is more than this. It represents, as well, a definitive benchmark of Catholic separateness from worldly morality, the touchstone for a contracultural piety. The zealous allegiance of Revivalists to Paul VI's encyclical is their pre-eminent badge of religious distinction. And the very fact that *Humanae Vitae* is a 'scandal and folly' to the modern temperament is taken as shining testimony to its wisdom. (If a world marred by turpitude finds it so outrageous, it must be right.)

The battle over contraception is a battle for the soul of the Catholic church; Revivalists aspire to save the church from the world, Progressives to save it from herself. For the latter, *Humanae Vitae* represents a futile attempt by a monarchic leadership, haunted by its twilight of power, to assert control over the centrifugal forces at play within the contemporary church. They think that any attempt by the hierarchy to impose sanctions for disobeying its teaching on birth control would result in massive defections from the church and, thus, be tantamount to institutional suicide.[42] In contrast, Revivalists, who demand a church with exacting boundaries, would welcome such sanctions as an instrument for winnowing out the golden grain from choking chaff.[43]

Revivalists believe that the church's hierarchical system of authority sustains and re-creates Catholicism's plausibility structure. Especially today, they argue, when even most bishops have been seduced by secularism and seem bound to leadership by applause meter, the papal office is the last dike protecting the church from the flood-waters of irreligion. It is for this reason that Pope John Paul II is the pre-eminent culture hero of North American Revivalists. They regard him as the embodiment of orthodoxy as well as their primary locus of support in the fight against irreligion and secularism. Devotion to the Holy See has heightened in recent years as North American Revivalists, especially in Canada, have become convinced of a creeping Gallicanism in their national churches. They believe that the majority of bishops too have been seduced by the blandishments of secularism and aspire to operate as independently as possible from Rome. Given the present pontiff's unaffected piety, uninhibited devotion to Mary, high esteem for motherhood and traditional family values, and his unbending response to dissent in the Netherlands and America, it is not surprising that John Paul ranks with Cardinal Ratzinger in the upper echelon of the Revivalist pantheon.[44]

ECCLESIOLA IN ECCLESIA

Thus, painted in broad strokes, is the basic contour of the Revivalist world-view. By preaching a theology that may be fairly described as 'non-historical orthodoxy,'[45] retreating into the past to reclaim a 'lost tradition' of Catholicism as an unchanging bastion undaunted by the vicissitudes of mundane history, and proposing ultramontanism as a panacea for the disarray of the contemporary church, Revivalists seek to draw up the wagons in a circle to protect against encroaching evil.

Although they are separate religious responses to the trauma of secularization, there do exist several suggestive points of comparison between Catholic Revivalism and Protestant fundamentalism. Both represent protests against modernizing trends within the wider culture and within their parent churches, both espouse an ideology of cultural decline, both attempt a puritan retrieval of core elements of their respective traditions, and both have cemented their distinctive identities through political activism.[46]

A fundamentalist movement of any genre presupposes of course a social situation in which a world-view once thought sacrosanct finds itself with a diminished currency and plausibility. As Frank J. Lechner has observed, the emergence of Protestant fundamentalism is incomprehensible unless viewed on the larger canvas of cultural change in which Western society was engulfed by the early decades of the twentieth century. As scientific explanations of the world, couched in a secularized post-millennialism, gained increased persuasiveness, traditional religious soteriology was relegated to a subordinate cultural status. As a countermovement to the ideology of *modernity*, Protestant fundamentalism defined itself in direct opposition to the cultural successes of secularism. The 'fundamentals of the faith' only had to be spelled out when they were no longer culturally assumed.[47]

Catholic Revivalism, similarly, cannot be understood apart from the volcano of Vatican II. By virtue of its authoritarian government and sacramental discipline, Catholicism was better equipped than most forms of Protestantism to maintain an appearance of imperviousness to the forces of change at work in the larger society. But the church could not, of course, produce Catholics who were fully insulated from the impulses of pluralism, scientism, and secularism, and adherence to its supernaturalist cosmology in the two decades prior to Vatican II was often as much a matter of external conformity as internalized belief. Thus, while the impulses of modernity within the church were partially contained, they nonetheless steadily accumulated and Vatican II provided the opportunity for their full-scale eruption. By mitigating its historical suspicion of democracy, freedom of conscience, and religious liberty, and also admitting its cluster of sacred symbols to a process of re-examination, the church emerged from the 'ghetto Catholicism' of Pius XII with one gigantic leap. And in the process, all of the parameters of Catholic separateness from profane culture were turned into question marks, the boundaries between church and world were opened. Delayed by half a century, Catholicism's confrontation with modernity is only now producing the kind of ideological fissures that have already been established as fixtures in the Protestant world. And Catholic Revivalism, much in the same manner as Protestant fundamentalism, may be viewed as a rearguard defence of a set of religious prescriptions which have lost their normative sway and appear threatened by extinction or, perhaps worse, by ridicule.

The parallel between Revivalism and fundamentalism does not end there. While both deplore the rise of secularism in the wider society, their dominant concern is its apparent spread within their own religious traditions. George Marsden has shown that the fiercest invective of fundamentalists in the first several decades of the twentieth century was reserved for fellow Protestants who had made peace with philosophical liberalism as well as the application of secular criteria of literary criticism to the scriptures, and who were thus thought to be corruptors *from within* of true Christianity.[48] Catholic Revivalists, likewise, have been preoccupied with the notion that liberal elements within the church constitute a 'Trojan horse in the City of God,'[49] bent on assaulting Catholic faith with the sword of secularism. Thus, they have called ceaselessly for punitive action against dissenters, publicly chastised bishops suspected of miscreant leaning, dismissed religious education curricula as secularist cant, decried Catholic colleges as breeding grounds for heresy, rebuked nuns who aspire to ordination, and railed against liturgical innovation. As the self-appointed vigilantes of Catholic Truth, Revivalists have set up a camp of war within a church they believe to be in ruins.[50]

The vision of the church to which Revivalists subscribe – triumphalist, exclusivist, and world-transcending – is aberrant in the context of North America's climate of denominational pluralism and liberal democracy. The story of Canadian and American Catholicism over the past century is partly one of continuous adaptation to this climate, of fashioning a common vocabulary with non-Catholic religions and attempting to prove the compatibility of the church with Canadian and American political structures and cultural agenda.[51] To the extent that North American Catholicism has successfully merged with the cultural mainstream, it has lost a certain combative edge and a sense of being an invader in enemy territory. To the Revivalist mind, this process of adaptation has been tantamount to emasculation: having surrendered to the wider society, the church has been spiritually neutered and cut off from its sacred lineage.[52]

Nowhere is this theme more pronounced than in the writing of James Hitchcock. Especially in the early years after the Second Vatican

Council, Hitchcock asserts, before Progressive Catholics in North America had re-routed their reforming zeal into a critique of capitalism, much that passed for church renewal was the product of a compulsory optimism concerning the values and future prospects of the dominant culture. In effect, he continues, the 'secular city' theology embraced by Progressives was a 'canonization of the banal,' an exaltation of wearied middle-class ideals. Rather than being a cutting-edge of cultural change, he says, Catholic Progressives have most often been greeters of the dawn in late afternoon, 'earnestly endorsing ideas whose proponents were in the process of abandoning them.' Thus, the new dispensation heralded by Progressives amounted only to bringing church and world together in holy wedlock, dissolving all tension between the two, and promoting a 'totally uncritical and placid acceptance of everything which culture or the state makes normal.' 'Someone has observed that, although the Church is now able, as a result of strenuous and often traumatic efforts, to speak to everyone, to employ a language which the world will comprehend, it now finds that it no longer has anything to say. More accurately, it has nothing to say which the world does not already know.'[53]

Part of the genius of Catholicism in past centuries, Revivalists contend, has been its radical strangeness, its defiant proclamation of truths the world would rather not hear. This is the genius credited by Chesterton (for whom Revivalists feel deep affection) with making Catholicism 'the only thing which saves a man from the degrading slavery of being a child of his own age.'[54] But today, claim Revivalists, it is dedicated lay Catholics who must rescue the church from spiritual lassitude and save her from the degrading slavery of being a child of this worst of all possible ages. Thus, writes Anne Roche, just as it befell a heroic laity to combat the fourth-century Arian heresy, so too in the present epoch must courageous and uncompromising lay Catholics slam the door shut against heresy, theological meandering, and mediocrity and take occupation of the Catholic high ground.

Now, in the face of the liberal establishment and the paralysed hierarchy, the laity have another chance to show that they are true to their baptism. We will perforce be less elegant in defense of orthodoxy than skilled theologians are in their assault on it ... When the dust clears, we fully intend to be occupying the historical ground of Roman Catholicism, accepting her entire system, receiving her Sacraments, obeying her bishops.

If there ever was a time for Counter-Reformation mentality it is now. Now, at the acknowledged end of Christian civilization with our society crumbling about us, with totalitarian and materialist alternatives offering themselves attractively, with many of the other Christian bodies giving up the struggle on divorce, purity, abortion, euthanasia, with the Catholic Church torn from within, now is the time for the Catholic to admit that Catholic Christianity is an extreme and total position, worth living and dying for, worth passing on to his children, worth defending against his priests.[55]

The present church, insist Revivalists, convulsed by revolution and with its priesthood and religious orders depleted, thus requires for its salvation a counter-revolution, a Catholic *jihad* centred upon the leadership of John Paul II and committed to a renaissance of papal authority and erstwhile norms of moral, doctrinal, and liturgical rectitude. In the newly retrenched, much shrunken, Catholicism, the church will be restored to her former ascetic vigour and delivered from her present cultural enslavement. Faithful lay Catholics have been returned to the catacombs, and there they must master the guile and resiliency of guerrilla warfare, for the very survival of Catholicism is at stake. And, says Anne Roche, they would be unwise to expect either support or understanding from the Progressive Catholic establishment. 'For today the Church asks of the Catholic laity, especially of married Catholics, a heroism and a lifelong commitment that it no longer dares to expect of the priest or nun ... It is the faithful Catholic layman ... who has unaccountably been left to defend authority and orthodoxy ... Therefore, his form of warfare must be the guerrilla skirmish that makes the government remember him and what he stands for. Even though he loses all the battles, he must not lose heart and he must not surrender. He must stay alive.'[56]

Given its self-conception as a heroic remnant called to revitalize the North American church, its *conventicle* ecclesiology, as well as its perfectionist aspirations and anti-cultural fortitude, Revivalism bears a close affinity to the *sectarian* type of religious organization as analysed by Troeltsch.[57] The conception of an inclusive church tolerating different levels of moral achievement and belief is anathema to the Revivalist mentality. Instead, the true church is an enclave of righteous believers who are known by their unfaltering obedience to Rome and self-identification with the Catholic past. Belief in an 'unchanging divine revelation ... that is above the ups and downs of cultures and the rhythm of history,' asserts von Hildebrand, is the foundation of Catholic faith.[58] And this revelation is true, insist Revivalists, regardless of its social utility, cultural appeal, or psychological beneficence. Those who do not or cannot accept it fully cannot legitimately call themselves Catholic.

Such is the crux of Revivalism. In attempting to define criteria of Catholic belonging within a narrow compass and thereby to separate the sheep from the goats, Revivalists advocate a qualified membership principle. While the mainstream North American church has been polluted by an ideological exchange with secularism, liberalism, feminism, and socialism, the burden and privilege of historical Catholicism has been taken over by a small band of the saintly – an *ecclesiola in ecclesia*[59] – that will ensure the passage of orthodoxy beyond this crooked generation.

There is great irony in the emergence of Revivalism in the church's post-conciliar era. Vatican II has been widely heralded as the council of lay emancipation, as the council that finally recognized the religious worth of the masses of ordinary Catholics. Revivalists have taken this interpretation of Vatican II in an altogether unanticipated direction. In rejecting the liberalization of Catholic discipline and dogma, which has been carried out at least in part ostensibly to 'lighten the spiritual load' of the laity, Revivalists are declaring their right, precisely as *lay* Catholics, to be unflinchingly conservative in both piety and morals. This is the principal reason why Revivalists are so exasperating to Catholic elites. For not only do they spurn the modernized church as something they had neither asked for nor wanted, but they defend their militant conservatism by expressly linking it to Vatican II's teaching on the 'apostolate of the laity.'[60] In other words, they take one of the favourite slogans of reform of Catholic Progressives, and by turning it on its head, convert it into a weapon of counter-reformation. The irony in this resides in the fact that the most zealous proponents of liberalization have to a large extent been nuns and priests who have rarely doubted that they were performing a service of generosity for the Catholic laity. To the Revivalist mind, however, the reforming elite has merely been guilty of installing a *nouveau* clericalism in place of the old.

The previous chapter described the conflict in the Canadian church between Revivalist and Progressive (or Social Justice) Catholics as a clash of orthodoxies. It is perhaps more fitting to describe this conflict as a clash of intra-Catholic status groups. All twenty-five subjects of this study's sample of Progressive Catholics are exponents of the new theology, new morality, and new ecclesiology that were discussed above and against which Revivalists are so fiercely opposed. Probably more significant is that sixteen of the twenty-five are members of religious orders and the remaining nine, while laypersons, qualify for admission to the Catholic elite by virtue of possessing a degree in theology. While the sample is small, it does indicate the prevalence of professed celibates within the ranks of Catholic Progressivism. Quite in contrast, there are very few priests and nuns *actively* involved in the pro-life movement in Toronto.

In conjunction with its theological dimension, then, the conflict within Canadian Catholicism between Revivalism and Progressivism is one of competing status groups. Progressives seek to remodel the church using the philosophical and political tools which they have acquired in their capacity as professionally trained theologians. Revivalists, by contrast, are more closely connected to the orbit of family, parish, and traditional devotion and feel displaced by alterations to the Catholic world-view. They also feel resentment that their own piety and contributions to the faith seem unrecognized and unappreciated in the reformed church. They are the Catholics who have clung tenaciously to ancient belief and doctrinal formulation; it is they who have bridled sexual passion and obeyed *Humanae Vitae*, raised children for the faith, and defended implausibilities such as papal infallibility and the divine Presence in the consecrated host. Rather than being rewarded for their perseverance and self-sacrifice, however, they are told that their piety and loyalty were perhaps redundant, that Catholicism is not after all a matter of such clear-cut definition and that the new pluriform church reserves no special place for, and indeed is embarrassed by, the spiritually fastidious. There is, however, one place where faith may still be expressed absolutely and without cultural stipulation: the pro-life movement.

In the Weberian sense of the term, then, Revivalists constitute a discontented *status group* within Canadian Catholicism.[61] They regard themselves as the unsung heroes of the church, the stalwart few who have held fast to the helm of faith at a time of chaos. Their reward within the church, however, is not honour and prestige, but rather ridicule and condescension. Letters to the editor of *Challenge*, the magazine which represents the voice of Canadian Revivalism, invariably feature overtones of status discontent. The following is a typical specimen:

... Finally, we need some respect – so that if we have a concern, we will not be patronized, not insulted, not ignored. After all, a certain kind of modernist Catholic is proud of bleating 'We are Church' – What about us? The ones without glamorous jobs and theology degrees? Are WE not 'Church'? And if we are, why do [the bishops] treat us and our beliefs like dirt?

What do the laity want?

Respect! The truth! Faithful clergy![62]

The status conflict between Progressives and Revivalists is not primarily one of intellectuals versus non-intellectuals. Although this dimension is present, Revivalism is not without its corps of intellectuals, most of whom are academics in fields other than theology. The conflict is more accurately understood as one of church functionaries (bishops, theologians, diocesan bureaucrats, priests, and nuns) versus estranged lay people (though Revivalism is also, of course, not without supporters among the clergy). In this vein, a rich irony of Revivalism is precisely its vigorous anti-clericalism. On the one hand, Revivalists claim solemn respect for the ordained priesthood and, indeed, are ready to shower with affection any priest who would make a declaration of solidarity with them. Yet on the other hand, they claim that the 'mutinous clergy' is in large measure responsible for the demolition of Catholic certitude and the alienation of faithful laity from the church.[63]

There is a sense in which this status discontent extends beyond Revivalism to include a wider proportion of the Canadian pro-life movement. As discussed in Chapter Four, Parish Catholic activists do not share the Revivalist viewpoint that the Canadian church is an apostate institution. Like the more militant Revivalists, however, Parish Catholics also feel that their contributions to the church as propagators of the faith through loyal parenthood have been disesteemed by the elite Catholic establishment. They believe that bishops, priests, and the church's bureaucratic 'middle management' look upon them as dupes for actually taking *Humanae Vitae* to heart and eschewing artificial birth control. Many Parish Catholic women feel that their status as mothers is being denigrated within the church by Progressive celibates whose interests are remote from the traditional Catholic family. Why, they ask, do Canadian Catholic elites seem to pour their energy into political causes while giving only paltry attention to the needs of Catholic family life? Participation in the pro-life movement affords these women an opportunity to affirm the family ideals which they believe have been neglected in the new social teaching of the Canadian church.[64]

CANADIAN CATHOLICISM: GHETTO OR DENOMINATION?

Theoretical analysis of religious organizations normally distinguishes the *denomination* from both the *church* and the *sect*. In contrast to the latter types of organization, the denomination rejects the concept of *extra ecclesiam nulla salus* in favour of a more inclusive ethos. Thus, the denomination functions according to principles of theological pluralism and toleration. Its boundaries are fluid and its organizational principles pragmatic as it seeks compatible coexistence with both its social environment and neighbouring religious bodies.[65]

In adjusting to Canadian patterns of pluralism, ecumenism, liberal democracy, and secularism, Revivalists contend, the Canadian church has taken on the complexion of a denomination. It has become so much a part of the shuffle of mainstream culture, they maintain, that being a Catholic in contemporary Canada is largely a redundancy. In its desire to accommodate the church to Canadian cultural life, they say, the Progressive Catholic establishment has made relics of traditional pieties and answers, turned the church into a repository of secular trends, and in the process promoted a *smorgasbord Catholicism* in which all might find something without the burden of wholesale commitment. So intertwined is the church with the Canadian Way of Life, Revivalists claim, that it is in danger of imitating the dominant culture even in its attitude toward the abortion question.

Extensive survey research by Canadian sociologist Reginald Bibby would seem to lend some support to this Revivalist critique. Rather than being fully committed to their respective religious traditions, Bibby argues, Canadians (Catholics just as much as Protestants) treat them much like retail outlets, taking from them isolated fragments which ultimately make little difference for either personal conduct or belief. Indeed, says Bibby, most self-professed Christians in Canada are barely distinguishable from non-believers in their cultural attitudes, ideals, and goals. As Peter Berger remarked about the cultural disposition of American Christians in the early 1960s, '[They] hold the same values as everyone else, but with more emphatic solemnity.'[66]

Far from resisting this movement from commitment to selective consumption, Bibby says, the Canadian churches have been only too willing to accommodate it, tailoring their religious offerings to whatever the market will bear. By being so 'graciously compliant' to the à la carte preferences of religious consumers, he observes, the churches have served up 'abridged versions' of their respective traditions which are little other than 'culture in sanctimonious clothing.'[67] They have demonstrated little inclination for either 'contradicting the times' or, as Pope John Paul II said in his 1984 visit to Canada, speaking about God 'without ever reducing the greatness of the message to the expectation of the listeners.'[68] Even in their new passion for social concern, asserts Bibby, the churches do not tell the secular culture anything it does not already believe according to its own terms. 'Rather than saying to culture, "This is what religion is," they have been much more inclined to say to culture, "What do you want religion to be?" – The result is that the gods have been fragmented with the blessing of the majority, the silence of many, and the protests of few. Rather than presenting religion as a system of meaning that insists on informing all of one's life, the groups have broken it down and offered it as a wide variety of belief, practice, program, and service items.'[69]

This trend toward specialized consumption, according to Bibby, is reflected by the 'devastating decline' (from 83 per cent in 1965 to 43 per cent in 1986) in the weekly attendance at mass of Canadian Catholics. Even the celebration of the Sunday Eucharist, described by the Canadian bishops as 'the centre and culmination of the whole life of the Catholic community,' has become a fragment that may or may not be selected from the church's diversified 'religious menu.' And the attitudes and beliefs of Canadian Catholics – concerning sexual ethics, quality of life, abortion, and other social issues – differ only slightly from those of other Canadians. As is the case with Canada's other dominant religious groups, maintains Bibby, the impact of Catholicism 'is consequently specific and limited, rather than general and comprehensive.' Canadian Catholicism has likewise 'taken a pluralistic view of religious belief and practice, leaving much up to the individual. Consequently, few beliefs and practices are regarded as normative.'[70]

Perhaps more striking than declining mass attendance is the fact that Canadian Catholics show only a slightly lower tendency than the general population to favour the legal availability of abortion. Roughly two in ten Catholics outside Quebec and three in ten Quebec Catholics, according to Bibby, are in favour of 'abortion on demand.'[71] Revivalists regard dissent on this subject as a Catholic 'point of no return,' as the moment when it becomes absurd to continue defining oneself as Catholic. They fear that Catholic teaching against abortion is in danger of becoming like the teaching against contraception, a dead letter which is honoured more in the breach than in the observance.

In this vein, a symbolic moment for Revivalists occurred in early 1986 when Maureen McTeer, the Catholic wife of a former Canadian prime minister, accepted an honorary directorship with the Canadian Abortion Rights Action League (CARAL). Revivalists looked upon this affair as a test case: would the bishops excommunicate McTeer and thus demonstrate the limits of Catholic dissent or would they merely look the other way? If the hierarchy was not prepared to enforce compliance on the crucial subject of abortion, they felt, then the sky would be the limit for what Canadian Catholics could believe and do. The preliminary indications were that the issue would not be resolved to the satisfaction of Revivalists. Bishop Adolphe Proulx of Gatineau-Hull, the diocese where McTeer lives, informed the *Toronto Star* that he had merely requested a meeting of clarification with her.[72]

It is extremely unlikely that the bishops would force a show-down with members of the Canadian laity over the abortion issue. Such a show-down would potentially reveal that many, and perhaps most, Canadian Catholics have ceased to regard the institutional church as a source of absolute moral authority. Indeed, *Humanae Vitae* proved perhaps better than anything else that Canadian Catholics, far from looking to the hierarchy for moral directives, practise their religion as a private affair.[73] Any attempt by the Canadian hierarchy to make adherence to the traditional teaching against abortion a necessary condition of Catholic belonging would just as likely be greeted by lay indifference and thereby further amplify the diminished control exercised by the bishops over the Canadian church. In this regard, Canadian sociologist Kenneth Westhues is correct when he observes that 'the more Catholics have themselves become involved in mainstream Canadian political and economic life, the less they have relied on the church as their intermediary and the more willing they have become to reduce it to the status of a voluntary association.'[74]

The *denominationalization* of Canadian Catholicism, or its reduction to a voluntary association, has profound implications for the interrelationship of Canada's religious and political cultures. In the previous chapter it was argued that the politics of ecumenism have placed severe constraints upon the political involvement of the Canadian hierarchy in the abortion question. Even if this were not the case, however, it is doubtful that the bishops would be capable of shaping in any appreciable way political decisions concerning abortion or any other publicly debated moral issue. In past generations it was precisely its control over the laity which gave the hierarchy leverage with which to bargain with federal and provincial governments in Canada. But as today's Catholics take from their religion only what they freely choose, it seems improbable that the bishops, even if they so desired, would be able to influence behaviour in the voting booth. This altered situation is neatly summarized by Westhues: 'In the present day, therefore, the Catholic Church in Canada appears to have lost, for the most part, its principal resource in negotiations with its host society, namely its moral authority over Catholic people. Governments realize that bishops cannot deliver the votes of Catholic people, and church and state have grown more separate ... This fact constitutes a grave concern for the modern church, as it seeks new ways of regaining relevance to principal sectors of Canadian society.'[75]

The decline of both episcopal authority and a Catholic consensus on abortion was most evident in February 1985 when only a fraction of Toronto Catholics heeded Cardinal Carter's call to participate in protests against the Morgentaler clinic. Not only did Carter's action force the movement to play its major bluff card of a massive church-orchestrated campaign against elective abortion clinics, but it also showed decisively that Canadian Catholics would not automatically answer the call of the hierarchy on this or likely any other issue. Particularly telling to Revivalists were the hostile and indifferent reactions accorded the protests by, respectively, leaders of Canada's liberal Protestant churches and the celibate Catholic elite. If silence on abortion were the price of denominationalism and ecumenism, they insisted, then it would be better for the Canadian church to adjourn to a sectarian ghetto of belief and practice where Catholics could be Catholic without compromise and without embarrassment.

PRO-LIFE ACTIVISM AND PURSUIT OF THE SACRED

Movements of religious protest frequently arise out of circumstances of economic privation or political dispossession.[76] With its predominantly middle-class background, Revivalism is obviously not a compensation in the spiritual realm for disprivilege in the mundane. Rather, as its name implies, it represents a revitalization movement among Catholics who feel spiritually disinherited from the post-Vatican II church. In addition, it would be inaccurate to portray Revivalism unequivocally as an enterprise of nostalgia, as a pious hangover from the halcyon days of pre-Vatican II Catholicism. One of the striking findings of this research is that some of the most ardent Revivalists are Catholic converts, who know of Pius XII only by rumour, and also young people under the age of thirty who are, effectively, children of the post-conciliar era.

Sociologists of religion have often noted that periods of social upheaval prove fertile ground for the emergence of religious groups of an authoritarian, introversionist stamp.[77] Thus, utopian sects in nineteenth-century America and New Religious Movements of more recent vintage have attracted recruits by promising an island of certitude within a sea of swirling confusion. It is tempting, but not entirely accurate, to similarly view Revivalism as a *fuga saeculi*, as a totalistic religious refuge from an unsettling age. For unlike the classical world-renouncing sect, Revivalists are not content with a merely cloistered virtue. In anti-abortion protest, they have discovered an extroverted spiritual mission that dovetails perfectly with their ideology of cultural decline and theory of Catholic vocation.

Max Weber contrasts virtuoso religiosity with the prosaic, unmusical religiosity practised by the religious masses. The possession by religious elites of special faculties (*charismata*) – whether of a pneumatic, moral, intellectual, or esthetical quality – that are either unavailable to or are rejected by the mass of believers is the primary impulsion behind the formation of separatist sects, specialized conventicles, and monastic communities. Moreover, notes Weber, virtuoso-religion exists in a state of tension with the institutional church, which claims complete jurisdiction over the administration of grace and the ethical sufficiency of its members. By making claim to a higher and perhaps exclusive spiritual status, 'carriers' of virtuoso-religion challenge the monopolistic authority of the official church.[78]

Virtuoso-religion often arises from the conviction that the church is stricken with spiritual lassitude and over-accommodation to profane culture, and that a nucleus of the righteous bears the seeds for its regeneration. Donatism, with its enthusiasm for martyrdom at a time when persecution of Christians had subsided, and Jansenism, with its ardour for ascetic discipline at a time of supposed laxity, are examples of this impulsion toward *aficionado* religious commitment, of the quest to consecrate a small corner of the church and thereby separate the spiritual virtuosi from the religiously vulgar or indifferent.[79] Revivalism is a contemporary manifestation of this *aficionado* tradition; its ritual of perfection is not martyrdom, self-mortification, or even for the most part abstinence from physical pleasures, but rather political protest on behalf of unborn life.

The 'elective affinity' between Catholic Revivalism and pro-life activism may also be described using a somewhat different language. Turner and Killian have observed that 'every social movement is shaped in part by the demand for gratifications unrelated to the movement's stated objectives.'[80] Joseph Gusfield, in a similar vein, has argued that social movements generally consist of both an instrumental and a symbolic component. Gusfield's *dramatist* approach to the analysis of social movements is thus intended to call attention to the symbolic dimension in which 'the object referred to has a range of meaning beyond itself.'[81] The activism of Revivalist Catholics is incompletely understood without an appreciation of its symbolic meaning.

The first part of this chapter explored the belief system, or theoretical dimension, of Revivalism. But, as Durkheim has shown, moral communities or religious groups require a common activity that serves as the collective expression of group identity as well as a basic source of group cohesion. Thus, religious ceremonial is both an expression of the consciousness of community and also a means for sustaining it.[82] It is proposed here that anti-abortion activism is the definitive public ceremonial – the popular ritual expression – of Revivalist Catholicism in Canada. It is the chief means by which Revivalists, as a marginalized status group within Canadian Catholicism, sacralize their group identity and define the boundaries of their common faith commitment.[83]

As civil rights activists within the pro-life movement have often noted, the confrontational and sanctimonious style of protest with which Revivalists seem intensely scripted may actually be self-defeating at a strictly political or instrumental level. In terms of its identity-bestowing capacity, however, this style of protest does have expressive importance and has thus been retained by Revivalists despite its dubious instrumental value. Robert K. Merton's conceptual distinction of manifest and latent functions can further clarify this point. Merton has argued that behaviour which serves no manifest or obvious function may persist precisely because it serves a latent, unrecognized one.[84] Apart from its avowed purpose of curtailing abortion, 'public witness' performs for its participants the latent (for the most part unintended and unacknowledged) function of producing and consolidating a contracultural religious identity. 'Public witness,' in other words, is more than simply a political tactic. When Revivalists engage in acts of civil disobedience and public demonstration, they leave behind the prosaic course of everyday existence and enter instead a more dramatic and more glamorous one where the boundaries between good and evil seem clearly defined and where religious heroism may be demonstrated. Far from being daunted by negative publicity, the religious crusader interprets it as persecution and uses it to vanquish doubt and reinforce determination. Thus, the trials and tribulations of anti-abortion activism evoke for Revivalists distant echoes from a more spiritually robust generation when standard-bearers of truth, then clothed in Jesuit robes, defended the faith by an ordeal of martyrdom. Pro-life activism, in short, is the new spiritual *frontier*.

The classification of all things into the mutually exclusive categories of the sacred and the profane, according to Durkheim, is decisive to the religious enterprise. From a somewhat different perspective, Mircea

Eliade has written that the two primordial modalities of experience – the sacred and the profane – have been divided throughout history by an insuperable abyss.[85] Modernity, however, has had debilitating consequences for this cosmic bifurcation of reality. Following Weber's thesis of the progressive 'disenchantment of the world,' culminating in a fully desacralized social order orchestrated by utilitarian reason, classical secularization theory holds that the sacred in complex, industrialized society is consigned to oblivion or, at the very least, to cultural irrelevance.[86] Whether a completely religionless society – one devoid of eruptions of the sacred – can exist is doubtful. But to Revivalist Catholics, the sacred, if it has not been fully eclipsed, has been subject to a process of progressive disorientation. It has lost for them its quality of pristine separateness. Through the church's gradual adoption of the agenda of secular society, with its various political and economic desiderata, the sacred has forfeited its exclusive domain and become enmeshed in the total gamut of socio-cultural reality. It can be found everywhere and, paradoxically, nowhere. To Revivalist Catholics, this commingling of sacred and secular has rendered the former precarious and, even worse, ambiguous.

There is a dialectical relationship between sacral and personal identities. When people endow certain conceptions, emotional states, and symbols with ultimate meaning, they in turn derive from these an essential ingredient of individual and group identity. Consequently, the disfranchisement of the sacred, or its estrangement from familiar conceptual and symbolic repositories, has constituted a crisis of identity for some Catholics. It is by anti-abortion protest that Revivalists implicitly attempt to counteract the diffusion of ultimacy throughout the Secular City and to resolve the fragmented consciousness of contemporary Catholicism. Through pro-life activism Revivalists seek to claim some segment of experience and belief as definitively and inexorably *Catholic* and beyond the shuffle of everyday existence.

It is precisely because unborn life is valorized by them as a hierophany – an unimpeachable manifestation of ultimacy – that Revivalists have adopted an absolutist and uncompromising political style. In Weberian language, they are committed to an 'ethic of ultimate ends.' Whereas the political conduct of civil rights activists within the pro-life movement is governed by responsibility for foreseeable consequences, that of Revivalists is directed toward the demonstration of exemplary virtue and to preservation of the 'flame of pure intentions.'[87] It is a vehicle for the consecration of a renewed Catholic identity.

Conclusion

The sheer complexity of the Canadian pro-life movement means that it cannot be understood by resorting to simplistic generalization or monocausal interpretation. Far from being a solid phalanx, the movement is composed of competing factions which have managed at best to coexist in an uneasy peace. As the first systematic investigation of the movement, this study has sought to come to terms with this complexity, with the mixed and sundry motivations underlying anti-abortion activism, and with the internal conflicts which have punctuated the movement's history. Toward this end it has distinguished the main types of pro-life activism and analysed the different emergent norms which are their bases.

More noteworthy than the movement's polymorphism, however, is the internal discord which anti-abortion protest represents for Canadian Catholicism. Indeed, it is with this matter, the tensions posed by the movement for the Canadian Catholic church, that the present study has been primarily concerned.

From a telescopic view, the movement appears both to operate with the blessing, if not always explicit mandate, of the institutional church and also to be a vehicle of consensus for Canadian Catholics. A closer view, however, reveals a completely contrary picture. The movement can only be considered a metaphor of Catholic unity in either a superficial or a highly nuanced sense. In its current dispensation, the movement functions for many of its participants as a conventicle of lay dissent against processes of modernization and liberalization within the Canadian church. Indeed, anti-abortion activism is a symbolic line of fracture separating Canadian Catholics of radically opposed faith commitments. Ironically, therefore, the very issue which is customarily thought to provide a unifying cement for Catholics is the point at which divisions within the Canadian church most vividly present themselves.

Whereas many, perhaps most, Canadian Catholics are caught in the dilemma of abortion's cultural ambiguity, its sense of tragic unavoidability, a specialized segment of the Catholic community has made anti-abortion protest the litmus test of authentic faith. Pro-life activism, Revivalists assert, is not merely an optional piety, a vocational spice, but rather is a prerequisite of Catholic belonging. It is the shibboleth of orthodoxy at a time when most other parameters of Catholic distinctiveness seem either uncertain or to have dissolved altogether. In their adherence to absolute value in an age of widespread relativism, Revivalists regard themselves as unsung heroes whose virtue will be recognized and finally celebrated by future generations of the faithful.

Whereas Revivalists regard opposition to abortion as the touchstone of genuine faith, Canadian Catholic elites, including most bishops, priests, and nuns, treat the issue with a circumspection bordering on avoidance. Although Catholic elites are generally uncomfortable with the trend toward greater abortion freedom, the pro-life cause is beyond the pale of the progressive ecumenism to which they are committed. Moreover, anti-abortionism is anomalous to the *nouveau* orthodoxy, designated here as *Social Justice* Catholicism, which has gained pre-eminence within the Canadian church. The pro-life movement, accordingly, has become the special domain of lay Catholics who feel both betrayed and disparaged by the leadership and current theological direction of the Canadian church.

This study has thus taken the totemic Catholic issue of abortion to demonstrate the high degree of ideological disarray which currently exists within the Canadian Catholic church. Contemporary divisions within Canadian, and by extension American, Catholicism are less formalized organizationally than are those that define North American Judaism. They are, nevertheless, just as pronounced in the realms of belief, piety, and style of religious commitment. With a hierarchical and centralized government which claims absolute jurisdiction over the symbols and apparatus of redemption, Catholicism retains the appearance of internal coherence and essential unanimity. This appearance, however, is deceptive. Much like Judaism, though less widely recognized, North American Catholicism consists of separate streams of belief and practice. Although these streams may flow from a common source and be linked by occasional tributaries, they travel divergent courses and pursue quite different destinations.

The ideological split in the Canadian church is exemplified by the mutual enmity between Revivalist and Social Justice Catholics. By canalizing their religious passion, frustration, and ideals into anti-abortion activism, Revivalists have made the pro-life movement emblematic of this larger ideological conflict. Whereas Social Justice Catholics hesitate to challenge the cultural orthodoxy of the pro-choice ethic, Revivalists relish the contracultural implications of anti-abortion protest. Through it they express not only moral abhorrence of abortion, but also their desire for a revitalized Catholicism, one of defiant, unembarrassed conviction and clear-cut definition. Anti-abortion protest is the Revivalist remedy for an androgynized Catholicism which, in the Revivalist view, has become all things to all people while ceasing to be anything of critical significance in itself.

Although given special accent here, Revivalist Catholics are not of course the sum of the Canadian pro-life movement. Civil rights and Parish Catholic activists as well as conservative Protestants impart to the movement an ideological pluralism which will not likely be lost, and conceivably may be extended, in subsequent years. Indeed, as this study has shown, generational differences even within Revivalism make it difficult to forecast the movement's future ideological direction. Nor can the eventual political outcome of the Canadian abortion debate by predicted with certainty. The future shape of the movement will largely be determined by its own internal power struggles and the social environment in which they occur.

It seems obligatory, considering the controversial nature of the subject-matter, to conclude this work by reasserting its intellectual standpoint. As promised at the outset, the study has remained agnostic on the moral question of abortion. As a strictly empirical investigation of the Canadian pro-life movement, it has attempted neither to condemn nor to champion the movement's central moral belief. Nor has it indulged in speculation over the future cultural status of the pro-life position. Considering the fluctuating fortunes of other political causes throughout history, causes as varied as abolitionism, temperance, and feminism, it would be inappropriate to pass historical judgment on anti-abortionism from the limited vantage point of the present. The nature of the world in which our descendants live will determine whether pro-life activists are adjudged to be prophets unrecognized in their own time or merely misguided sentimentalists. This study has thus attempted, from the restricted horizon of a single scholar, merely to analyse an important social movement which has shown no indication of either tempering its moral convictions or surrendering its political goals.

Afterword

The present study has taken the reader almost to the eve of a historic event of profound bearing on the future of the Canadian abortion debate. On 28 January 1988 the Supreme Court of Canada upheld Dr Henry Morgentaler's 1984 Ontario jury acquittal and struck down as unconstitutional the country's 1969 abortion law. In its epochal judgment (*The Queen* v. *Morgentaler et al.*), the court ruled that a law forcing women to seek hospital permission for an abortion violates the Charter of Rights and Freedoms guarantee of a right to 'life, liberty, and the security of the person.' By one dramatic judicial stroke, therefore, abortion was taken out of the criminal code and recognized as a private matter between a woman and her physician.

While unmistakably a severe blow to anti-abortion activists, the Supreme Court judgment was not an unmixed triumph for pro-choice advocates. First, despite striking down the criminal code restrictions on access to abortion, the court left open the possibility for enactment of a new law which, while respecting the autonomy guaranteed women by the charter, would provide protection for the unborn at a stage of fetal development deemed appropriate by Parliament. The prospect of an impending legislative battle over the thorny question of fetal rights thus removed some of the lustre from pro-choice celebrations. And second, far from surrendering their cause in light of the Supreme Court decision, leading anti-abortion activists immediately served notice that they intended, using all available means, to intensify the protest against legalized abortion. Indeed, the irrepressibility of the anti-abortion movement, its defiant pledge to persevere in spite of any setback imaginable, signified that the Supreme Court ruling had profoundly changed the circumstances of, but almost certainly had not concluded, the Canadian battle over abortion.

It is not possible here to assess the political implications of the Supreme Court decision, or even fully to assess its early impact upon the anti-abortion movement. In keeping with the central theme of this study, the following brief discussion focuses rather more narrowly upon the repercussions of the decision for Canadian Catholicism.

The feelings of betrayal and outrage expressed widely within the Catholic community in the immediate aftermath of the Supreme Court ruling underscored more vividly than perhaps ever before the heavy investment of the Canadian church in the abortion issue. In a media release issued on 28 January 1988 G. Emmett Cardinal Carter, archbishop of Toronto, denounced the ruling as 'a disaster' and promised that the efforts of Canadian Catholics 'to protect the rights of the unborn [would] continue unabated.'[1] And one month later, in a letter addressed to Prime Minister Brian Mulroney and members of Parliament, Carter decried the 'state of lawlessness' arising from the court's ruling and demanded that the government begin drafting permanent legislation that would 'respect human life at all stages.' Catholics of good conscience, the cardinal wrote, would be satisfied only with a law which protected unborn life from the moment of conception onwards. Advertising that his letter had been endorsed by the Ontario Conference of Catholic Bishops and by leading anti-abortion groups across the country, and also that he had instructed it be read in all 208 parishes of the Toronto archdiocese, the cardinal warned that 'We are pledged to deploy our influence and all of our strength to obtain this result.'[2]

Equally resolute, though far gentler in approach, was the pastoral statement of April 1988 issued by James Hayes, archbishop of Halifax and president of the Canadian Conference of Catholic Bishops. In *Faithful to the Future*, Archbishop Hayes observed that the Supreme Court decision had presented Canadian Catholics simultaneously with 'a crisis and an opportunity.' 'It is now both necessary and possible,' he advised, 'to create new legislation which will recognize the right to life of the most voiceless and vulnerable in our society.' The archbishop insisted that increased acceptance of abortion bespeaks a moral failure of far-reaching proportion in Canadian society. 'The society which accepts abortion as a solution to present problems (whether personal or social),' he wrote, 'is also a society which abuses its children, lays waste the environment, risks nuclear war and implements economic policies in which the immediate benefits to some will be dearly paid for by many in the future.' In concluding his statement, the archbishop encouraged Catholics to share their 'faith in the future and [their] commitment to the unborn with the politicians of Canada and with all Canadians.'[3]

Accustomed as they were to fighting the issue alone, many veteran Catholic activists were unprepared for this windfall of episcopal support. The more cynical among them discounted it as mere posturing, and doubted that the bishops would actually be drawn into political confrontation over the Supreme Court ruling. In the wake of the controversy created by the ruling, they reasoned, it was virtually a ritual requirement that the bishops fly the pro-life flag.

Especially perplexing to Revivalist Catholic activists was the passionate response of Cardinal Carter. It was Carter after all who seven years earlier had incurred their wrath by endorsing the Charter of Rights and Freedoms despite its silence on the question of fetal rights. Now that the Supreme Court had struck down the 1969 abortion law on the ground that it violated the charter, it seemed to some Revivalist activists that the cardinal's display of indignation was merely an attempt to save face. There were, however, other Catholics in the movement who both welcomed and accepted the sincerity of Cardinal Carter's involvement, but even some of them doubted that it would bring more than a quite temporary and primarily symbolic benefit to the anti-abortion cause.

Of far greater significance than any episcopal statement was the impassioned reception accorded the Supreme Court decision by the *Catholic New Times*. As the principal literary organ of Canada's Progressive or Social Justice Catholics, the *New Times* had previously shown limited interest in both the abortion issue and the pro-life movement, and thus seemed an unlikely bet to rally to the movement's side at its latest hour of crisis. And yet in a powerful editorial published in February 1988, the *New Times* condemned the Supreme Court decision as a shameful betrayal of 'the most voiceless and powerless of all minorities.' Equally shameful, according to the editorial, was the 'lack of moral sensitivity' exhibited by pro-choice supporters in their unrestrained jubilation over the decision. And in a startling departure from its habitual ecumenism, the *New Times* upbraided the United Church of Canada for heartily endorsing the decision as 'the first step towards a truly just system of access for women who wish to make a responsible choice about abortion.' On the question of abortion, the editorial advised, '[We] must say, to our friends in the United Church, that divided we stand.'[4]

In a subsequent editorial, published in June 1988 and signed by all four members of the newspaper's editorial committee, the *New Times* admonished both those Catholics who had adopted 'a popular liberal position' on abortion and others whose customary silence on the issue perhaps reflected a greater commitment to tolerance than to justice. 'It would be disastrous, for our country and for our church,' the newspaper's readership was told, 'if the social virtue of tolerance [were] invoked to legitimate the decertification of the unborn as human beings.' Declaring its conviction that the church's teaching on abortion 'speaks with prophetic clarity in the midst of the murky morality of liberal capitalism,' the *New Times* exhorted its readers to align themselves with the pro-life movement. 'If we do not take a clear and determined stand on abortion now,' said the editorial, 'we will soon find that the ground for all our efforts at social justice will have disappeared from under our feet.' For far too long, it added, have Progressive Catholics used the obvious shortcomings of the pro-life movement as justification for remaining uninvolved in the fight against abortion. Despite its extremist tendencies, advised the editorial, the movement deserved the respect of all Catholics both for its 'passionate conviction' and for having 'borne [with courage] the political heat of the day on the issue of abortion.' Refusing to exempt even itself from the charge of complacency, the *New Times* confessed that 'Over the years ... we have not spoken strongly enough or often enough. We underestimated the political influence of the pro-choice lobby and overestimated the resources of the pro-life movement to carry the burden of this struggle. We also underestimated the moral plasticity of the consumer culture which was so easily reshaped after the decision to partially legalize abortion twenty years ago. It is more socially acceptable now to treat human beings as disposable commodities than it was twenty years ago. We were mistaken in our judgment.'[5]

This unprecedented appeal by the *New Times* for Catholic solidarity on the abortion issue seemed at first sight to augur a new era for the

Canadian pro-life movement. With its well-established reputation for social radicalism, the *New Times* offered the movement a voice strikingly different from that which it had for so long been dominated. Henceforward, if nothing else, the anti-abortion cause could not so readily or categorically be stigmatized as right-wing.

Early indications, however, suggest it improbable that the movement will be transformed as a result of the unexpected support given it by the *New Times*. So ingrained is their mistrust of the movement in general and of Revivalist Catholics in particular that Progressive Catholics have thus far been reluctant to heed the appeal of their newspaper for greater commitment to the anti-abortion cause. Those few who have heeded it have a presence within the movement neither sufficiently strong nor, in all likelihood, sufficiently durable to alter the movement's congenital conservatism. Survival itself will be challenge enough for them in a movement which has seldom in the past tolerated pluralism within its own ranks.

If the Supreme Court decision of January 1988 induced a momentary truce, traditional hostilities between Revivalist Catholic activists and their bishops resurfaced several months later in the course of debate over new Canadian abortion legislation. In May 1988 the federal government introduced a resolution which offered members of Parliament a choice of three options for a new abortion law. The first option or Amendment A would have prohibited abortion except when, in the opinion of two qualified medical practitioners, the mother's life or health would be endangered by continuation of the pregnancy; the second option or Amendment B would have allowed women virtually full freedom of choice; and Amendment C, the government's main option, would have permitted abortion in the unspecified early stages of pregnancy with certain restrictions in the later stages.

In a letter sent that June to members of Parliament in the name of the Canadian Conference of Catholic Bishops (CCCB), Archbishop James Hayes advised that all three options were 'objectionable from the standpoint of Catholic teaching' but that Amendment A was 'the least objectionable.' Although it was not a perfect solution, the archbishop suggested, Amendment A would at least impose significant restrictions on abortion and could therefore in good conscience be supported by Catholic legislators.[6] Almost immediately, the bishops drew heavy fire from the Revivalist Catholic wing of the pro-life movement. In a news release Campaign Life Coalition (CLC)[7] denounced the CCCB's position as a 'betrayal of both nation and church.' Instead of demanding full legal protection for the unborn, CLC president Jim Hughes said the bishops had given their blessing to a proposed law that almost certainly would be more lenient than the erstwhile 1969 law. Once again, in the view of Revivalist Catholic activists, had their bishops demonstrated an unwillingness to take an unequivocal stand on behalf of unborn life.[8]

As it turned out, the federal government's main resolution or option C and various amendments to it were voted on and defeated by the House of Commons on 28 July 1988; the question of a new abortion law remained unresolved.[9] But the stage had been set for yet another battle over abortion within Canadian Catholicism. Despite their continued displeasure with the Supreme Court decision, it seems doubtful that the bishops would campaign for an outright ban on abortion. Not only would such a campaign stand little prospect of political success, but it would seriously jeopardize the ideals of ecumenism and democratic pluralism which the CCCB has for so long been concerned to foster. A far more likely scenario, and one in fact already indicated by the CCCB's guarded endorsement of Amendment A, is that the bishops would be satisfied with a compromise law which placed some limitations on abortion and provided at least ostensible safeguards for the fetus. Much like the defunct 1969 law, such a compromise solution would reflect enough of the Catholic viewpoint on abortion to be at least palatable. Moreover, public opinion polls conducted since the Supreme Court decision reveal that a majority of Canadians continue to support some restrictions on abortion.[10] It would therefore be possible for the bishops to push for a compromise law without communicating the impression that they aspired to impose a peculiarly Catholic morality upon the wider society. For Catholic Revivalists within the pro-life movement, however, abortion remains an issue which transcends considerations of either political feasibility or popular taste. They will be satisfied with nothing less from their bishops than an implacable crusade for legislation outlawing abortion. There seems little doubt, therefore, that the abortion issue, famous enough for producing deep societal fissions, will remain a source of internal dissension for Canadian Catholicism.

On the broader national scene, the issue has retained a high public profile since the Supreme Court decision of January 1988. Although pleased that the ensuing year-and-a-half of debate had not resulted in a new law, pro-choice advocates still complained that accessibility to abortion services remained restricted in certain regions of the country.[11] Pro-life supporters, for their part, earned headlines for conducting massive demonstrations against abortion clinics in Toronto and Vancouver.[12] And in March 1989, the Supreme Court of Canada once again captured the national spotlight, this time for refusing to rule on a constitutional challenge which argued that the fetus is a person with legal rights.[13] It would seem that in some respects the Canadian debate over abortion has only just begun.

Research Appendix

As initially conceived, this study was intended to be a sociological examination of the conflict between the Canadian pro-life and pro-choice movements. Preliminary interviews with pro-life activists, however, suggested that the internal tensions posed by the pro-life movement for Canadian Catholicism represented a story significant enough to be told in its own right. Accordingly, it was decided to focus almost entirely upon the pro-life movement and especially upon its specifically Catholic aspects.

Formal interviewing for the project was undertaken during a twelve-month period beginning in February 1985 when public furore over Toronto's Morgentaler clinic was at its highest level. Since the study sought to understand the pro-life movement in historical perspective, interviews were conducted with activists whose various peaks of activism spanned the movement's roughly twenty years of existence. The selection procedure for interviewing may be described as partly random and partly strategic. Most sample subjects were asked to participate in the project simply on the basis of their ready availability on the picket line, in the Campaign Life offices, or in other spheres of movement activity. Other subjects, however, were specifically targeted and sought out for interviews, either because they were recommended through movement channels as ideal candidates for participation in the project or because they had once played prominent roles but were no longer as active in the movement.

The author introduced himself to prospective interviewees as a doctoral candidate from the University of Toronto involved in a major research project on the Canadian pro-life movement. Almost all subjects seemed impressed by the author's reassurance that the project would be written in the interests of fairness and objectivity. Only one person declined a request for an interview. Anonymity and confidentiality were promised to all interviewees.

The interviews themselves varied in length from one to two-and-a-half hours and were held either at movement locales, restaurants, or the residences of subjects. Only once, with a married couple, did interviews involve more than one subject. Given the *qualitative*[1] direction of the project, with emphasis upon empathic understanding rather than replicability, interviews were semi-scheduled, relatively open-ended, and designed to minimize the inhibitions of respondents.[2] All interviews did, however, elicit responses to the following prescribed themes:

1 Biographic and demographic information.
2 Activism profile (organizational affiliations, level of commitment to the movement).
3 Moral career (that is, both predisposing and precipitating conditions for joining the movement).
4 Personal authority and public strategy (that is, private legitimations for holding the anti-abortion position and preferred strategy for public presentation of this position).
5 Future prospects (that is, political hopes, aspirations, and goals).
6 Attitudes toward contemporary popular culture in Canada.
7 Religiosity (beliefs, practices, affiliations).

Interviews with the availability sample of one hundred and eleven pro-life subjects provided the empirical basis for the activist typology which was elaborated in Chapter Four. In addition, the author conducted ten further interviews with people not included in the availability sample for the specific purpose of reconstructing the movement's history. The private files and archival materials which several of these subjects made available to the author greatly facilitated the writing of the first three chapters.

In 1986 and 1987 the author conducted further interviews with an availability sample of twenty-five Progressive, or Social Justice, Catholics for the purpose of clarifying the relationship of this new Catholic orthodoxy to the abortion issue and the pro-life movement. These respondents were likewise promised confidentiality and anonymity.

For purposes of more general analysis, interviews were also conducted with an assortment of individuals unaffiliated with either the pro-life movement or with Social Justice Catholicism. Because these correspondents were similarly guaranteed anonymity, quotations taken from these interviews for this study are necessarily unattributed.

Throughout the two years of research for the project, the author also performed content analysis of movement literature. In addition to works listed in the bibliography, literature analysed included what may be described as movement ephemera, a congeries of fugitive sources such as pamphlets, broadsheets, newsletters, magazines, and demonstration sheets.

The author, furthermore, undertook approximately one hundred and twenty hours of participant observation at a spectrum of movement functions and activities.[3] The author's identity and research intentions were by this point generally known throughout movement circles, and thus participant observation was not performed on a covert basis.[4]

The concentration of research in the Toronto area gives this study a decidedly regional flavour. This is not necessarily, however, an admission of parochialism. Toronto is in many respects a microcosm of the larger movement and, by most criteria, the epicentre of anti-abortionism in Canada. In order to test the broader applicability of this study's research findings, the author attended the Fourteenth Annual Alliance for Life Conference (Lethbridge, 2–4 July 1986). Participant observation and interviewing conducted there revealed lines of intra-movement division strikingly similar to those discovered in Toronto.

The author, furthermore, attended the 1986 National Right to Life Convention (Denver, 12–14 June) for the purpose of assessing points of similarity and difference between the Canadian and American pro-life movements. The comparative discussion undertaken in Chapter Three is largely the fruit of this research.

In short, the research strategy of this study falls within the familiar boundaries of the type of field research most commonly identified with the 'Chicago school' of sociology.[5]

Notes

INTRODUCTION

1 For a useful bibliography of theological literature on abortion, see Maureen Muldoon, *Abortion: An Annotated Indexed Bibliography* (New York: E. Mellen Press 1980). See also June O'Connor, 'The Debate Continues: Recent Works on Abortion,' *Religious Studies Review* 11, 2 (1985): 105–14. For a comprehensive listing, up to and including 1984, of studies in the sociology of religion on the abortion issue, see Anthony J. Blasi and Michael W. Cuneo, *Issues in the Sociology of Religion: A Bibliography* (New York and London: Garland Publishing, Inc. 1986), 17–21.

2 See Max Weber, 'Science as a Vocation,' in H.H. Gerth and C. Wright Mills, eds., *From Max Weber: Essays in Sociology* (New York: Oxford University Press 1980), 129–56; and Max Weber, 'The Meaning of "Ethical Neutrality" in Sociology and Economics,' in E.A. Shils and H.A. Finch, eds., *The Methodology of the Social Sciences* (New York: The Free Press 1949), 1–47.

3 William Walker, 'Supreme Court Decision Backs Morgentaler: Up to MPs Whether to Try New Approach on Abortion,' *Toronto Star* 29 January 1988: A1, A4

4 *Roman Catholicism: The Search for Relevance* (Oxford: Basil Blackwell 1980), 239

CHAPTER ONE

1 For a valuable historical resource on the controversy over abortion in

Canada, see Carol Mazur and Sheila Pepper, *Women in Canada: A Bibliography, 1965–1982* (Toronto: OISE Press 1984), 1–5.

2 For a more complete discussion of the 1969 abortion law, see Diana Dimmer and Loreta Zubas, 'Update on the Abortion Law in Canada,' paper prepared for the National Association of Women and the Law, Ottawa, August 1985.

3 *Criminal Code, Revised Statutes of Canada*, 1970, Chapter C–34, Section 251

4 An overview of the parliamentary debate preceding passage of the 1969 abortion law may be found in Alphonse de Valk, *Morality and Law in Canadian Politics: The Abortion Controversy* (Montreal: Palm Publishers 1974), 99–126.

5 *Hansard*, 6 May 1969, p. 8397

6 See, for example, Sue Hierlihy, 'Ottawa Inquest Exposes Rubber-Stamp Abortions,' *The Interim* 4, 4 (June 1986): 3.

7 See John T. Noonan, Jr, *A Private Choice: Abortion in America in the Seventies* (New York: The Free Press 1979).

8 See Colin Francome, *Abortion Freedom: A Worldwide Movement* (Boston: George Allen & Unwin 1984).

9 David Andrusko, ed., *To Rescue the Future: The Pro-Life Movement in the 1980s* (Toronto: Life Cycle Books 1983), v. On this theme from an American perspective, see C. Everett Koop and Francis A. Schaeffer, *Whatever Happened to the Human Race?* (Westchester, Ill.: Crossway Books 1983).

10 For a feminist critique of the 1969 law, see Sharon Walls, 'Abortion and Improved Abortion Services,' unpublished discussion paper for the Victoria Caucus of Women and the Law, September 1982. For a more general feminist perspective, see Beverly Wildung Harrison, *Our Right to Choose: Toward a New Ethic of Abortion* (Boston: Beacon Press 1983).

11 De Valk, *Morality and Law in Canadian Politics*, 51

12 (Berkeley: University of California Press 1984). For a different estimation of American anti-abortion activists, see James R. Kelly, 'Beyond the Stereotypes: Interviews with Right-to-Life Pioneers,' *Commonweal*, 20 November 1981: 654–9.

13 Canadian pro-life groups historically have operated with shoe-string financing. In 1977–8 the Coalition for the Protection of Human Life survived on a twelve-month budget of $62,750. (Coalition *Budget* –

1 June 1977–31 May 1978.) On the financial independence of the movement from the institutional Catholic church, see Anne Collins, *The Big Evasion: Abortion, the Issue That Won't Go Away* (Toronto: Lester & Orpen Dennys 1985), 41, 262.

14 See, for example, Connie Paige, *The Right to Lifers: Who They Are, How They Operate, Where They Get Their Money* (New York: Summit Books 1983), 75.

15 On this point, the author acknowledges indebtedness to staff officers of the Canadian Conference of Catholic Bishops, interviewed in Ottawa on 18 September 1986.

16 Alphonse de Valk, *The Worst Law Ever* (Edmonton: Life Ethics Centre 1979), 8

17 James R. Kelly, 'Towards Complexity: The Right to Life Movement,' unpublished paper, 1986, p. 25. See also F.S. Jaffe, B.L. Lindheim, and P.R. Lee, *Abortion Politics: Private Morality and Public Policy* (New York: McGraw-Hill 1981), 73–85.

18 *Pro-Life News Canada*, published in Winnipeg, Manitoba, had a 1985 circulation of about forty thousand. The Alliance also publishes a French-language newsletter, *Actualité Vie.*

19 *The Story of Birthright: The Alternative to Abortion* (Libertyville, Ill.: Prow Books 1973), 5

20 Ibid., 108–13

21 The individual referred to is Ian Gentles. See Eugene R. Fairweather and Ian Gentles, eds., *The Right to Birth* (Toronto: Anglican Book Centre 1976).

22 Tension between local or regional groups and the national office was a prominent feature of the Fourteenth Annual Alliance for Life Conference (Lethbridge, 2–4 July 1986), which the author attended as a participant-observer.

23 This quotation is taken from *The Uncertified Human* masthead.

24 See James D. Hunter, 'Operationalizing Evangelicalism: A Review, Critique, and Proposal,' *Sociological Analysis* 42 (1981): 363–72.

25 All of these conservative Protestant groups have produced like-minded statements against abortion. For a typical example, see the Pentecostal Assemblies of Canada Position Paper, *The Christian Alternative to Abortion* (Toronto 1984).

26 See John H. Simpson and Henry MacLeod, 'The Politics of Morality in

Canada,' in R. Stark, ed., *Religious Movements: Genesis, Exodus, and Numbers* (New York: Paragon House 1985), 224–6.

27 S.D. Clark, 'The Religious Sect in Canadian Politics,' in *The Developing Canadian Community* (Toronto: University of Toronto Press 1968), 144

28 See, for example, Bruce Alton, ed., *The Abortion Question* (Toronto: Anglican Book Centre 1983); Phyllis Creighton, ed., *Abortion, An Issue for Conscience* (Toronto: The Anglican Church of Canada 1974); Ruth Evans, ed., *Abortion: A Study* (Toronto: United Church of Canada 1971); and the United Church of Canada, *Report of the Commission on Abortion to the Twenty-Eighth General Council*, 11 February 1980.

29 *Report of the Committee on the Operation of the Abortion Law* (Ministry of Supply and Services 1977): 211–12. This document is often referred to as the Badgley Committee Report.

30 Ibid., 287

31 Coalition for the Protection of Human Life, *A Brief to the Ontario Legislature* (first draft), October 1977: 3

32 Ibid., 4–5

33 Coalition for the Protection of Human Life, *A Brief to the Ontario Legislature* (second draft), November 1977: 4, 1; Letter from Coalition Executive to All Registered Lobbyists and Presidents of All Pro-Life Groups in Ontario, 3 November 1977

34 Ibid., 4a

35 Ibid., 8

36 Letter from Rev Brad H. Massman to Ms Margaret Turner, Coalition for Life, 28 November 1977

37 Coalition for Life, *National Newsletter* 4, 1 (January 1978): 1–2

38 Letter from Thomas J. Keating (State Deputy, Knights of Columbus, Ontario State Council) to Executive Committee, Coalition for Life, 13 December 1977

39 A. Romaniuc, *Fertility in Canada: From Baby-boom to Baby-bust* (Ottawa: Ministry of Supply and Services 1984), 52

40 Ibid., 52–3. See also M. Boyd and D. Gillieson, 'Canadian Attitudes on Abortion: Results of the Gallup Polls,' *Canadian Studies in Population* 2 (1975): 63.

41 Karl Mannheim, *Ideology and Utopia*, translated by Louis Wirth and Edward Shils (New York and London: Harcourt Brace Jovanovich 1936), 274–6

42 This term appeared several times in the correspondence generated by

the 1977 Coalition brief.

43 This phrase was coined by William I. Thomas and Dorothy S. Thomas in *The Child in America: Behavior Problems and Programs* (New York: Knopf 1928), 572.

44 Neil J. Smelser, *Theory of Collective Behavior* (New York: The Free Press 1962), 270–381

45 Orrin E. Klapp, *Collective Search For Identity* (New York: Holt, Rinehart and Winston 1969), 274

46 'Campaign Charted to Identify Pro-Life Election Candidates,' *Western Catholic Reporter* 13, 13 (November 28, 1977); 'Abortion Foes Hatching Political Blitz,' *Edmonton Journal*, 24 November 1977, C6

47 Coalition for Life, *Minutes of Executive Meeting*, 28 April 1978

48 Coalition for Life, *President's Report*, Fifth Annual General Meeting (Winnipeg, Manitoba), 26 May 1978

49 James R. Kelly, 'Towards Complexity: The Right to Life Movement,' 18

CHAPTER TWO

1 See *Minutes of Proceedings and Evidence*. Standing Committee of Health and Welfare, House of Commons, first session; twenty-seventh Parliament 1966. For a more extended treatment of some of the matters raised in this chapter, see Michael W. Cuneo, 'Keepers of the Faith: Lay Militants, Abortion, and the Battle for Canadian Catholicism,' in Roger O'Toole, ed., *Sociological Studies of Roman Catholicism* (New York: Edwin Mellen Press 1989), 146–62.

2 This brief is included in the booklet entitled *Contraception, Divorce, Abortion: Three Statements by Canadian Catholic Conference* (Ottawa: Canadian Catholic Conference 1968), 12–19.

3 Ibid., 17

4 Ibid., 6

5 Ibid., 6

6 Ibid., 15

7 Ibid., 15

8 Ibid., 15. For the quotation from the *Decree on the Apostolate of the Laity*, see Walter M. Abbott, SJ, ed., *The Documents of Vatican II* (New York: The American Press 1966), 498.

9 Ibid., 14, 16

10 Ibid., 16

11 Ibid., 17
12 Alphonse de Valk, 'Understandable but Mistaken: Law, Morality and the Catholic Church in Canada, 1966–1969,' *Canadian Catholic Historical Association, Study Sessions* 49 (1982): 102
13 Canadian Catholic Conference, *Contraception, Divorce, Abortion*, 18
14 Ibid., 23
15 Ibid., 22
16 'Delay in Reforms Urged – R.C. Bishops Preparing Fight on Abortion,' *Globe and Mail*, 7 April 1967, 1
17 'Religion and the Quest for a National Identity: The Background in Canadian History,' in Peter Slater, ed., *Religion and Culture in Canada/Religion et Culture au Canada* (Canadian Corporation for Studies in Religion 1977), 18
18 'Religion and Canada: A Historical Perspective,' paper presented to the Canadian Society for the Study of Religion, 1973; cited in Roger O'Toole, 'Some Good Purpose: Notes on Religion and Political Culture in Canada,' *Annual Review of the Social Sciences of Religion* 6 (1982): 181
19 Quoted in Reginald Whitaker, 'Reason, Passion and Interest: Pierre Trudeau's Eternal Liberal Triangle,' *Canadian Journal of Political and Social Theory* 4, 1 (1980): 5–31
20 A.M. Greeley, *The Denominational Society* (Glenview, Ill.: Scott, Foresman 1972), 1
21 John Webster Grant, *The Church in the Canadian Era* (Toronto: McGraw-Hill Ryerson 1972), 160–83
22 See N. Keith Clifford, 'His Dominion: A Vision in Crisis,' in Slater, ed., *Religion and Culture*, 24–41.
23 De Valk, 'Understandable but Mistaken,' 88
24 See the editorial 'Recipe for Workable Laws' (14 October 1966).
25 'Now the Job Is to be Done, Let it be Done Right' (21 December 1967)
26 Editorial, 'A Clear Distinction' (April 1968)
27 For a detailed report of the Catholic bishops' role in this debate, see Alphonse de Valk, *Morality and Law in Canadian Politics: The Abortion Controversy* (Montreal: Palm Publishers 1974), 61–6.
28 Canadian Catholic Conference, *Contraception, Divorce, Abortion*, 26–7. The Vatican II reference to abortion is from the *Pastoral Constitution on the Church in the Modern World*, Article 51. See Abbott, ed., *The Documents of Vatican II*, 256.

29 CCC, *Contraception, Divorce, Abortion*, 27
30 Ibid., 29
31 De Valk, *Morality and Law in Canadian Politics*, 73
32 Ibid., 77
33 Ibid., 80
34 Ibid., 82
35 De Valk, 'Understandable but Mistaken,' 107
36 Ibid., 107–8
37 Ibid., 108
38 Abbott, ed., *The Documents of Vatican II*, 287–8. Staff officers of the Canadian Conference of Catholic Bishops advised the author that this passage from *Gaudium et Spes* was a main guideline for the bishops in their political deliberations during the 1960s (Interview, Ottawa, 18 September 1986).
39 See Abbott, ed., *The Documents of Vatican II*, 672–96.
40 Alphonse de Valk, *Abortion: Christianity, Reason and Human Rights* (Edmonton: Life Ethics Centre 1982), 2
41 De Valk, *Morality and Law in Canadian Politics*, 84
42 Canadian Catholic Conference, *Statement Reaffirming CCC Position on Abortion*, Issued by the Executive Committee in the Name of the Administrative Board (Ottawa, 5 December 1968), 2
43 Canadian Catholic Conference, *Statement on Abortion*, Plenary Assembly (Ottawa, 9 October 1970), 1
44 On the negative reaction within the Canadian church to *Humanae Vitae*, see Anne Roche Muggeridge, *The Desolate City: The Catholic Church in Ruins* (Toronto: McClelland and Stewart 1986), 96–7.
45 Ibid., 98
46 See, for example, Vincent N. Foy, *A Commentary on the Canadian Bishops' Statement on the Encyclical Humanae Vitae* (Toronto 1968).
47 See Roche Muggeridge, *The Desolate City*, 98–9; and the editorial 'We Are a Truly Canadian Church,' Canadian *Catholic Register* (5 October 1968).
48 Alphonse de Valk, 'Our Bishops on Humane Vitae,' *The Interim* 4, 6 (September 1986): 12
49 Canadian Catholic Conference, *Statement on the Formation of Conscience* (Ottawa, 1 December 1973), 6, 12
50 Donald DeMarco, *The Contraceptive Mentality* (Edmonton: Life Ethics Centre 1982), 3

51 Ibid., 9
52 Joseph Boyle, 'Contraception and Natural Family Planning,' *International Review of Natural Family Planning* 4, 4 (1980): 311–12
53 DeMarco, *The Contraceptive Mentality*, 6
54 Ibid., 12
55 The intra-uterine device (IUD) is universally deplored by movement participants, on the ground that it is an abortifacient and may thus cause the death of a very young embryo.
56 The main North American missionary for the 'contraceptive mentality' thesis is Fr Paul Marx, founder and president of the Washington-based lobbying organization Human Life International. *HLI Reports*, the organization's principal informational organ, is published seventeen times annually and is familiar to many Canadian Catholic activists. The Canadian office of Human Life International is located in Laval, Quebec. See Paul Marx, *The Death Peddlers: War on the Unborn* (Collegeville, Minn.: Saint John's University Press 1971).
57 De Valk, 'Understandable but Mistaken,' 107
58 Alphonse de Valk, *The Worst Law Ever* (Edmonton: Life Ethics Centre 1979), 14

CHAPTER THREE

1 See Erving Goffman, *Presentation of Self in Everyday Life* (Garden City, NY: Anchor 1959).
2 For the distinction between *expressive* and *instrumental* behaviour in social movements, see R.E. Park and E.W. Burgess, *Introduction to the Science of Sociology* (Chicago: University of Chicago Press 1924), 870–4.
3 The movement's most controversial tactic at the turn of the decade was its campaign to win membership control over hospital administrative boards.
4 A. Romaniuc, *Fertility in Canada: From Baby-boom to Baby-bust* (Ottawa: Ministry of Supply and Services 1984), 53
5 See, for example, Campaign Life's *Election Issue '78 – The Protection of Unborn Children in Canada* (A Pro-Life Presentation to Candidates Seeking Election to the House of Commons; Toronto 1978).
6 By the late 1970s Campaign Life strategists were talking seriously of forming an independent political party. The short-lived Pro-Life Party of Canada, founded in early 1983, was the first step in this direction.

See Kathleen Toth, 'A Message from the President,' *The Interim* 1, 1 (March 1983): 5.

7 As examples of the kind of 'educational material' favoured by the movement, see Nick Thimmesch, *When Abortion Fails: The Unborn's Uncertain Destiny* (Toronto: Life Cycle Books n.d.); and *Life or Death* (Cincinnati: Hayes Publishing Co. n.d.).

8 Alphonse de Valk, *Abortion Politics: Canadian Style* (Edmonton: Life Ethics Centre 1982), 7–8

9 There were, however, dissenters from this strategy. On Joe Borowski, the most prominent of these, see Anne Collins, *The Big Evasion: Abortion, the Issue That Won't Go Away* (Toronto: Lester & Orpen Dennys 1985), 1–12.

10 On the secularization of Canadian public life, see John Webster Grant, 'Religion and the Quest for a National Identity: The Background in Canadian History,' in Peter Slater, ed., *Religion and Culture in Canada/Religion et Culture au Canada* (Canadian Corporation for Studies in Religion 1977), 18–20.

11 Mary Meehan, *Commonweal*, 20 November 1981: 650; cited in Alphonse de Valk, *Abortion: Christianity, Reason and Human Rights* (Edmonton: Life Ethics Centre 1982), 3

12 The author attended a public debate at which the pro-life spokeswoman's attempt to introduce pictorial evidence of fetal development was greeted with derision by most of the audience. (Debate between Dr Henry Morgentaler and Gwen Landolt, Erindale College, Mississauga, Ontario, 1 April 1985)

13 Max Weber, 'Science as a Vocation,' in H.H. Gerth and C. Wright Mills, eds., *From Max Weber: Essays in Sociology* (New York: Oxford University Press 1980), 143

14 For parallel intra-movement conflicts in the United States, see James R. Kelly, 'Towards Complexity: The Right to Life Movement,' unpublished paper, 1986, 21.

15 Bernard N. Nathanson, 'Deeper into Abortion,' *New England Journal of Medicine* 291 (28 November 1974): 1189

16 B.N. Nathanson (with Richard N. Ostling), *Aborting America* (Garden City, NY: Doubleday 1979), 187–217; and B.N. Nathanson, *The Abortion Papers* (New York: Frederick Fell 1983), 177–209

17 C. Gwendolyn Landolt, 'The Borowski Case – (What's It All About),' *The Interim* 1, 3 (May 1983): 1, 3

18 'Lunatic Spectacle in Regina,' *Toronto Star*, 12 May 1983
19 The remainder of this chapter attempts to analyse the pro-life movement in Toronto by the concentrated ethnographic method which Geertz, borrowing a term from Gilbert Ryle, calls 'thick description.' See Clifford Geertz, 'Thick Description: Toward an Interpretive Theory of Culture,' in *The Interpretation of Cultures* (New York: Basic Books 1973), 3–30. For a historian's defence of such an approach, see Lawrence Stone, *The Past and the Present* (Boston: Routledge & Kegan Paul 1981), 86.
20 Patricia Horsford, *Globe and Mail*, 12 March 1981
21 Campaign Life, 'Canada in Crisis,' Canadian *Catholic Register*, Election Supplement, 14 March 1981. Section 15(1) of the proposed Charter of Rights and Freedoms promised to forbid 'discrimination based on race, national or ethnic origin, colour, sex, age or disability.' This *equality guarantee* became law on 17 April 1985. See Carol Goar, 'Few Governments Ready to Guarantee Equality as Charter Takes Force,' *Toronto Star*, 16 April 1985, A1, A5.
22 Letter from Fr Brad H. Massman, Director of Office of Communications (Archdiocese of Toronto), to Archdiocesan Priests, 30 March 1981
23 Letter to the Editor, *Globe and Mail*, 25 April 1981
24 Gwen Smith, 'Priests Told to Eschew Literature: Pro-Lifers Bitter over Carter Order on Militant Group,' *Globe and Mail*, 30 April 1981, 1, 2
25 Ibid. See also Claire Hoy, 'He Wants to Have it Both Ways,' *Toronto Sun*, 29 April 1981: 8. Writing in the liberal *Catholic New Times*, Janet Somerville suggested that Carter's disciplining of Campaign Life was both justified and overdue. See 'Split over Cardinal's Support for Charter of Rights,' 26 April 1981: 11.
26 On the funding of Ontario Separate Schools question, see Claire Hoy, *Bill Davis* (Toronto: Methuen 1985), 264–76.
27 G. Emmett Cardinal Carter, 'Charter of Rights' (4 April 1981)
28 *Toronto Star*, 11 April 1981
29 G. Emmett Cardinal Carter, 'Cardinal Carter Issues Clarifying Statement,' *Globe and Mail*, 29 April 1981
30 'Anti-Abortionists Write Pope to Condemn Carter,' *Toronto Star*, 30 April 1981, 1, 7
31 Letter from Campaign Life (signed by members of the Toronto and national executives) to His Holiness John Paul II (Vatican City, Europe), 12 May 1981

32 Ibid.
33 Memorandum from G. Emmett Cardinal Carter to Fr Brad Massman, Archdiocesan Director of Communications, 22 April 1981
34 Letter from Fr E. Colleton (Campaign Life) to Dr John Sullivan, 2 June 1981
35 See *Hansard*, House of Commons Debates, 7 April 1981. When asked in Parliament if the proposed charter would be prejudicial to the rights of the unborn, Mr Jean Chretien (Minister of Justice) quoted Cardinal Carter's 4 April statement on the charter and said, 'I am sure this statement from His Excellency will go a long way in assuring ... that the opinion of the government is well founded and consistent.'
36 Letter from Campaign Life (Mr Jim Hughes, Chairman, CL Toronto and Area; Mr Paul Dodds, Chairman, CL Ontario; Mrs Kathleen Toth, President, CL Canada) to the Catholic Bishops of Canada, 20 May 1981
37 Ibid. In late May 1981 the Canadian Conference of Catholic Bishops did unsuccessfully petition Prime Minister Trudeau for inclusion of a clause which would guarantee the charter's neutrality on the rights of the unborn. The Ontario Conference of Catholic Bishops made a similar request in a brief delivered to the Special Joint Committee on the Constitution. In the view of Campaign Life, however, this show of concern was merely cosmetic. See *Information*, Bulletin of the Canadian Conference of Catholic Bishops, #OPI–234, 28 May 1981; and Earl Amyotte, 'Charter No Help to Unborn,' *The Interim* 1, 1 (March 1983): 4.
38 See, for example, Alphonse de Valk, 'Abortion Politics Canadian Style,' in Paul Sachdev, ed., *Abortion Readings and Research* (Toronto: Butterworth 1981), 5–15.
39 See J.T. Noonan, Jr, *A Private Choice* (New York: The Free Press 1979).
40 See Tom Sinclair-Faulkner, 'Canadian Catholics: At Odds on Abortion,' *The Christian Century*, 9 September 1981, 870.
41 In the 1985 Ontario provincial election campaign, for example, Campaign Life found very few candidates willing publicly to espouse the anti-abortion position. See, for example, Trish Crawford, 'Morgentaler's Clinic Fuels Abortion Issue: All Three Leaders Back Improved Access to Abortion – Delighting Pro-Choice Forces but Dismaying Pro-Life Lobby,' *Toronto Star*, 11 April 1985, A19.
42 For a competent account of Morgentaler's legal odyssey, see the National Film Board documentary, *Democracy on Trial: The Morgentaler*

Affair. See also Eleanor Pelrine, *Morgentaler: The Doctor Who Couldn't Turn Away* (Toronto: Gage 1975).

43 These phrases were used by Dr Morgentaler at a public debate attended by the author (Erindale College, 1 April 1985).

44 In April 1985 the Ontario Court of Appeal overturned the jury acquittal and ordered a retrial on Morgentaler's first charges. In 1986 Morgentaler appealed this decision to the Supreme Court of Canada. On 28 January 1988 the Supreme Court upheld Morgentaler's 1984 acquittal, ruling that Canada's 1969 abortion law is unconstitutional because it violates the charter guarantee of a right to 'life, liberty and the security of the person.' See 'Step-by-Step History of Morgentaler Fight,' *Toronto Star*, 29 January 1988, A12.

45 Michael McAteer, 'Carter Urges Faithful to Join Abortion Protest,' *Toronto Star*, 12 February 1985, A6

46 Stanley Oziewicz, 'Carter Supports Protest Against Abortion Clinic: Cardinal's Action Draws Ire,' *Globe and Mail*, 12 February 1985, 1, 2

47 'Futile Protest,' *Toronto Star*, 13 February 1985, A20

48 Pat McNenly, 'Metro Churches Split on Abortion Protest,' *Toronto Star*, 18 February 1985, A14

49 Stanley Oziewicz, 'Don't Push own Abortion Beliefs, Rabbis Urge,' *Globe and Mail*, 21 February 1985, M4

50 Brian McAndrew, 'Pro-Life Group Gears Up for Mass Protest,' *Toronto Star*, 16 February 1985, A6

51 Pro-Life Action Committee (Advertisement), 'Citizens of Ontario,' *Globe and Mail*, 14 February 1985, 10

52 Dana Flavelle, 'Morgentaler Backers to Hold Rally on Friday,' *Toronto Star*, 17 February 1985, A3

53 Linda Barnard, 'Prayers Ring Out to End Abortions,' *Toronto Sun*, 18 February 1985, 4

54 Paul Bilodeau, 'Pro-Life Activists Parade at Morgentaler Clinic,' *Toronto Star*, 19 February 1985, A7; and Murray Campbell, '300 Rally at Morgentaler Clinic to Start Week of Demonstrations,' *Globe and Mail*, 19 February 1985, M5. The description of the February 1985 protests is based entirely on the author's personal field notes.

55 Michele Mandel, 'Anti-Abortion Protest Grows,' *Toronto Sun*, 20 February 1985, 14; Kathy English, 'Ranks of Protesters Grow Outside Abortion Clinic,' *Toronto Star*, 20 February 1985, A12

56 Kathy English, 'Pro-Life Rally Gains Strength as 900 Protest,' *Toronto Star*, 21 February 1985, A6; and Murray Campbell, 'Students from Separate Schools Give Protest Air of a Pep Rally,' *Globe and Mail*, 21 February 1985, M1

57 'Thousands Block Street outside Abortion Clinic,' *Globe and Mail*, 22 February 1985, 1, 2; Kathy English and Chris Welner, '3000 Protesters Demand Abortion Clinic be Closed,' *Toronto Star*, 22 February 1985, A1; Michele Mandel, 'Protesters Turn Rowdy at Anti-Abortion Rally,' *Toronto Sun*, 22 February 1985, 4

58 Murray Campbell, 'Rally of Morgentaler Supporters Decries Role of Church,' *Globe and Mail*, 23 February 1985, M1

59 Paul Bilodeau, 'Pro-Life Activists Parade at Morgentaler Clinic,' *Toronto Star*, 19 February 1985, A7

60 *Toronto Sun*, 22 February 1985, 10; 25 February 1985, 11; 4 March 1985, 10; *Toronto Star*, 27 February 1985, A22; 2 March 1985, B3; *Globe and Mail*, 5 March 1985, 6

61 The response of the Toronto news media to Carter's involvement in the protests was overwhelmingly negative. See, for example, Laura Sabia, 'Cross to Bear,' *Toronto Sun*, 26 February 1985, 12; Michael McAteer, 'United Churchman Raps Catholic Abortion Stand,' *Toronto Star*, 24 February 1985, A2; Lynda Hurst, 'Reverend's Abortion Stand a Humane One,' *Toronto Star*, 26 February 1985, B1; 'Religion and Argument,' *Globe and Mail*, 13 March 1985, 6; Tom Harpur, 'Name-Calling, Violence Have no Place in Abortion Issue,' *Toronto Star*, 3 March 1985, A16; and Allan Golombek, 'Clergy Meddling, Morgentaler Says,' *Toronto Sun*, 5 March 1985, 26. Only two Toronto newspaper columnists supported Carter's role. See Barbara Amiel, 'Words without Wisdom,' *Toronto Sun*, 19 February 1985, 12; and Claire Hoy, 'Gutless on the Hill,' *Toronto Sun*, 21 February 1985, 4.

62 Interview, Chancery Office (Toronto), 6 May 1985. The same diocesan official was specifically troubled by the following reported remarks of Ruth Evans, deputy-secretary of Christian development for the United Church of Canada: 'A particular church at this point is engaged in demonstrations which lead to great trouble. We know in the United States that demonstrations outside clinics have led to fire-bombings. I see this as a spiralling of that kind of violence.' See Rosie DiManno, 'Pro-Life Groups Losing Battle, Opponent Says,' *Toronto Star*, 22 Febru-

ary 1985, A14. See also Elaine Carey, 'Church Spokesmen Worry that Marches May Create Serious Rifts in Community,' *Toronto Star*, 2 March 1985, B5.

63 Kathy English and Paula Todd, '5,000 March in Support of Abortion,' *Toronto Star*, 23 February 1985, A1

64 On 'cognitive dissonance,' see L. Festinger, H.W. Riecken, and S. Schachter, *When Prophecy Fails* (New York: Harper Torchbooks 1964).

65 Women's Network for Life leaflet, *Women's Demonstration against Morgentaler Clinic* (17 December 1984). See also Rosemary Bottcher, 'Pro-Abortionists Poison Feminism,' in Gail Grenier Sweet, ed., *Pro-Life Feminism* (Toronto: Life Cycle Books 1985), 45.

66 See the newsletter, *Sisterlife*, which is published by Feminists for Life of America from the organization's main office in Kansas City, Mo.

67 For use of the term 'cognitive minority,' see P.L. Berger, *A Rumor of Angels* (Garden City, NY: Doubleday 1969), 7.

68 Walter Stefaniuk, 'Pro-Lifers Plan Office beside Morgentaler Clinic,' *Toronto Star*, 6 March 1985, A2; and John H. Simpson and Henry MacLeod, 'The Politics of Morality in Canada,' in R. Stark, ed., *Religious Movements* (New York: Paragon House 1985), 228

69 *Liberation* (formerly *Encounter*) 13, 4 (Dec 1984–Feb 1985), published by the Ken Campbell Evangelistic Association; Choose Life Canada (advertisement), *Toronto Star*, 23 February 1985, A15

70 Interview, staff members of The Way Inn, 20 March 1986

71 See David Little, 'Announcing the Catholic Foundation for Human Life,' *The Interim* 2, 2 (April 1984): 13. The foundation was founded by Mr Little and is based in Moncton, New Brunswick.

72 See Seymour Martin Lipset, 'Canada and the United States – A Comparative View,' *Canadian Review of Sociology and Anthropology* 1 (1964): 173–85.

73 What is a point of contention within the Canadian movement is whether or not civil disobedience can legitimately involve violence. See 'Violence, Abortionists and Anger,' *The Interim* 2, 11 (February 1985): 4; and 'Our February Editorial,' *The Interim* 3, 2 (April 1985): 4.

74 On the Prolife Nonviolent Action Project, see John Cavanaugh-O'Keefe, *Nonviolence Is an Adverb* (Gaithersburg, Md. 1985). On Human Life International, see Fr Paul Marx, *Not Even a 'Little Bit' of Abortion* (Washington, DC n.d.). On Prolifers for Survival, see the

following brochures written by Juli Loesch, all published in Chapel Hill, NC 1985: *Acts of Aggression, Imagining the Real*, and *On Nuclear Weapons*. See also the bi-monthly newspaper *P.S. (Prolifers for Survival)*. On the Pro-Life Direct Action League, see *The Unborn Speak ... 'Doesn't MY Life Count for Something?'* (St Louis, n.d.). On the Pro-Life Action League, see Joseph M. Scheidler, *Closed: 99 Ways to Stop Abortion* (Toronto: Life Cycle Books 1985).

75 (Gaithersburg, Md.: Prolife Nonviolent Action Project 1984), 15

76 Quoted in E. Michael Jones, 'Abortion Mill Rescue: Are Sit-ins the Answer?' *Fidelity* 6, 8 (July–August 1987): 34

77 Ibid., 33. See Charles Rice, *Fifty Questions on Abortion, Euthanasia, and Related Issues* (Notre Dame, Ind.: Cashel Institute 1986). See also Monica M. Migliorino, 'Report from Rats' Alley: Down and Out with the Unborn in Chicago and Milwaukee,' *Fidelity* 6, 8 (July–August 1987): 38–45.

78 See J.C. Willke, MD, 'From the President's Desk: A Place for Public Witness?' *National Right to Life News*, 15 May 1986, 3, 8.

79 At the 1986 NRLC convention in Denver, attended by the author as a participant-observer, John Cavanaugh-O'Keefe of the Prolife Nonviolent Action Project was forcibly evicted from the convention site for distributing 'subversive' anti-abortion literature.

80 See John C. Willke, MD (NRLC President), *1986 Convention Handout*, Denver, 27 May 1986.

81 Indeed, when the Supreme Court of Canada, in January 1988, struck down the Canadian abortion law, several activists suggested to the author that it would be necessary to push the movement toward greater radicalism.

82 The Canadian movement's propensity for radicalism has risen to the increasing extent that it has felt cut off from culturally *acceptable* means of attaining its political goals. See Robert K. Merton, *Social Theory and Social Structure*, revised and enlarged edition (Glencoe, Ill.: The Free Press 1957), 176–84.

83 Like their Catholic allies, Reformed activists believe that human life begins at *conception*.

84 Mr John Valk, Centre for Religious Studies (University of Toronto), assisted the author with this paragraph.

85 The Honourable Ian Scott, QC (Attorney-General), *Statement – Re: Demonstrators at the Morgentaler Clinic*, 22 August 1985

86 Letter from G. Emmett Cardinal Carter to the Honourable Ian Scott, 22 August 1985

87 Letter from G. Emmett Cardinal Carter to Campaign Life and Toronto and Area Right to Life, 22 August 1985

88 Lynda Hurst, 'Anti-Abortion Pickets' Arrogance Is Staggering,' *Toronto Star*, 27 August 1985, B1

89 Letter from Norma Scarborough (President, Canadian Abortion Rights Action League) to the Honourable Ian Scott, 21 August 1985

90 Bill Walker, '5-Picket Limit Urged outside Abortion Clinic,' *Toronto Star*, 23 August 1985, A6; and Lynda Hurst, 'Anti-Abortion Pickets' Arrogance is Staggering'

91 Diana Coulter, 'Abortion Clinic Foes Ignore Picket-Limit Deal,' *Toronto Star*, 24 August 1985, A6

92 Ciaran Ganley, 'Campaign Life Slams Scott,' *Toronto Sun*, 23 August 1985, 5

93 Bill Walker, '5-Picket Limit Urged outside Abortion Clinic'

94 Gordon Brockhouse, 'Giant Rally a "Success",' *The Interim* 3, 8 (November 1985): 1, 2

95 The Family Coalition Party, with strong ties to the anti-abortion movement, was founded in 1986. In its promotional brochure, the party is described as 'a coalition of those who realize that the old parties no longer defend the foundational philosophy for an acceptable society.' *Introducing ... the Family Coalition Party* (Toronto: FCP 1987).

CHAPTER FOUR

1 R.H. Turner and L.M. Killian, *Collective Behavior* (3rd ed.; Englewood Cliffs, NJ: Prentice-Hall, Inc. 1987), 255

2 For a critique of media stereotypes such as this, see Michael Higgins, 'Abortion Issue Calls for Restraint by the Media,' *Toronto Star*, 20 February 1988, M13.

3 James R. Kelly, 'Beyond the Stereotypes: Interviews with Right-to-Life Pioneers,' *Commonweal* (20 November 1981): 654–5. See also James R. Kelly, 'Turning Liberals into Fascists: A Case Study of the Distortion of the Right-to-Life Movement,' *Fidelity* 6, 8 (July–August 1987): 17–22; and Dave Andrusko, 'Zealots, Zanies and Assorted Kooks: How the Major Media Interprets the Pro-Life Movement,' in Andrusko, ed., *To*

Rescue the Future: The Pro-Life Movement in the 1980s (Toronto: Life Cycle Books 1983), 183–200.

4 See, for example, Andrew H. Merton, *Enemies of Choice* (Boston: Beacon Press 1981); Marilyn M. Falik, 'Ideology and Abortion Policy Politics' (Unpublished PhD dissertation, New York University 1975); Stephen L. Markson, 'Citizens United for Life: Status Politics, Symbolic Reform and the Anti Abortion Movement' (Unpublished PhD dissertation, University of Massachusetts 1979); and Susan E. Mason, 'The "Pro-Family" Ideology of the 1970s' (Unpublished PhD dissertation, Columbia University 1981).

5 Turner and Killian, *Collective Behavior*, 231

6 Kristin Luker, *Abortion and the Politics of Motherhood* (Berkeley: University of California Press 1984). Luker's book investigates *both* pro-life and pro-choice activists. For scholarly appraisements, see Carole Joffe, 'The Meaning of the Abortion Conflict,' *Contemporary Sociology* 14, 1 (1985): 26–8; and James R. Kelly, 'Tracking the Intractable: A Survey on the Abortion Controversy,' *Cross Currents* (Summer/Fall 1985): 212–18.

7 Kelly, ibid., 214

8 Luker, *Abortion and the Politics of Motherhood*, 197

9 Ibid., 205

10 Joseph R. Gusfield, *Symbolic Crusade* (Urbana, Ill.: University of Illinois Press 1966)

11 Many of the delegates who attended the 1986 NRLC convention in Denver, for example, did not fit Luker's profile.

12 An investigation of regional variations within the Canadian movement would require a separate study.

13 See Max Weber, ' "Objectivity" in Social Science and Social Policy,' in E.A. Shils and H.A. Finch, eds., *The Methodology of the Social Sciences* (New York: The Free Press 1949), 90–103.

14 See R.E. Park and E.W. Burgess, *Introduction to the Science of Sociology* (Chicago: University of Chicago Press 1924).

15 Turner and Killian, *Collective Behavior*, 3, 7–8

16 Ibid., 243

17 For use of these terms, see ibid., 297–8.

18 For use of the term 'keynoting,' see ibid., 84.

19 See Cardinal Joseph Bernardin, *The Seamless Garment* (Kansas City:

National Catholic Reporter Publishing Co. 1984); and Francis X. Meehan, *Abortion and Nuclear War: Two Issues, One Moral Cause* (Liguori, Mo.: Liguori Publications 1984).

20 See, for example, Mary Parthun, *The Psychological Effects of Induced Abortion*; and Heather Morris and Lorraine Williams, *Physical Complications of Abortion*. These two reports are published in the same volume, under the title *Abortion's Aftermath* (Toronto: Human Life Research Institute 1985).

21 This is Bryan Wilson's term. See his *Contemporary Transformations of Religion* (Oxford: Oxford University Press 1976), 16.

22 In the mid-1970s civil rights activists infuriated many in the movement by organizing a symposium on abortion (St Michael's College, University of Toronto) at which both sides of the controversy were allowed equal time for presentation of their views.

23 See Marshall Fightlin, 'Post Abortion Counselling: A Pro-Life Task,' in Andrusko, *To Rescue the Future*, 273–9.

24 For a cautious feminist reappraisal of abortion, see Kathleen McDonnell, *Not an Easy Choice* (Toronto: Women's Press 1984).

25 See 'The Report on Therapeutic Abortion Services in Toronto (Powell Report),' unpublished report commissioned by the Ontario Ministry of Health (Toronto: January 1987). See also Denise Harrington, 'Report Describes Abortion Stigma,' *Toronto Star*, 30 January 1987, A4.

26 Katrina Maxtone-Graham, *Pregnant by Mistake* (New York: Liveright 1973); and Linda Bird Francke, *The Ambivalence of Abortion* (New York: Dell 1979)

27 The new, more conservative Coalition for the Protection of Human Life publishes a quarterly newspaper, *Vitality*, from its Ottawa headquarters.

28 The Toronto-based Human Life Research Institute was founded in 1984. Among reports published by the institute are the following: Dr L.L. de Veber and Jessica Pegis, *Heroin vs. Morphine: The Current Debate*, 1985; John Gallagher, *Is the Human Embryo a Person?* 1985; Ian Gentles, *The Law and Abortion*, 1985; and Jessica Pegis, L.L. de Veber, and Ian Gentles, *Sex Education: A Review of the Literature from Canada, the United States, Britain and Sweden*, 1986.

29 See Anne Collins, *The Big Evasion* (Toronto: Lester & Orpen Dennys 1985), 204–7.

30 Ellen Tabisz, 'A Farewell Word,' *Pro-Life News*, May 1983, 10
31 Cited in Collins, *The Big Evasion*, 206
32 For a more extensive discussion of this theme, see Brigitte Berger and Peter L. Berger, *The War over the Family* (Garden City, NY: Anchor 1983).
33 See, for example, Sabina McLuhan, 'All in the Family,' *The Interim* 4, 4 (June 1986): 27.
34 Tahi L. Mottl, 'The Analysis of Countermovements,' *Social Problems* 27 (1980): 620
35 On neo-traditionalism in the United States, see R.C. Liebman and R.W. Wuthnow, eds., *The New Christian Right* (New York: Aldine 1983).
36 Berger and Berger, *The War over the Family*, 24–39
37 Ibid., 38–9
38 See Reginald W. Bibby, *Fragmented Gods: The Poverty and Potential of Religion in Canada* (Toronto: Irwin 1987), 27–8.
39 Collins, *The Big Evasion*, 191–2. For a feminist analysis of groups such as REAL Women, see Andrea Dworkin, *Right-Wing Women* (New York: Wideview/Perigee 1983).
40 Grace Petrasek, 'REAL Women and Election '84,' *The Interim* 2, 6 (September 1984): 17
41 On the idealization of the 1950s by contemporary cultural conservatives, see Douglas T. Miller and Marian Nowak, *The Fifties: The Way We Really Were* (Garden City, NY: Doubleday 1977).
42 This term is used in Jerome C. Himmelstein, 'The New Right,' in Liebman and Wuthnow, *The New Christian Right*, 16.
43 In 1983 Ontario MPP John Sweeney was quoted in the Toronto media as saying that the Holocaust had begun 'in the abortion clinics of Europe.' See Collins, *The Big Evasion*, 196.
44 *Rachel Weeping* (Kansas City: Andrews and McMeel 1982), 141
45 (St Louis: Landmark Press 1983)
46 See R.N. Bellah, 'Civil Religion in America,' *Daedalus* 96 (1967): 1–21.
47 J.T. Noonan, Jr, *A Private Choice* (New York: The Free Press 1979)
48 For use of this term, see Peter L. Berger and Thomas Luckmann, *The Social Construction of Reality* (New York: Penguin Books 1976), 110–46.
49 Luker, *Abortion and the Politics of Motherhood*, 151–2. See also Donald Granberg, 'The Abortion Activists,' *Family Planning Perspectives* 13, 4 (1981): 158–61.

50 Luker, *Abortion and the Politics of Motherhood*, 154
51 The term 'contraculture' is coined in J.M. Yinger, 'Contraculture and Subculture,' *American Sociological Review* 25 (1960): 625–45.
52 See Alphonse de Valk, 'Open Letter to Catholic Bishops: Let's Put Our House in Order,' *The Interim* 2, 9 (December 1984): 8–9.
53 There are only a few priests and nuns actively involved in anti-abortion protest in the Toronto area.
54 For use of this term, see I.M. Zeitlin, *The Social Condition of Humanity* (New York: Oxford University Press 1981), 149–52.
55 Fr Paul Marx, 'Explaining the Contraceptive Mentality,' *The Interim* 6, 1 (April 1987): 27
56 In Weberian terms, the world-view of Revivalists is based on *substantive* rather than *formal* rationality. See Max Weber, *The Theory of Social and Economic Organization*, translated by A.M. Henderson and Talcott Parsons (New York: The Free Press 1964), 185.
57 See P.L. Berger, *The Sacred Canopy* (Garden City, NY: Anchor 1967).
58 On Opus Dei, see Jose V. Casanova, 'The First Secular Institute: The Opus Dei as a Religious Movement–Organization,' *Annual Review of the Social Sciences of Religion* 6 (1982): 243–85.
59 For the distinction between Apollonian and Dionysian religiosity, see Ruth Benedict, *Patterns of Culture* (Boston: Houghton Mifflin 1959), 79.
60 Berger and Luckmann, *The Social Construction of Reality*, 39
61 On religious movements of counter-modernization, see Robert Wuthnow et al., *Cultural Analysis* (Boston: Routledge & Kegan Paul 1984), 68–9.
62 Robert A. Stallings, 'Patterns of Belief in Social Movements: Clarifications from an Analysis of Environmental Groups,' *Sociological Quarterly* 14 (1973): 477
63 This distinction is discussed by Gerhard Lenski in *The Religious Factor* (Garden City, NY: Doubleday 1961).
64 For discussion in a different context of the *expressive* dimension of political activism, see Roger O'Toole, *The Precipitous Path* (Toronto: Peter Martin 1977), 72–4.
65 See Turner and Killian, *Collective Behavior*, 296.
66 Herbert Blumer, 'Collective Behavior,' in A.M. Lee, ed., *New Outline of the Principles of Sociology* (New York: Barnes and Noble 1953), 206, 208
67 See Roger Straus, 'Changing Oneself: Seekers and the Creative Trans-

formation of Experience,' in John Lofland, ed., *Doing Social Life* (New York: Wiley 1976), 252–72.

CHAPTER FIVE

1 On *causal pluralism* in Weber's sociology, see H.H. Gerth and C. Wright Mills, eds., *From Max Weber: Essays in Sociology* (New York: Oxford University Press 1980), 34–5.

2 See Max Weber, *The Sociology of Religion*, translated by E. Fischoff (Boston: Beacon Press 1963), 1.

3 Reinhard Bendix, 'Memoir of My Father,' *The Canadian Review of Sociology and Anthropology* 2, 1 (1965): 1. See also Dennis H. Wrong, 'The Oversocialized Conception of Man in Modern Society,' *American Sociological Review* 26, 2 (1961): 183–93; and James T. Hannon, 'The Use of Life History Research to Study the Development of Political and Religious Commitments,' paper read at the Forty-ninth Annual Meeting of the Association for the Sociology of Religion (Chicago, 22 August 1987).

4 This is an expression used by several contributors in Gail Grenier Sweet, ed., *Pro-Life Feminism* (Toronto: Life Cycle Books 1985).

5 The social teaching of the Canadian Catholic bishops is examined in Chapter Six, 150–6.

6 For further discussion on this point, see Kristin Luker, *Abortion and the Politics of Motherhood* (Berkeley: University of California Press 1984), 163–7.

7 See Marcene Marcoux, *Cursillo: Anatomy of a Movement* (New York: Lambeth Press 1982).

8 See William James, *The Varieties of Religious Experience* (New York: Mentor 1958).

9 (Allen, Texas: Argus Communications 1981)

CHAPTER SIX

1 Adam Exner, Roman Catholic Archbishop of Winnipeg, is the most notable exception. See Matt Maychak, 'Bishop Leads Thousands in Anti-Abortion March,' *Toronto Star*, 8 March 1985, A2.

2 On this theme, see Richard P. McBrien, *Do We Need the Church?* (London: Collins 1969).

3 See Michael Czerny, 'Puebla: Step into the 1980s,' *The Ecumenist* 18, 1 (1979): 1–5.

4 Gregory Baum, 'The Shift in Catholic Social Teaching,' in G. Baum and D. Cameron, *Ethics and Economics: Canada's Catholic Bishops on the Economic Crisis* (Toronto: James Lorimer 1984), 20

5 Ibid., 20–1

6 Ibid., 32–3. See also Donal Dorr, *Option for the Poor: A Hundred Years of Vatican Social Teaching* (Maryknoll, NY: Orbis Books 1983).

7 For the documents of the Medellín Conference, see Joseph Gremillion, ed., *The Gospel of Peace and Justice* (Maryknoll, NY: Orbis Books 1976), 445–76. For the final document of the Puebla Conference, see J. Eagleson and P. Scharper, eds., *Puebla and Beyond* (Maryknoll, NY: Orbis Books 1979).

8 Baum, 'The Shift in Catholic Social Teaching,' 25. See also Arthur F. McGovern, *Marxism: An American Christian Perspective* (Maryknoll, NY: Orbis Books 1981), 118–20.

9 Gregory Baum, *The Priority of Labor: A Commentary on Laborem Exercens* (New York: Paulist Press 1982)

10 Cardinal Flahiff's address is published in a booklet, *Witness to Justice: Some Statements by the Canadian Catholic Bishops* (Toronto: Canadian Catholic Organization for Development and Peace n.d.), 1–3.

11 Gregory Baum, 'Values and Society,' *The Ecumenist* 17, 2 (1979): 25–31

12 *Witness to Justice*, 22–3

13 Ibid., 23–4

14 Ibid., 30–1

15 See Gregory Baum, *Catholics and Canadian Socialism* (Toronto: James Lorimer 1980).

16 *Witness to Justice*, 30–1

17 Ibid., 23, 24, 28

18 Ibid., 29

19 E.F. Sheridan, SJ, ed., *Do Justice!: The Social Teaching of the Canadian Catholic Bishops (1945–1986)* (Toronto: The Jesuit Centre for Social Faith and Justice 1987), 356. This is the most complete collection of social statements by the Canadian Catholic bishops.

20 *Ethical Reflections* received widespread attention in the national media for several weeks following its release.

21 Sheridan, *Do Justice!*, 402

22 See Duncan Cameron, 'Do Canada's Bishops Make Economic Sense?' in Baum and Cameron, *Ethics and Economics*, 94–150; and Kenneth Westhues, 'The Option for (and against) the Poor,' *Grail* 3, 1 (1987): 23–38.

23 The prelate in question was Cardinal Carter, archbishop of Toronto. See Baum, 'The Shift in Catholic Social Teaching,' 82–3.

24 Sheridan, *Do Justice!*, 402

25 Baum, 'The Shift in Catholic Social Teaching,' 51

26 Ibid., 60

27 See Bill McSweeney, *Roman Catholicism: The Search for Relevance* (Oxford: Basil Blackwell 1980), 198–08.

28 *Catholic New Times*, a national newspaper published bi-weekly in Toronto, is the chief organ of Progressive Catholicism in Canada.

29 See Alphonse de Valk, *Morality and Law in Canadian Politics* (Montreal: Palm Publishers 1974), 61–6.

30 James R. Kelly, 'Towards Complexity: The Right to Life Movement,' unpublished paper, 1986, 36

31 Sister Mary Jo Leddy, although uninvolved personally in the pro-life movement, is one Social Justice Catholic who has made her opposition to abortion public. See Mary Jo Leddy and James H. Olthuis, 'Thoughtful Perspectives on Abortion,' *Catalyst* 6, 10 (November 1983): 4–5; and Michael W. Higgins and Douglas R. Letson, *Portraits of Canadian Catholicism* (Toronto: Griffin House 1986), 67–8.

32 All twenty-five subjects are actively involved in 'social justice ministry' in the Toronto area.

33 In 'The Shift in Catholic Social Teaching' (p. 19), for example, Gregory Baum describes abortion as a matter of 'personal ethics.'

34 Emile Durkheim, *Suicide: A Study in Sociology*, translated by J.A. Spaulding and G. Simpson (London: Routledge & Kegan Paul 1952)

35 See Kathleen J. Ferraro and John M. Johnson, 'How Women Experience Battering: The Process of Victimization,' *Social Problems* 30, 3 (1983): 325–33.

36 James C. Mohr, *Abortion in America: The Origins and Evolution of National Policy* (New York: Oxford University Press 1978)

37 For an investigation of inter-denominational strife over the issue of contraception, see Kenneth W. Underwood, *Protestant and Catholic* (Boston: Beacon Press 1957).

38 See Gregory Baum, 'Liberation Theology and "The Supernatural",' *The Ecumenist* 19, 6 (1981): 86.

39 See, for example, Gregory Baum, 'Abortion: An Ecumenical Dilemma,' in Edward Batchelor, ed., *Abortion: The Moral Issues* (New York: The Pilgrim Press 1982), 38–47.

40 See the Canadian Society for the Defense of Tradition, Family and Property (TFP), 'Where Is Canada Heading? [advertisement],' *The Interim* 5, 1 (March 1987), 26–7.

41 On this point, see Mary Jo Neitz, 'Family, State, and God: Ideologies of the Right-to-Life Movement,' *Sociological Analysis* 42, 3 (1981): 265–76.

42 See, for example, Alphonse de Valk, 'The Sexual Revolution, Feminism and the Churches (Part x): Catholic Bishops of Canada,' *The Interim* 5, 9 (December 1987): 17.

43 For a theological analysis of conflicting ecclesiological models within Catholicism, see Avery Dulles, *Models of the Church* (Garden City, NY: Image Books 1978).

44 See, for example, the following editorials on the issue published by *Catholic New Times*: 'Don't Sign the Abortion Ad' (13 October 1985, 5); 'The Abortion Debate Is Bedevilled' (9 December 1984, 5); and 'Placing Pro-Life Protests in Context' (10 March 1985, 5).

45 Michael Ryan, *Solidarity: Christian Social Teaching and Canadian Society* (London, Ont.: Guided Study Programs in the Catholic Faith, 1986); and A. Huntly, J. Morin, and M. Sfeir, *Political and Social Rights and Human Dignity* (Dubuque, Iowa: Wm. C. Brown Co. n.d.). The latter work has the imprimatur of G. Emmett Cardinal Carter.

46 M. Czerny and J. Swift, *Getting Started on Social Analysis in Canada* (Toronto: Between the Lines 1984), 17

47 Canadian Conference of Catholic Bishops (Administrative Board), *Ethical Reflections on Respect for Life* (Ottawa, 7 September 1983), 1

48 Canadian Conference of Catholic Bishops, *To Love and Serve Life* (Ottawa, April 1986), 1

49 Bishop Remi De Roo, *Cries of Victims – Voice of God* (Ottawa: Novalis 1986), 147

50 See, for example, *Therefore Choose Life ...* (Toronto: Ontario Conference of Catholic Bishops, 15 August 1983).

51 De Roo, *Cries of Victims*, 86, 89, 115

52 Episcopal Commission for Social Affairs, *Witness to Justice: A Society to be Transformed – Working Instruments* (Ottawa 1979)

53 Statements included in this booklet are *Sharing Daily Bread, Northern Development: At What Cost?, From Words to Action*, and *A Society to be Transformed*.
54 Sheridan, *Do Justice!*, 5–12
55 *Compass* is published six times annually in Toronto by the Jesuit Fathers of Upper Canada.
56 See De Roo, *Cries of Victims*, 35–6. See also Scott Symons, 'Did Moral Bankruptcy of Canada Prompt Bishops to Speak Out?' *Globe and Mail*, 19 April 1983, 7.
57 Some French-Canadian commentators accused the bishops of promoting 'a clericalism of the left.' See Baum, 'The Shift in Catholic Social Teaching,' 76–7.
58 The author expresses indebtedness for this observation to Ms Madeline Attallah of Toronto, who performed a content analysis of the Canadian print media's response to *Ethical Reflections*. See, for example, Senator Keith Davey, 'Ottawa's Answer to the Bishops,' *Toronto Star*, 8 January 1983, B4.
59 See, for example, Robert MacIntosh, 'The Bishops and the Economy,' *Toronto Star*, 8 January 1983, B4.
60 *Globe and Mail*, 22 January 1983; cited in Baum, 'The Shift in Catholic Social Teaching,' 61. See also Fergus Coyle, 'Treat Unemployment as Crisis United Church Ministers Urge,' *Toronto Star*, 28 January 1983.
61 Canada's major Christian denominations, according to Reginald W. Bibby, comprise a 'monopolized mosaic' on the Canadian religious scene. See Bibby's *Fragmented Gods* (Toronto: Irwin 1987), 48–9.
62 Pat McNenly, 'Clergy's Crusade on Sunday Shopping Gains Support,' *Toronto Star*, 2 February 1988, A16; and '4 Churches United in Battle Over Shopping,' *Toronto Star*, 1 February 1988, A1, A16
63 See, for example, *Pornography Kit* (Toronto: United Church Division of Mission 1985).
64 See John R. Williams, ed., *Canadian Churches and Social Justice* (Toronto: Anglican Book Centre and L. Lorimer 1984); and R.C. Hutchinson, 'Ecumenical Witness in Canada: Social Action Coalitions,' *International Review of Mission* 71 (1982): 344–52.
65 The major churches, according to John H. Simpson, have historically regarded themselves as privileged *agents* 'from within' in the maintenance, and sometimes reformation, of Canada's *collective order*. See J.H. Simpson, 'Federal Regulation and Religious Broadcasting,' in W.

Westfall et al., eds., *Religion/Culture: Comparative Canadian Studies* (Ottawa: Association for Canadian Studies 1985), 161–2; and J.H. Simpson and H. MacLeod, 'The Politics of Morality in Canada,' in R. Stark, ed., *Religious Movements* (New York: Paragon House 1985), 229, 233.

66 C. Wright Mills, *The Sociological Imagination* (New York: Oxford University Press 1959), 15

67 See Roger O'Toole, 'Society, the Sacred and the Secular: Sociological Observations on the Changing Role of Religion in Canadian Culture,' in Westfall et al., eds., *Religion/Culture*, 109, 115.

68 Foreword to Bibby, *Fragmented Gods*, ix

69 See N.K. Clifford, 'His Dominion: A Vision in Crisis,' in P. Slater, ed., *Religion and Culture in Canada/Religion et Culture au Canada* (Canadian Corporation for Studies in Religion 1977), 24–41.

70 See Michael McAteer, 'Christians at the Crossroads: Canada's Christians at a Turning Point,' *Toronto Star*, 16 April 1987, A20; and Michael McAteer, 'United Church Membership Down Another 9,000 in 1986,' *Toronto Star*, 25 June 1987, A13.

71 Bibby, *Fragmented Gods*, 14

72 Ibid., 21

73 John Webster Grant, *The Church in the Canadian Era* (Toronto: McGraw-Hill Ryerson 1972), 204

74 See Dan Donovan, *A Lasting Impact: John Paul II in Canada* (Toronto: Novalis 1985). On the intensive media coverage accorded John Paul II's 1984 visit to Canada, see Michael McAteer, 'Runcie and John Paul: A Study in Differences,' *Toronto Star*, 5 October 1985, L14.

75 Outside of the pope's 1984 Canadian tour, it is doubtful that any religious events of the 1980s have so thoroughly engaged the Canadian print media as did the 1985 and 1987 synods of Catholic bishops in Rome.

76 This paragraph draws from conversations between the author and denominational officials of the United, Anglican, and Presbyterian churches. See also Denyse Handler, 'Agreeing to Disagree: Catholic/United Church Dialogue,' *The Canadian Catholic Review* 4, 8 (1986): 20–1.

77 See C.B. Sissons, *Church and State in Canadian Education* (Toronto: Ryerson 1959).

78 Michael McAteer, 'Fight's Not Over, Church Leaders Say,' *Toronto Star*, 1 July 1987, A12; Michael McAteer, 'Churches Urged to Battle

Death Penalty,' *Toronto Star*, 3 May 1987, A22; and Pat McNenly, 'High-Profile Cast to Speak Out at Rally against Death Penalty,' *Toronto Star*, 4 May 1987, A1, A9

79 See Alan Christie and Michael McAteer, 'Davis "Saddened" by Archbishop's "Hitler" Charge on School Funding,' *Toronto Star*, 26 April 1985, 1, 8; John Ferri, 'Fight Catholic Funding, Garnsworthy Urges,' *Toronto Star*, 1 June 1985, A3; and Louise Brown, 'United Church Warns of Tensions on School Funding,' *Toronto Star*, 23 February 1985, A6.

80 See William Westfall, 'The Dominion of the Lord: An Introduction to the Cultural History of Protestant Ontario in the Victorian Period,' *Queen's Quarterly* 83 (1976): 47–70.

81 Michael Higgins, 'Back when King Billy Rode Tall in the Saddle,' *Toronto Star*, 12 July 1986, L10. See also Peter Howell, 'Carter Regrets "Hostility",' *Toronto Sun*, 15 September 1985, 48.

82 Cited in De Roo, *Cries of Victims*, 95. See also Baum, 'The Shift in Catholic Social Teaching,' 62.

83 De Roo, ibid., 99–104. See also Tony Clarke, 'Communities for Justice,' *The Ecumenist* 19 (1981): 17–25.

84 For the term 'counterfeit of faith,' see Eric Voegelin, *New Science of Politics* (Chicago: University of Chicago Press 1972), 123, 129.

85 De Roo, *Cries of Victims*, 114

86 On *Octogesima Adveniens*, see Baum, *The Priority of Labor*, 81.

87 See Pope John Paul II's Apostolic Exhortation, *The Role of the Christian Family in the Modern World (Familiaris Consortio)* (Boston: St Paul Editions 1982).

88 See, for example, Fr Jonathan Robinson, *Papal Teaching Today and the State of the Faith* (Toronto: The Catholic Register 1985).

89 The theme of cultural decadence is pervasive in Revivalist literature. For typical examples, see Larry Henderson's 'A Tale of Two Cultures,' and E.C. Farrell's 'The 1960s – A Look Back,' in *Challenge* 13, 7 (April 1987): 12, 18–19.

90 See, for example, *Our Lady Speaks to Her Beloved Priests* (7th English ed.; Milan: The Marian Movement of Priests 1983).

91 Colin Francome, *Abortion Freedom* (Boston: George Allen & Unwin 1984)

92 For a similar argument from a non-Revivalist standpoint, see George Grant, *Technology and Justice* (Toronto: Anansi 1986), 117–30.

93 See above, 71–3

94 See, for example, Alphonse de Valk, 'Sexual Revolution, Feminism and the Churches,' *The Interim* 4, 6 (September 1986): 10–12; and Donna Steichen, 'From Convent to Coven: Catholic Neo-Pagans at the Witches' Sabbath,' *Fidelity* 5, 1 (December 1985): 27–37.

CHAPTER SEVEN

1 See Michael Hill, *A Sociology of Religion* (London: Heinemann 1973), 107–9. For amplification of much of the present chapter's discussion, see Michael W. Cuneo, 'Soldiers of Orthodoxy: Revivalist Catholicism in North America,' *Studies in Religion/Sciences Religieuses* 17, 3 (1988): 347–63.

2 In addition to works specifically cited, the following magazines and periodicals were identified by the author as *Revivalist* and subjected to content analysis over the two-year publishing span of 1985–6: *Fidelity* (South Bend, Indiana); *The Wanderer* (St Paul, Minnesota); *The Interim* (Toronto, Ontario); and *Challenge* (Winnipeg, Manitoba).

3 See, for example, William Dinges, 'Catholic Traditionalism,' in J. Fichter, ed., *Alternatives to American Mainline Churches* (New York: Rose of Sharon 1983), 137–58.

4 See, for example, Patrick M. Arnold, 'The Rise of Catholic Fundamentalism,' *America* 156, 14 (April 11, 1987): 297–02.

5 James Mooney, *The Ghost Dance Religion* (Washington: Bureau of American Ethnology Annual Report 1892–3). The term is employed in another and entirely unrelated context by Jay Dolan in his study of evangelicalism in nineteenth-century American Catholicism. See Jay P. Dolan, *Catholic Revivalism: The American Experience, 1830–1900* (Notre Dame: University of Notre Dame Press 1978).

6 Anthony F.C. Wallace, 'Revitalization Movements,' *American Anthropologist* 58 (1956): 279

7 Ibid., 279

8 Ibid., 275

9 See Charles Fracchia, *Second Spring* (New York: Harper & Row 1980).

10 This is the case, for example, with even so perceptive an observer as Bill McSweeney. See his *Roman Catholicism: The Search for Relevance* (Oxford: Basil Blackwell 1980), 196–232.

11 William Dinges, 'Catholic Traditionalism in America: A Study of the Remnant Faithful' (Unpublished PhD dissertation, University of Kansas 1983)

12 See M. Timothy Iglesias, 'CUF and Dissent: A Case Study in Religious Conservatism,' *America* 156, 14 (April 11, 1987): 303–7. Catholics United for the Faith (CUF) is an American Revivalist organization.

13 On the subject of popular religiosity, see Peter W. Williams, *Popular Religion in America* (Englewood Cliffs, NJ: Prentice-Hall 1980).

14 Louis C. Bouyer, *The Decomposition of Catholicism*, translated by C.U. Quinn (Chicago: Franciscan Herald 1969), 54

15 This observation is impressionistic and is based mainly on the author's research in Toronto.

16 See, for example, James Likoudis and Kenneth P. Whitehead, *The Pope, the Council, and the Mass* (West Hanover, Mass.: Christopher Publishing House 1981).

17 See Anne Roche, *The Gates of Hell: The Struggle for the Catholic Church* (Toronto: McClelland and Stewart 1975).

18 James Hitchcock, *The Decline and Fall of Radical Catholicism* (New York: Herder and Herder 1971), 95, 130, 180. See also Dietrich von Hildebrand, *Trojan Horse in the City of God* (Chicago: Franciscan Herald Press 1967), 9, 39, 44.

19 See Michael Hill, *The Religious Order* (London: Heinemann 1973).

20 Von Hildebrand, *Trojan Horse*, 9, 189–90, 255; and Iglesias, 'CUF and Dissent,' 307. The 'horizontalizing' effects of *aggiornamento* are attributed by Revivalists to the secularizing pressures at work in the larger culture. See, for example, D. von Hildebrand, *The Devastated Vineyard* (Chicago: Franciscan Herald Press 1973), 250.

21 In a sermon given in Rome on 29 June 1972, Pope Paul VI said that 'Satan's smoke has made its way into the temple of God through some crack' (*L'Osservatore Romana* [English edition], 10 July 1972).

22 Michael W. Cuneo, 'Conservative Catholicism in North America: Pro-Life Activism and the Pursuit of the Sacred,' *Pro Mundi Vita* [Europe-North America Dossier no. 36] (Brussels: Pro Mundi Vita 1987)

23 The term 'new theology' is used here as a schematic convenience; obviously the sheer breadth and complexity of contemporary Catholic theology defies unilineal categorization. For insightful treatments, from a North American vantage point, of innovative Catholic theology in the post-conciliar era, see the following: David Tracy, *Blessed Rage for Order* (New York: Crossroad 1981); David Tracy, *The Analogical Imagination* (New York: Crossroad 1981); Richard P. McBrien, *Do We Need the Church?* (London: Collins 1969); and Andrew M. Greeley, *The New Agenda* (Garden City, NY: Doubleday 1973). In the last work, see

especially the foreword by Gregory Baum, 11–34. For a sociological discussion of the victory of the 'new theology,' see McSweeney, *Roman Catholicism*, chs. 4–7. On the role played by Vatican II in making phenomenology and the social sciences central to Catholic theologizing, see John F. Kobler, *Vatican II and Phenomenology* (Dordrecht: Martinus Nijhoff 1985).

24 Von Hildebrand, *Trojan Horse*, xi; James Hitchcock, *Catholicism and Modernity: Confrontation or Capitulation?* (Ann Arbor: Servant Books 1979), 38

25 Hitchcock, *Catholicism and Modernity*, 13. See also Msgr George A. Kelly, *The Battle for the American Church* (Garden City, NY: Doubleday 1979), 471; and Michael Novak, *Confession of a Catholic* (San Francisco: Harper & Row 1983), 78.

26 See, for example, Larry Henderson, *The Hot Seat* (Toronto: The Catholic Register 1986).

27 Hitchcock, *Catholicism and Modernity*, 35. See also Novak, *Confession of a Catholic*, 114–15.

28 Hitchcock, *Catholicism and Modernity*, 35. See also Hitchcock's *What Is Secular Humanism?* (Ann Arbor: Servant Books 1982), 61–79. For the notion of 'therapeutic culture,' see Philip Rieff, *The Triumph of the Therapeutic* (New York: Harper Torchbooks 1968).

29 See, for example, E. Michael Jones, 'Requiem for a Magazine: The Sodomization of the Catholic Press in Saskatchewan,' *Fidelity* 6, 3 (February 1987): 22–36.

30 For a Revivalist critique of the contemporary ethical theory known as 'proportionalism,' see Msgr George A. Kelly, *The Crisis of Authority* (Chicago: Regnery Gateway 1982), 62, 64.

31 See Paul Johnson, *Pope John Paul II and the Catholic Restoration* (Ann Arbor: Servant 1981); and Ralph Wiltgen, *The Rhine Flows into the Tiber* (New York: Hawthorn 1967).

32 Hitchcock, *Decline and Fall*, 56, 64

33 Kelly, *The Battle for the American Church*, viii, 53, 241, 472, 490; Hitchcock, *Decline and Fall*, 99, 170; and Hitchcock, *Catholicism and Modernity*, 98, 101

34 Roche, *Gates of Hell*, 13–14

35 Peter Hebblethwaite, *The Runaway Church* (New York: The Seabury Press 1975)

36 Kelly, *The Battle for the American Church*, 355

37 Roche, *Gates of Hell*, 22, 26

38 Hitchcock, *Catholicism and Modernity*, 101
39 Roche, *Gates of Hell*, 27–9
40 Anne Roche Muggeridge, *The Desolate City: The Catholic Church in Ruins* (Toronto: McClelland and Stewart 1986), 75
41 Kelly, *The Battle for the American Church*, 239
42 See, for example, Andrew M. Greeley and Mary Durkin, *How To Save the Catholic Church* (New York: Viking 1984).
43 Kelly, *Crisis of Authority*, 58–9; and Hitchcock, *Decline and Fall*, 42. See also D. von Hildebrand, *The Encyclical Humanae Vitae: A Sign of Contradiction* (Chicago: Franciscan Herald Press 1969).
44 See Joseph Cardinal Ratzinger (with Vittorio Messori), *The Ratzinger Report*, translated by S. Attanasio and G. Harrison (San Francisco: Ignatius Press 1985).
45 For the term 'non-historical orthodoxy,' see Michael Novak, *The Open Church* (New York: Macmillan 1964), 56–71.
46 Protestant fundamentalism and Catholic Revivalism have found their political catalysts, respectively, in anti-evolutionism and anti-abortionism.
47 Frank J. Lechner, 'Fundamentalism and Sociocultural Revitalization in America: A Sociological Interpretation,' *Sociological Analysis* 46, 3 (1985): 243–59
48 G.M. Marsden, *Fundamentalism and American Culture* (New York: Oxford University Press 1980)
49 Von Hildebrand, *Trojan Horse*
50 This theme is developed extensively by Anne Roche Muggeridge in *The Desolate City*.
51 See, for example, the chapter on John Courtney Murray in C.E. Curran, *American Catholic Social Ethics* (Notre Dame: University of Notre Dame Press 1982), 172–232; and Gregory Baum, 'Catholic Foundation of Human Rights,' *The Ecumenist* 18, 1 (1979): 6–12.
52 Revivalists would argue that Herberg's thesis, regarding the submersion during the 1950s of North America's major religious traditions into the American Way of Life, remains valid for contemporary Catholicism. See Will Herberg, *Protestant, Catholic, Jew* (Garden City, NY: Doubleday 1956).
53 Hitchcock, *Catholicism and Modernity*, 217. See also Hitchcock, *Decline and Fall*, 90, 146, 150, 158.
54 G.K. Chesterton, *The Catholic Church and Conversion* (New York: Macmillan 1926), 93
55 Roche, *Gates of Hell*, 36–7

56 Ibid., 93, 220
57 Ernst Troeltsch, *The Social Teaching of the Christian Churches*, 2 vols., translated by O. Wyon (London: George Allen and Unwin 1931)
58 Von Hildebrand, *Trojan Horse*, 4
59 Wach employs the concept of *ecclesiola in ecclesia* to characterize non-schismatic groups that protest against alleged compromise and laxity within the larger ecclesiastical body. See Joachim Wach, *Sociology of Religion* (Chicago: University of Chicago Press 1944), 173–205.
60 The 'apostolate of the laity' is frequently emphasized, for example, in *Lay Witness*, the national newsletter of Catholics United for the Faith (New Rochelle, NY).
61 On the concept of 'status groups,' see Max Weber, 'Class, Status, Party,' in H.H. Gerth and C. Wright Mills, eds., *From Max Weber: Essays in Sociology* (New York: Oxford University Press 1980), 181.
62 *Challenge* 13, 9 (June 1987): 21
63 Ibid., 20
64 Six sample subjects are members of the Canadian Organization of Catholic Women for Life, Faith and Family (COCWLFF), an intra-church lobbying group founded in 1985 for the purpose of arresting the influence of feminism upon Canadian Catholicism. See Kathleen Toth, 'Active Program Outlined for COCWLFF, Says New President,' *Challenge* 13, 3 (December 1986): 9. On the continuing dialogue between Catholic feminists and the Canadian bishops, see Elisabeth J. Lacelle, 'Women in the Catholic Church of Canada,' *The Ecumenist* 23, 4 (1985): 49–54.
65 David A. Martin, 'The Denomination,' *British Journal of Sociology* 12, 1 (1962): 1–14
66 Peter L. Berger, *The Noise of Solemn Assemblies* (New York: Doubleday 1961); cited in Reginald W. Bibby, *Fragmented Gods: The Poverty and Potential of Religion in Canada* (Toronto: Irwin 1987), 169
67 Bibby, *Fragmented Gods*, 134, 236, 254
68 Quoted in ibid., 263
69 Ibid., 111
70 Ibid., 17, 126, 151. See also *The Meaning of Sunday in a Pluralistic Society* (Ottawa: Canadian Conference of Catholic Bishops 1986), 3.
71 Bibby, *Fragmented Gods*, 161–3. A survey conducted for the *Globe and Mail* in 1985 found that 47 per cent of Canadian Catholics, and 53 per cent of all Canadians, favour abortion-on-demand. See M. Adams, D. Dasko, and Y. Corbeil, 'The Globe–CROP Poll: Slim Majority of

Canadians Favors Free Choice, Poll Finds,' *Globe and Mail*, 15 June 1985, 1, 12. The Globe–CROP poll provoked the following editorial comments in the Canadian *Catholic Register*, 29 June 1985, 4: 'Conclusion: our Church is in serious trouble. Only a very strong campaign by the responsible Church authorities, re-inforcing [Catholic teaching against abortion], can counter the influence of the world, the flesh and the devil. We do not see such a campaign developing.'

72 See Michael McAteer, 'Abortion and Backlash against McTeer,' *Toronto Star*, 22 February 1986, L10; and Anthony Hawkins, 'Maureen McTeer: "Abortion Posting Shameful",' *The Interim* 4, 1 (March 1986): 14.

73 On the widespread use by Catholic women of church-condemned birth control techniques, see T.R. Balakrishnan, J.F. Kantner, and J.D. Allingham, *Fertility and Family Planning in a Canadian Metropolis* (Montreal: McGill–Queen's University Press 1975).

74 'The Adaptation of the Roman Catholic Church in Canadian Society,' in S. Crysdale and L. Wheatcroft, eds., *Religion in Canadian Society* (Toronto: Macmillan 1976), 303

75 Ibid., 303–4

76 See, for example, H. Richard Niebuhr, *The Social Sources of Denominationalism* (New York: Meridan 1975).

77 See, for example, C.Y. Glock and R.N. Bellah, eds., *The New Religious Consciousness* (Berkeley: University of California Press 1976); and Michael Barkun, *Crucible of the Millennium* (Syracuse: Syracuse University Press 1986).

78 Max Weber, 'The Social Psychology of the World Religions,' in Gerth and Mills, eds., *From Max Weber*, 287–8

79 See Ronald A. Knox, *Enthusiasm* (Oxford: Clarendon Press 1950).

80 R.H. Turner and L.M. Killian, *Collective Behavior* (3rd ed.; Englewood Cliffs, NJ: Prentice-Hall 1987), 274

81 *Symbolic Crusade* (Urbana, Ill.: University of Illinois Press 1966), 163

82 Emile Durkheim, *The Elementary Forms of the Religious Life*, translated by J.W. Swain (New York: The Free Press 1965). See also J. Wach, *Sociology of Religion*, 27–34.

83 On the identity-bestowing capacity of religious activity, see Hans Mol, *Identity and the Sacred* (New York: The Free Press 1976).

84 *Social Theory and Social Structure* (Glencoe, Ill.: The Free Press 1957), 60–84

85 *The Sacred and the Profane*, translated by W.R. Trask (New York: Harcourt Brace Jovanovich 1959), 14
86 See Bryan R. Wilson, *Religon in Secular Society* (London: C.A. Watts 1966).
87 Max Weber, 'Politics as a Vocation,' in Gerth and Mills, eds., *From Max Weber*, 120–7

AFTERWORD

1 See Dan Smith, 'Cardinal Carter Calls Court Ruling "Uncivilized," ' *Toronto Star*, 29 January 1988, A1.
2 G. Emmett Cardinal Carter, *Statement to the Right Hon. the Prime Minister of Canada and the Members of the Federal Parliament*, 29 February 1988
3 Archbishop James M. Hayes, *Faithful to the Future: Pastoral Statement on Abortion*, April 1988
4 'This Is a Time to Weep,' *Catholic New Times*, 21 February 1988, 5. The United Church had endorsed the Supreme Court decision in an official communiqué released on 28 January 1988.
5 'An Open Letter to Socially Concerned Catholics: Resist Abortion – Now!' *Catholic New Times*, 26 June 1988, 5. See also 'The Abortion Dilemma: Our Readers Respond,' *Catholic New Times*, 24 July 1988, 7.
6 Archbishop James M. Hayes, *Statement by CCCB President to Members of Parliament*, June 1988. This statement had been approved by the permanent council of the CCCB at its meeting of 15–16 June 1988.
7 Campaign Life Coalition (CLC) was formed by a 1986 merger of Campaign Life and the Ottawa-based Coalition for the Protection of Human Life.
8 Michael McAteer, 'Bishops' Stance on Abortion Bid "a Betrayal" Group Charges,' *Toronto Star*, 29 June 1988, A25; and Doreen Beagan, 'Pro-Lifers Say Shocked by Letter,' Canadian *Catholic Register*, 16 July 1988, 3. Cardinal Carter subsequently, on 26 July 1988, sent a personal statement to all members of the House of Commons and the Senate in which he condemned the government's abortion resolution. For the complete text of this statement, see 'Cardinal Sends Commons, Senate Abortion Message,' Canadian *Catholic Register*, 6 August 1988, 6.
9 Graham Fraser, 'MPs Vote Down Abortion Resolution,' *Globe and Mail*, 29 July 1988, A1, A5

10 See, for example, David Vienneau, 'Poll finds 59% Favor Limits on Abortion,' *Toronto Star*, 20 June 1988, A3.

11 André Picard, 'One Year after Abortion Law Struck Down, Little Has Changed,' *Globe and Mail*, 28 January 1989, A3

12 Janet Somerville, 'Pro-Lifers Turn to "Rescue" Tactics,' *Catholic New Times*, 5 February 1989, 3; and Robert Matas, 'B.C. Judge Unmoved by Heat of Anti-Abortion Arguments,' *Globe and Mail*, 1 March 1989, A1, A2

13 Pro-life activist Joe Borowski had asked the court to find that the fetus is a person with a constitutional right to life, liberty, and security of person and the right to equal protection of the law. The court decided that it would not be in the public interest to rule on fetal rights without an abortion law in place. See 'Abortion Issue Back in PM's Lap: Top Court Refuses to Rule,' Halifax *Mail–Star*, 10 March 1989, 1, 2.

RESEARCH APPENDIX

1 See Howard Schwartz and Jerry Jacobs, *Qualitative Sociology* (New York: The Free Press 1979).

2 See Norman K. Denzin, *The Research Act* (Chicago: Aldine 1970), ch. 6; Raymond L. Gordon, *Interviewing* (Homewood, Ill.: Dorsey Press 1969); and S. Richardson, B. Snell, and P.L. Kendall, *The Interview: Its Forms and Functions* (New York: Basic Books 1965).

3 On the method of participant-observation, see Glenn Jacobs, ed., *The Participant Observer* (New York: George Braziller 1970); John Lofland, *Analyzing Social Settings* (Belmont, Calif.: Wadsworth Publishing 1971), ch. 5; and Severyn T. Bruyn, *The Human Perspective in Sociology* (Englewood Cliffs, NJ: Prentice-Hall 1966).

4 See I. C. Jarvie, 'The Problem of Ethical Integrity in Participant Observation,' *Current Anthropology* 10 (1969): 505–8.

5 Buford M. Junker, *Field Work* (Chicago: University of Chicago Press 1960)

Bibliography

GENERAL REFERENCES

Abbott, Walter M., ed. *The Documents of Vatican II*. New York: The America Press 1966

Alton, Bruce, ed. *The Abortion Question*. Toronto: Anglican Book Centre 1983

Badgley Committee. *Report of the Committee on the Operation of the Abortion Law*. Ottawa: Ministry of Supply and Services 1977

Balakrishnan, T.R., J.F. Kantner, and J.D. Allingham. *Fertility and Family Planning in a Canadian Metropolis*. Montreal: McGill-Queen's University Press 1975

Barkun, Michael. *Crucible of the Millennium*. Syracuse: Syracuse University Press 1986

Baum, Gregory. 'Catholic Foundation of Human Rights.' *The Ecumenist* 18, 1 (1979): 6–12

– 'Values and Society.' *The Ecumenist* 17, 2 (1979): 25–31

– *Catholics and Canadian Socialism*. Toronto: James Lorimer 1980

– 'Liberation Theology and "The Supernatural,"' *The Ecumenist* 19, 6 (1981): 81–7

– *The Priority of Labor: A Commentary on Laborem Exercens*. New York: Paulist Press 1982

– 'Abortion: An Ecumenical Dilemma.' In Edward Batchelor, ed., *Abortion: The Moral Issues*, 38–47. New York: Pilgrim Press 1982

Baum, Gregory, and Duncan Cameron. *Ethics and Economics: Canada's Catholic Bishops on the Economic Crisis*. Toronto: James Lorimer 1984

Bellah, Robert N. 'Civil Religion in America.' *Daedalus* 96 (1967): 1–21

Bendix, Reinhard. 'Memoir of My Father.' *The Canadian Review of Sociology and Anthropology* 2, 1 (1965): 1–18

Benedict, Ruth. *Patterns of Culture*. Boston: Houghton Mifflin 1959

Berger, Peter L. *The Sacred Canopy*. Garden City, NY: Anchor 1967

Berger, Peter L., and Brigitte Berger. *The War over the Family*. Garden City, NY: Anchor 1983

Berger, Peter L., and Thomas Luckmann. *The Social Construction of Reality*. New York: Penguin Books 1976

Bibby, Reginald W. *Fragmented Gods: The Poverty and Potential of Religion in Canada*. Toronto: Irwin 1987

Bird Francke, Linda. *The Ambivalence of Abortion*. New York: Dell 1979

Blasi, Anthony J., and Michael W. Cuneo. *Issues in the Sociology of Religion: A Bibliography*, 17–21. New York: Garland Publishing 1986

Blumer, Herbert. 'Collective Behavior.' In A.M. Lee, ed., *New Outline of the Principles of Sociology*, 178–208. New York: Barnes and Noble 1953

Bouyer, Louis C. *The Decomposition of Catholicism*, translated by C.U. Quinn. Chicago: Franciscan Herald 1969

Boyd, M., and D. Gillieson. 'Canadian Attitudes on Abortion: Results of the Gallup Polls.' *Canadian Studies in Population* 2 (1975): 63

Bruyn, Severyn T. *The Human Perspective in Sociology*. Englewood Cliffs, NJ: Prentice-Hall 1966

Canadian Conference of Catholic Bishops. *Contraception, Divorce, Abortion*. Ottawa: CCC 1968

– *Statement Reaffirming CCC Position on Abortion*. Ottawa: CCC 1968

– *Statement on Abortion*. Ottawa: CCC 1970

– *Witness to Justice: A Society to be Transformed – Working Instruments*. Ottawa: Episcopal Commission for Social Affairs 1979

– *Ethical Reflections on the Economic Crisis*. Ottawa: CCCB 1983

– *Ethical Reflections on Respect for Life*. Ottawa: CCCB 1983

– *To Love and Serve Life*. Ottawa: CCCB 1986

– *The Meaning of Sunday in a Pluralistic Society*. Ottawa: CCCB 1986

– *Witness to Justice: Some Statements by the Canadian Catholic Bishops*. Toronto: CCODP n.d.

Casanova, Jose V. 'The First Secular Institute: The Opus Dei as a Religious Movement-Organization.' *Annual Review of the Social Sciences of Religion* 6 (1982): 243–85

Chesterton, G.K. *The Catholic Church and Conversion*. New York: Macmillan 1926

Clark, S.D. 'The Religious Sect in Canadian Politics.' In his *The Developing Canadian Community*, 131–46. Toronto: University of Toronto Press 1968

Clarke, Tony. 'Communities for Justice.' *The Ecumenist* 19 (1981): 17–25

Clifford, N.K. 'His Dominion: A Vision in Crisis.' In Peter Slater, ed., *Religion and Culture in Canada/Religion et Culture au Canada*, 23–41. Canadian Corporation for Studies in Religion 1977

Collins, Anne. *The Big Evasion: Abortion, the Issue That Won't Go Away*. Toronto: Lester & Orpen Dennys 1985

Creighton, Phyllis, ed. *Abortion, An Issue for Conscience*. Toronto: The Anglican Church of Canada 1974

Cuneo, Michael W. 'Conservative Catholicism in North America: Pro-Life Activism and the Pursuit of the Sacred.' *Pro Mundi Vita* 36 (1987): 3–28

– 'Soldiers of Orthodoxy: Revivalist Catholicism in North America.' *Studies in Religion/Sciences Religieuses* 17, 3 (1988): 347–63

Curran, Charles E. *American Catholic Social Ethics*, 172–232. Notre Dame: University of Notre Dame Press 1982

Czerny, Michael, and Jamie Swift. *Getting Started on Social Analysis in Canada*. Toronto: Between the Lines 1984

Denzin, Norman K. *The Research Act*. Chicago: Aldine 1970

De Roo, Bishop Remi. *Cries of Victims – Voice of God*. Ottawa: Novalis 1986

De Valk, Alphonse. *Morality and Law in Canadian Politics: The Abortion Controversy*. Montreal: Palm Publishers 1974

– 'Abortion Politics Canadian Style.' In Paul Sachdev, ed., *Abortion Readings and Research*, 5–15. Toronto: Butterworths 1981

– 'Understandable but Mistaken: Law, Morality and the Catholic Church in Canada, 1966–1969.' *Canadian Catholic Historical Association, Study Sessions* 49 (1982): 87–109

Dinges, William. 'Catholic Traditionalism.' In J. Fichter, ed., *Alternatives to American Mainline Churches*, 138–58. New York: Rose of Sharon 1983

– 'Catholic Traditionalism in America: A Study of the Remnant Faithful.' Unpublished PhD dissertation, University of Kansas 1983

Donovan, Dan. *A Lasting Impact: John Paul II in Canada*. Toronto: Novalis 1985

Dorr, Donal. *Option for the Poor: A Hundred Years of Vatican Social Teaching*. Maryknoll, NY: Orbis Books 1983

Dulles, Avery. *Models of the Church*. Garden City, NY: Image Books 1978

Durkheim, Emile. *Suicide: A Study in Sociology*, translated by J.A. Spaulding and G. Simpson. London: Routledge & Kegan Paul 1952

– *The Elementary Forms of the Religious Life*, translated by J.W. Swain. New York: The Free Press 1965

Dworkin, Andrea. *Right-Wing Women*. New York: Wideview/Perigee 1983

Eagleson, J., and P. Scharper, eds. *Puebla and Beyond*. Maryknoll, NY: Orbis Books 1979

Eliade, Mircea. *The Sacred and the Profane*, translated by W.R. Trask. New York: Harcourt Brace Jovanovich 1959

Evans, Ruth, ed. *Abortion: A Study*. Toronto: United Church of Canada 1971

Falik, Marilyn M. 'Ideology and Abortion Policy Politics.' Unpublished PhD dissertation, New York University 1975

Ferraro, Kathleen J., and John M. Johnson. 'How Women Experience Battering: The Process of Victimization.' *Social Problems* 30, 3 (1983): 325–33

Festinger, L., H.W. Riecken, and S. Schachter. *When Prophecy Fails*. New York: Harper Torchbooks 1964

Fracchia, Charles. *Second Spring*. New York: Harper & Row 1980

Francome, Colin. *Abortion Freedom: A Worldwide Movement*. Boston: George Allen & Unwin 1984

Geertz, Clifford. *The Interpretation of Cultures*, 3–30. New York: Basic Books 1973

Glock, C.Y., and R.N. Bellah, eds. *The New Religious Consciousness*. Berkeley: University of California Press 1976

Goffman, Erving. *Presentation of Self in Everyday Life*. Garden City, NY: Anchor 1959

Gordon, Raymond L. *Interviewing*. Homewood, Ill.: Dorsey Press 1969

Granberg, Donald. 'The Abortion Activists.' *Family Planning Perspectives* 13, 4 (1981): 158–61

Grant, George. *Technology and Justice*, 117–30. Toronto: Anansi 1986

Grant, John W. *The Church in the Canadian Era*. Toronto: McGraw-Hill Ryerson 1972

– 'Religion and the Quest for a National Identity: The Background in Canadian History.' In Peter Slater, ed., *Religion and Culture in Canada/Religion et Culture au Canada*, 7–21. Canadian Corporation for Studies in Religion 1977

Greeley, Andrew M. *The Denominational Society*. Glenview, Ill.: Foresman 1972

– *The New Agenda*. Garden City, NY: Doubleday 1973

Greeley, Andrew M., and Mary Durkin. *How to Save the Catholic Church*. New York: Viking 1984

Gremillion, Joseph, ed. *The Gospel of Peace and Justice*. Maryknoll, NY: Orbis Books 1976

Gusfield, Joseph R. *Symbolic Crusade: Status Politics and the American Temperance Movement*. Urbana, Ill.: University of Illinois Press 1966

Handler, Denyse. 'Agreeing to Disagree: Catholic/United Church Dialogue.' *The Canadian Catholic Review* 4, 8 (1986): 20–1

Harrison, Beverly Wildung. *Our Right to Choose: Toward a New Ethic of Abortion*. Boston: Beacon Press 1983

Hebblethwaite, Peter. *The Runaway Church*. New York: The Seabury Press 1975

Herberg, Will. *Protestant, Catholic, Jew*. Garden City, NY: Doubleday 1956

Higgins, Michael W., and Douglas R. Letson. *Portraits of Canadian Catholicism*. Toronto: Griffin House 1986

Hill, Michael. *A Sociology of Religion*. London: Heinemann 1973

– *The Religious Order*. London: Heinemann 1973

Hoy, Claire. *Bill Davis*, 264–76. Toronto: Methuen 1985

Hunter, James D. 'Operationalizing Evangelicalism: A Review, Critique, and Proposal.' *Sociological Analysis* 42 (1981): 363–72

Hutchinson, R.C. 'Ecumenical Witness in Canada: Social Action Coalitions.' *International Review of Mission* 71 (1982): 344–52

Jacobs, Glenn, ed. *The Participant Observer*. New York: George Braziller 1970

Jaffe, F.S., B.L. Lindheim, and P.R. Lee. *Abortion Politics: Private Morality and Public Policy*. New York: McGraw-Hill 1981

James, William. *The Varieties of Religious Experience*. New York: Mentor 1958

Jarvie, I.C. 'The Problem of Ethical Integrity in Participant Observation.' *Current Anthropology* 10 (1969): 505–08

Joffe, Carole. 'The Meaning of the Abortion Conflict.' *Contemporary Sociology* 14, 1 (1985): 26–8

Junker, Buford M. *Field Work*. Chicago: University of Chicago Press 1960

Kelly, James R. 'Beyond the Stereotypes: Interviews with Right-to-Life Pioneers.' *Commonweal* (20 November 1981): 654–9

– 'Tracking the Intractable: A Survey on the Abortion Controversy.' *Cross Currents* (Summer/Fall 1985): 212–18

– 'Turning Liberals into Fascists: A Case Study of the Distortion of the Right-to-Life Movement.' *Fidelity* 6, 8 (1987): 17–22

Klapp, Orrin E. *Collective Search For Identity*. New York: Holt, Rinehart and Winston 1969

Knox, Ronald A. *Enthusiasm*. Oxford: Clarendon Press 1950

Kobler, John F. *Vatican II and Phenomenology*. Dordrecht: Martinus Nijhoff 1985

Lacelle, Elisabeth J. 'Women in the Catholic Church of Canada.' *The Ecumenist* 23, 4 (1985): 49–54

Lechner, Frank J. 'Fundamentalism and Sociocultural Revitalization in America: A Sociological Interpretation.' *Sociological Analysis* 46, 3 (1985): 243–59

Leddy, Mary Jo, and James H. Olthuis. 'Thoughtful Perspective on Abortion.' *Catalyst* 6, 10 (November 1983): 4–5

Lenski, Gerhard. *The Religious Factor*. Garden City, NY: Doubleday 1961

Liebman, R.C., and R. Wuthnow, eds. *The New Christian Right*. New York: Aldine 1983

Lipset, Seymour Martin. 'Canada and the United States – A Comparative View.' *Canadian Review of Sociology and Anthropology* 1 (1964): 173–85

Lofland, John. *Analyzing Social Settings*. Belmont, Calif.: Wadsworth Publishing 1971

Luker, Kristin. *Abortion and the Politics of Motherhood*. Berkeley: University of California Press 1984

Marcoux, Marcene. *Cursillo: Anatomy of a Movement*. New York: Lambeth Press 1982

Markson, Stephen L. 'Citizens United for Life: Status Politics, Symbolic Reform and the Anti Abortion Movement.' Unpublished PhD dissertation, University of Massachusetts 1979

Marsden, George M. *Fundamentalism and American Culture*. New York: Oxford University Press 1980

Martin, David A. 'The Denomination.' *British Journal of Sociology* 12, 1 (1962): 1–14

Mason, Susan E. 'The "Pro-Family" Ideology of the 1970s.' Unpublished PhD dissertation, Columbia University 1981

Maxtone-Graham, Katrina. *Pregnant by Mistake*. New York: Liveright 1973

Mazur, Carol, and Sheila Pepper. *Women in Canada: A Bibliography*, 1–5. Toronto: OISE Press 1984

McBrien, Richard P. *Do We Need the Church?* London: Collins 1969

McDonnell, Kathleen. *Not an Easy Choice*. Toronto: Women's Press 1984

McSweeney, Bill. *Roman Catholicism: The Search for Relevance*. Oxford: Basil Blackwell 1980

Merton, Andrew H. *Enemies of Choice*. Boston: Beacon Press 1981

Merton, Robert K. *Social Theory and Social Structure*, revised and enlarged edition. Glencoe, Ill.: The Free Press 1957

Miller, Douglas T., and Marian Nowak. *The Fifties: The Way We Really Were*. Garden City, NY: Doubleday 1977

Mills, C. Wright. *The Sociological Imagination*. New York: Oxford University Press 1959

Mohr, James C. *Abortion in America: The Origins and Evolution of National Policy*. New York: Oxford University Press 1978

Mol, Hans. *Identity and the Sacred*. New York: The Free Press 1976

Mooney, James. *The Ghost Dance Religion*. Washington: Bureau of American Ethnology Annual Report 1892–3

Mottl, Tahi L. 'The Analysis of Countermovements.' *Social Problems* 27 (1980): 620–35

Muldoon, Maureen. *Abortion: An Annotated Indexed Bibliography*. New York: E. Mellen Press 1980

Neitz, Mary Jo. 'Family, State, and God: Ideologies of the Right-to-Life Movement.' *Sociological Analysis* 42, 3 (1981): 265–76

Noonan, John T., Jr. *A Private Choice: Abortion in America in the Seventies*. New York: The Free Press 1979

Novak, Michael. *The Open Church*. New York: Macmillan 1964

O'Connor, June. 'The Debate Continues: Recent Works on Abortion.' *Religious Studies Review* 11, 2 (1985): 105–14

O'Toole, Roger. 'Some Good Purpose: Notes on Religion and Political Culture in Canada.' *Annual Review of the Social Sciences of Religion* 6 (1982): 177–215

– 'Society, the Sacred and the Secular: Sociological Observations on the Changing Role of Religion in Canadian Culture.' In William Westfall, Louis Rousseau, Fernand Harvey, and John Simpson, eds., *Religion/Culture: Comparative Canadian Studies*, 99–117. Ottawa: Association for Canadian Studies 1985

O'Toole, Roger, ed. *Sociological Studies of Roman Catholicism*. New York: E. Mellen Press 1989

Paige, Connie. *The Right to Lifers: Who They Are, How They Opeate, Where They Get Their Money*. New York: Summit Books 1983

Park, R.E., and E.W. Burgess. *Introduction to the Science of Sociology*. Chicago: University of Chicago Press 1924

Pelrine, Eleanor. *Morgentaler: The Doctor Who Couldn't Turn Away*. Toronto: Gage 1975

Richardson, S., B. Snell, and P.L. Kendall. *The Interview: Its Forms and Functions*. New York: Basic Books 1965

Rieff, Philip. *The Triumph of the Therapeutic*. New York: Harper 1968

Romaniuc, A. *Fertility in Canada: From Baby-boom to Baby-bust*. Ottawa: Ministry of Supply and Services 1984

Ryan, Michael. *Solidarity: Christian Social Teaching and Canadian Society*. London, Ont.: Guided Study Programs in the Catholic Faith 1986

Schwartz, Howard, and Jerry Jacobs. *Qualitative Sociology*. New York: The Free Press 1979

Sheridan, E.F., ed. *Do Justice! The Social Teaching of the Canadian Catholic Bishops (1945–1986)*. Toronto: The Jesuit Centre for Social Faith and Justice 1987

Simpson, John H. 'Federal Regulation and Religious Broadcasting.' In William Westfall, Louis Rousseau, Fernand Harvey, and John Simpson, eds., *Religion/Culture: Comparative Canadian Studies*, 152–63. Ottawa: Association for Canadian Studies 1985

Simpson, John H., and Henry MacLeod. 'The Politics of Morality in Canada.' In R. Stark, ed., *Religious Movements: Genesis, Exodus, and Numbers*, 221–40. New York: Paragon House 1985

Sinclair-Faulkner, Tom. 'Canadian Catholics: At Odds on Abortion.' *The Christian Century*, 9 September 1981, 870–1

Sissons, C.B. *Church and State in Canadian Education*. Toronto: Ryerson 1959

Smelser, Neil J. *Theory of Collective Behavior*. New York: The Free Press 1962

Stone, Lawrence. *The Past and the Present*. Boston: Routledge & Kegan Paul 1981

Straus, Roger. 'Changing Oneself: Seekers and the Creative Transformation of Experience.' In J. Lofland, ed., *Doing Social Life*, 252–72. New York: Wiley 1976

Tracy, David. *Blessed Rage for Order*. New York: Crossroad 1981

– *The Analogical Imagination*. New York: Crossroad 1981

Turner, R.H., and L.M. Killian. *Collective Behavior*, 3rd ed. Englewood Cliffs, NJ: Prentice-Hall 1987

Voegelin, Eric. *New Science of Politics*. Chicago: University of Chicago Press 1972

Wach, Joachim. *Sociology of Religion*. Chicago: University of Chicago Press 1944

Wallace, Anthony F.C. 'Revitalization Movements.' *American Anthropologist* 58 (1956): 264–81

Weber, Max. 'The Meaning of "Ethical Neutrality" in Sociology and Economics.' In E.A. Shils and H.A. Finch, eds., *The Methodology of the Social Sciences*, 1–47. New York: The Free Press 1949

– ' "Objectivity" in Social Science and Social Policy.' In E.A. Shils and H.A. Finch, eds., *The Methodology of the Social Sciences*, 50–112. New York: The Free Press 1949

– *The Sociology of Religion*, translated by E. Fischoff. Boston: Beacon Press 1963

– *The Theory of Social and Economic Organization*, translated by A.M. Henderson and T. Parsons. New York: The Free Press 1964

– 'Science as a Vocation.' In H.H. Gerth and C. Wright Mills, eds., *From Max Weber: Essays in Sociology*, 129–56. New York: Oxford University Press 1980

– 'Class, Status, Party.' In H.H. Gerth and C. Wright Mills, eds., *From Max Weber: Essays in Sociology*, 180–95. New York: Oxford University Press 1980

– 'The Social Psychology of the World Religions.' In H.H. Gerth and C. Wright Mills, eds., *From Max Weber: Essays in Sociology*, 267–301. New York: Oxford University Press 1980

Westfall, William. 'The Dominion of the Lord: An Introduction to the Cultural History of Protestant Ontario in the Victorian Period.' *Queen's Quarterly* 83 (1976): 47–70

Westhues, Kenneth. 'The Adaptation of the Roman Catholic Church in Canadian Society.' In S. Crysdale and L. Wheatcroft, eds., *Religion in Canadian Society*, 290–306. Toronto: Macmillan 1976

– 'The Option for (and against) the Poor.' *Grail* 3, 1 (1987): 23–38

Whitaker, Reginald. 'Reason, Passion and Interest: Pierre Trudeau's Eternal Liberal Triangle.' *Canadian Journal of Political and Social Theory* 4, 1 (1980): 5–31

Williams, John R., ed. *Canadian Churches and Social Justice*. Toronto: Anglican Book Centre and L. Lorimer 1984

Wilson, Bryan R. *Religion in Secular Society*. London: C.A. Watts 1966

Wrong, Dennis H. 'The Oversocialized Conception of Man in Modern Society.' *American Sociological Review* 26, 2 (1961): 183–93

Wuthnow, Robert, James Davison Hunter, Albert Bergesen, and Edith Kurzweil. *Cultural Analysis*. Boston: Routledge & Kegan Paul 1984

Yinger, J.M. 'Contraculture and Subculture.' *American Sociological Review* 25 (1960): 625–45

TORONTO NEWSPAPER REFERENCES

Adams, M., D. Dasko, and Y. Corbeil. 'The Globe-CROP Poll.' *Globe and Mail*, 15 June 1985, 1, 12

Amiel, Barbara. 'Words without Wisdom.' *Toronto Sun*, 19 February 1985, 12

Barnard, Linda. 'Prayers Ring Out to End Abortions.' *Toronto Sun*, 18 February 1985, 4

Beagan, Doreen. 'Pro-Lifers Say Shocked by Letter.' Canadian *Catholic Register*, 16 July 1988, 3

Bilodeau, Paul. 'Pro-Life Activists Parade at Morgentaler Clinic.' *Toronto Star*, 19 February 1985, A7

Brown, Louise. 'United Church Warns of Tensions on School Funding.' *Toronto Star*, 23 February 1985, A6

Campbell, Murray. '300 Rally at Morgentaler Clinic to Start Week of Demonstrations.' *Globe and Mail*, 19 February 1985, M5

– 'Students from Separate Schools Give Protest Air of a Pep Rally.' *Globe and Mail*, 21 February 1985, M1

– 'Rally of Morgentaler Supporters Decries Role of Church.' *Globe and Mail*, 23 February 1985, M1

Carey, Elaine. 'Church Spokesmen Worry that Marches May Create Serious Rifts in Community.' *Toronto Star*, 2 March 1985, B5

Carter, Cardinal G. Emmett. 'Cardinal Carter Issues Clarifying Statement.' *Globe and Mail*, 29 April 1981

Christie, Alan, and Michael McAteer. 'Davis "Saddened" by Archbishop's "Hitler" Charge on School Funding.' *Toronto Star*, 26 April 1985, 1, 8

Coulter, Diana. 'Abortion Clinic Foes Ignore Picket-Limit Deal.' *Toronto Star*, 24 August 1985, A6

Coyle, Fergus. 'Treat Unemployment as Crisis United Church Ministers Urge.' *Toronto Star*, 28 January 1983, A8

Crawford, Trish. 'Morgentaler's Clinic Fuels Abortion Issue.' *Toronto Star*, 11 April 1985, A19

Davey, Senator Keith. 'Ottawa's Answer to the Bishops.' *Toronto Star*, 8 January 1983, B4

DiManno, Rosie. 'Pro-Life Groups Losing Battle, Opponent Says.' *Toronto Star*, 22 February 1985, A14

English, Kathy. 'Ranks of Protesters Grow Outside Abortion Clinic.' *Toronto Star*, 20 February 1985, A12

– 'Pro-Life Rally Gains Strength as 900 Protest.' *Toronto Star*, 21 February 1985, A6

English, Kathy, and Chris Welner. '3,000 Protesters Demand Abortion Clinic Be Closed.' *Toronto Star*, 22 February 1985, A1

English, Kathy, and Paula Todd. '5,000 March in Support of Abortion.' *Toronto Star*, 23 February 1985, A1

Ferri, John. 'Fight Catholic Funding, Garnsworthy Urges.' *Toronto Star*, 1 June 1985, A3

Flavelle, Dana. 'Morgentaler Backers to Hold Rally on Friday.' *Toronto Star*, 17 February 1985, A3

Fraser, Graham. 'MPs Vote Down Abortion Resolution.' *Globe and Mail*, 29 July 1988, A1, A5

Ganley, Ciaran. 'Campaign Life Slams Scott.' *Toronto Star*, 23 August 1985, 5

Golombek, Allan. 'Clergy Meddling, Morgentaler Says.' *Toronto Sun*, 5 March 1985, 26

Harpur, Tom. 'Name-Calling, Violence Have No Place in Abortion Issue.' *Toronto Star*, 3 March 1985, A16

Higgins, Michael. 'Back When King Billy Rode Tall in the Saddle.' *Toronto Star*, 12 July 1986, L10

– 'Abortion Issue Calls for Restraint by the Media.' *Toronto Star*, 20 February 1988, M13

Howell, Peter. 'Carter Regrets "Hostility."' *Toronto Sun*, 15 September 1985, 48

Hoy, Claire. 'He Wants to Have It Both Ways.' *Toronto Sun*, 29 April 1981, 8

– 'Gutless on the Hill.' *Toronto Sun*, 21 February 1985, 4

Hurst, Lynda. 'Anti-Abortion Pickets' Arrogance Is Staggering.' *Toronto Star*, 27 August 1985, B1

MacIntosh, Robert. 'The Bishops and the Economy.' *Toronto Star*, 8 January 1983, B4

Mandel, Michele. 'Anti-Abortion Protest Grows.' *Toronto Sun*, 20 February 1985, 14

– 'Protesters Turn Rowdy at Anti-Abortion Rally.' *Toronto Sun*, 22 February 1985, 4

McAndrew, Brian. 'Pro-Life Group Gears up for Mass Protest.' *Toronto Star*, 16 February 1985, A6

McAteer, Michael. 'Carter Urges Faithful to Join Abortion Protest.' *Toronto Star*, 12 February 1985, A6

– 'United Churchman Raps Catholic Abortion Stand.' *Toronto Star*, 24 February 1985, A2

– 'Christians at the Crossroads: Canada's Christians at a Turning Point.' *Toronto Star*, 16 April 1987, A20

– 'Churches Urged to Battle Death Penalty.' *Toronto Star*, 3 May 1987, A22

– 'Bishops' Stance on Abortion Bid "a Betrayal" Group Charges.' *Toronto Star*, 29 June 1988, A25

McNenly, Pat. 'Metro Churches Split on Abortion Protest.' *Toronto Star*, 18 February 1985, A14

– 'Clergy's Crusade on Sunday Shopping Gains Support.' *Toronto Star*, 2 February 1988, A16

Oziewicz, Stanley. 'Don't Push Own Abortion Beliefs, Rabbis Urge.' *Globe and Mail*, 21 February 1985, M4

Picard, André. 'One Year After Abortion Law Struck Down, Little Has Changed.' *Globe and Mail*, 28 January 1989, A3

Sabia, Laura. 'Cross to Bear.' *Toronto Sun*, 26 February 1985, 12

Smith, Dan. 'Cardinal Carter Calls Court Ruling "Uncivilized." ' *Toronto Star*, 29 January 1988, A1

Smith, Gwen. 'Priests Told to Eschew Literature: Pro-Lifers Bitter over Carter Order on Militant Group.' *Globe and Mail*, 30 April 1981, 1, 2

Somerville, Janet. 'Pro-Lifers Turn to "Rescue" Tactics.' *Catholic New Times*, 5 February 1989, 3

Vienneau, David. 'Poll Finds 59% Favor Limits on Abortions.' *Toronto Star*, 20 June 1988, A3

Walker, Bill. '5-Picket Limit Urged Outside Abortion Clinic.' *Toronto Star*, 23 August 1985, A6

– 'Supreme Court Decision Backs Morgentaler: Up to MPs Whether to Try New Approach on Abortion.' *Toronto Star*, 29 January 1988, A1, A4

PRO-LIFE MOVEMENT REFERENCES (CANADIAN AND AMERICAN)

Amyotte, Earl. 'Charter No Help to Unborn.' *The Interim* 1, 1 (March 1983): 4

Andrusko, Dave, ed. *To Rescue the Future: The Pro-Life Movement in the 1980s*. Toronto: Life Cycle Books 1983

Bernardin, Cardinal Joseph. *The Seamless Garment*. Kansas City: National Catholic Reporter Publishing 1984

Bottcher, Rosemary. 'Pro-Abortionists Poison Feminism.' In Gail Grenier Sweet, ed., *Pro-Life Feminism*, 45–7. Toronto: Life Cycle Books 1985

Brennan, William. *The Abortion Holocaust: Today's Final Solution*. St Louis: Landmark Press 1983

Brockhouse, Gordon. 'Giant Rally a "Success."' *The Interim* 3, 8 (November 1985): 1, 2

Burtchaell, James T. *Rachel Weeping: The Case against Abortion*. Kansas City: Andrews and McMeel 1982

Cavanaugh-O'Keefe, John. *No Cheap Solutions*. Gaithersburg, Md.: Prolife Nonviolent Action Project 1984

– *Nonviolence Is an Adverb*. Gaithersburg, Md.: Prolife Nonviolent Action Project 1985

De Valk, Alphonse. *The Worst Law Ever*. Edmonton: Life Ethics Centre 1979

– *Abortion: Christianity, Reason and Human Rights*. Edmonton: Life Ethics Centre 1982

– *Abortion Politics: Canadian Style*. Edmonton: Life Ethics Centre 1982

– 'Open Letter to Catholic Bishops: Let's Put Our House in Order.' *The Interim* 2, 9 (December 1984): 8–9

– 'Our Bishops on Humanae Vitae.' *The Interim* 4, 6 (September 1986): 12

– 'The Sexual Revolution, Feminism and the Churches (Part X): Catholic Bishops of Canada.' *The Interim* 5, 9 (December 1987): 17

De Veber, L.L., and Jessica Pegis. *Heroin vs. Morphine: The Current Debate*. Toronto: Human Life Research Institute 1985

Fairweather, Eugene R., and Ian Gentles, eds. *The Right to Birth*. Toronto: Anglican Book Centre 1976

Gallagher, John. *Is the Human Embryo a Person?* Toronto: Human Life Research Institute 1985

Gentles, Ian. *The Law and Abortion*. Toronto: Human Life Research Institute 1985

Hierlihy, Sue. 'Ottawa Inquest Exposes Rubber-Stamp Abortions.' *The Interim* 4, 4 (June 1986): 3

Jones, E. Michael. 'Abortion Mill Rescue: Are Sit-ins the Answer?' *Fidelity* 6, 8 (July–August 1987): 28–37

Koop, C. Everett, and Francis A. Schaeffer. *Whatever Happened to the Human Race?* Westchester, Ill.: Crossway Books 1983

Kremer, E.J., and E.A. Synan, eds. *Death before Birth: Canada and the Abortion Question*. Toronto: Griffin House 1974

Landolt, C. Gwendolyn. 'The Borowski Case (What's It All About).' *The Interim* 1, 3 (May 1983): 1, 3

Little, David. 'Announcing the Catholic Foundation for Human Life.' *The Interim* 2, 2 (April 1984): 13

Loesch, Juli. *Acts of Aggression*. Chapel Hill, NC: Prolifers for Survival 1985

– *Imagining the Real*. Chapel Hill, NC: Prolifers for Survival 1985

Marx, Paul. *The Death Peddlers: War on the Unborn*. Collegeville, Minn.: Saint John's University Press 1971

– 'Explaining the Contraceptive Mentality.' *The Interim* 6, 1 (April 1987): 27

McLuhan, Sabina. 'All in the Family.' *The Interim* 4, 4 (June 1986): 27

Meehan, Francis X. *Abortion and Nuclear War: Two Issues, One Moral Cause*. Liguori, Mo.: Liguori Publications 1984

Migliorino, Monica M. 'Report from Rats' Alley: Down and Out with the Unborn in Chicago and Milwaukee.' *Fidelity* 6, 8 (July–August 1987): 38–45

Morris, Heather, and Lorraine Williams. *Physical Complications of Abortion*. Toronto: Human Life Research Institute 1985

Nathanson, Bernard N. (with R.N. Ostling). *Aborting America*. Garden City, NY: Doubleday 1979

– *The Abortion Papers*. New York: Frederick Fell 1983

Parthun, Mary. *The Psychological Effects of Induced Abortion*. Toronto: Human Life Research Institute 1985

Pegis, Jessica, L.L. de Veber, and Ian Gentles. *Sex Education: A Review of the Literature from Canada, the United States, Britain and Sweden*. Toronto: Human Life Research Institute 1986

Petrasek, Grace. 'REAL Women and Election '84.' *The Interim* 2, 6 (September 1984): 17
Powell, John. *Abortion: The Silent Holocaust*. Allen, Texas: Argus Communications 1981
Rice, Charles. *Fifty Questions on Abortion, Euthanasia, and Related Issues*. Notre Dame, Ind.: Cashel Institute 1986
Scheidler, Joseph M. *Closed: 99 Ways to Stop Abortion*. Toronto: Life Cycle Books 1985
Summerhill, Louise. *The Story of Birthright: The Alternative to Abortion*. Libertyville, Ill.: Prow Books 1973
Sweet, Gail Grenier, ed. *Pro-Life Feminism*. Toronto: Life Cycle Books 1985
Tabisz, Ellen. 'A Farewell Word.' *Pro-Life News* (May 1983): 10
Thimmesch, Nick. *When Abortion Fails: The Unborn's Uncertain Destiny*. Toronto: Life Cycle Books n.d.
Toth, Kathleen. 'A Message from the President.' *The Interim* 1, 1 (March 1983): 5
Willke, J.C. 'From the President's Desk: A Place for Public Witness?' *National Right to Life News*, 15 May 1986, 3, 8

REVIVALIST CATHOLIC REFERENCES

Arnold, Patrick M. 'The Rise of Catholic Fundamentalism.' *America* 156, 14 (11 April 1987): 297–302
Cowden-Guido, Richard. *John Paul II and the Battle for Vatican II: Report from the Synod*. Manassas, Va.: Trinity Communications 1986
DeMarco, Donald. *Sex and the Illusion of Freedom*. Kitchener, Ont.: Mission House Publications 1981
– *The Contraceptive Mentality*. Edmonton: Life Ethics Centre 1982
De Valk, Alphonse. 'Sexual Revolution, Feminism and the Churches.' *The Interim* 4, 6 (September 1986): 10–12
Farrell, E.C. 'The 1960s – A Look Back.' *Challenge* 13, 7 (April 1987): 18–19
Hawkins, Anthony. 'Maureen McTeer: "Abortion Posting Shameful."' *The Interim* 4, 1 (March 1986): 14
Henderson, Larry. *The Hot Seat*. Toronto: The Catholic Register 1986
– 'A Tale of Two Cultures.' *Challenge* 13, 7 (April 1987): 12
Hitchcock, James. *The Decline and Fall of Radical Catholicism*. New York: Herder and Herder 1971
– *Catholicism and Modernity: Confrontation or Capitulation?* Ann Arbor: Servant Books 1979

– *What Is Secular Humanism?* Ann Arbor: Servant Books 1982
– *Years of Crisis: Collected Essays, 1970–1983*. San Francisco: Ignatius Press 1985
Iglesias, M. Timothy. 'CUF and Dissent: A Case Study in Religious Conservatism.' *America* 156, 14 (11 April 1987): 303–7
Johnson, Paul. *Pope John Paul II and the Catholic Restoration*. Ann Arbor: Servant Books 1981
Jones, E. Michael. 'Requiem for a Magazine: The Sodomization of the Catholic Press in Saskatchewan.' *Fidelity* 6, 3 (February 1987): 22–36
Kelly, George A. *The Battle for the American Church*. Garden City, NY: Doubleday 1979
– *The Crisis of Authority*. Chicago: Regnery Gateway 1982
Likoudis, James, and Kenneth P. Whitehead. *The Pope, the Council, and the Mass*. West Hanover, Mass.: Christopher Publishing House 1981
Martin, Malachi. *The Jesuits*. New York: Simon & Schuster 1987
Miceli, Vincent P. *The Antichrist*. Harrison, NY: Roman Catholic Books 1981
Novak, Michael. *Confession of a Catholic*. San Francisco: Harper & Row 1983
Ratzinger, Joseph Cardinal (with Vittorio Messori). *The Ratzinger Report*, translated by S. Attanasio and G. Harrison. San Francisco: Ignatius Press 1985
Robinson, Jonathan. *Papal Teaching Today and the State of the Faith*. Toronto: The Catholic Register 1985
Roche Muggeridge, Anne. *The Gates of Hell: The Struggle for the Catholic Church*. Toronto: McClelland and Stewart 1975
– 'Love among the Ruins.' *Today Magazine (Toronto Star)*, 10 April 1982, 8–10, 16
– *The Desolate City: The Catholic Church in Ruins*. Toronto: McClelland and Stewart 1986
Steichen, Donna. 'From Convent to Coven: Catholic Neo-Pagans at the Witches' Sabbath.' *Fidelity* 5, 1 (December 1985): 27–37
Von Hildebrand, Dietrich. *Trojan Horse in the City of God*. Chicago: Franciscan Herald 1967
– *The Encyclical Humanae Vitae: A Sign of Contradiction*. Chicago: Franciscan Herald 1969
– *The Devastated Vineyard*. Chicago: Franciscan Herald 1973
Wiltgen, Ralph. *The Rhine Flows into the Tiber*. New York: Hawthorn 1967

Index